Historical Problems:
Studies and Documents

Edited by

PROFESSOR G. R. ELTON
University of Cambridge

15

MEDIEVAL MONARCHY IN ACTION

In the same series

MEDIEVAL MONARCHY IN ACTION

The German Empire from Henry I to Henry IV

Boyd H. Hill Jr

Professor in the Department of History
University of Colorado

LONDON : GEORGE ALLEN AND UNWIN LTD
NEW YORK : BARNES AND NOBLE BOOKS

British ISBN 0 04 943017 3 Cased
           0 04 943018 1 Paper

Published in the U.S.A. by
Harper & Row Publishers Inc.
Barnes & Noble Import Division

American ISBN 389–04652–3

Printed in Great Britain
in 10 point Plantin
by Alden & Mowbray Ltd
at the Alden Press, Oxford

PREFACE

This book might equally well have been subtitled 'The German *Emperors* from Henry I to Henry IV', for it concentrates on what these rulers did. My orientation is admittedly very old-fashioned and calls for some explanation. M. I. Finley has rightly criticized those modern histories of Rome which 'proceed through each reign in turn, from Augustus on, centring the account on the emperors themselves, their acts and their qualities, distinguishing and judging. Which of them, if any, merits such concentrated attention is rarely asked. Given a king, historians and their readers alike become mesmerized.'[1]

My main purpose in collecting these sources was to present certain documents of the tenth and eleventh centuries which had not appeared before in English – the royal and imperial diplomas of that period.[2] To be sure, the deeds of the Saxon and Salian dynasties yield information about economics, social classes, and institutions, but most of all they tell what the emperors were doing. I do not claim that these diplomas tell *everything* they did, and still less that everything they did (even if derivable from the documents) would constitute the 'history' of the German empire, but I think that *anything* they did officially is significant for the topic. I hasten to add that the diplomas are not all of equal significance. Some are simple grants of land which could be multiplied many times over in every reign. Others are unique, like the *Ottonianum*, which has received special attention from historians because of what it tells us about papal–imperial relations.

Even a small collection of diplomas, such as the one that follows, reveals the diversity of the problems which the emperors faced, though not necessarily what they actually accomplished. I have tried to include diplomas which deal with every geographical part of the empire as well as with every reign from Henry I to Henry IV. I have also included

[1] 'A Profitable Empire', *The New York Review of Books*, 29 January 1970, p. 52.
[2] To my knowledge, not more than five of those in my collection have appeared before in English.

documents which are not, strictly speaking, diplomas, though they are published in the *Monumenta* series called *Diplomatum regum et imperatorum Germaniae*, such as epistles and *placita*, the records of court trials at which the emperor presided. My problem was not what to include but what to leave out, for the inclusion of any diploma of a German emperor could probably be rationalized in a collection of this sort. In addition to the diplomas, I have included certain non-diplomatic sources which have a direct bearing on the activities of the emperors. I do not pretend that my choice is not an arbitrary one, but I hope that it is none the less useful as an introduction to the period.

For those who read German there is now an excellent collection of sources, beginning with the Franks and going up to the fall of Constantinople, in *Geschichte in Quellen*, II, *Mittelalter*, ed. Wolfgang Lautemann, Munich, 1970. It contains more than 700 selections with the greatest variety of literary genres, some of which are not represented in my collection: for instance, monastic annals, saints' lives, and papal registers. The scope of my book is much narrower, and I have leaned towards complete documents rather than excerpts.

Unless otherwise indicated, the translations are my own. I have not really translated the diplomas in this volume into English but rather into a diplomatic language that can be readily understood by native speakers of English but which does not actually exist as a spoken dialect. Undoubtedly the style of the finished product could have been much improved if I had taken the license to convert the Latin phraseology into current popular idiom, but I felt that this would do too much violence to the historical content. My aim is not to make tenth-century texts palatable to twentieth-century readers: their own interest in the subject matter must do that for them. I have sought rather to present literal translations that will give students a close approximation to the diplomas, but I have not spared them the effort of energetic study of the material.

Eugene Nida, a proponent of free translation of ancient texts, suggests that the very subject matter of past civilizations can be translated into terms that will make immediate sense to modern readers. As an example he cites J. B. Phillips's rendering of Romans 16:16, 'greet one another with a holy kiss', as 'give one another a hearty handshake all around'.[3] This translation is 'dynamic' and 'natural' and has now become the vogue. 'A translation of dynamic equivalence aims at complete naturalness of expression, and tries to relate the receptor to modes of behavior relevant within the context of his own culture; it does not insist that

---

[3] *Toward a Science of Translating*, Leiden, 1964, p. 160.

he understand the cultural patterns of the source-language context in order to comprehend the message'.[4]

I believe that this approach, though doubtless successful in luring unsophisticated peoples into reading the message of the Gospels, represents a falsification of the source. It would be more helpful to the student of history to offer a literal rendering and to supply whatever footnotes are needed by way of explanation. This is what I have tried to do, and in this I am not alone. E. H. Warmington in his translation of Old Latin inscriptions has reproduced the jargon of ancient laws so that the result sounds like legal English, an appropriate vehicle for the subject and one that is familiar to the reader.[5] This pedantic adherence to the original also seems to characterize most translations of English constitutional documents that I have seen. How would one put the following into modern parlance so that the content is immediately comprehensible to a student of the 1970s?

'In assizes of darrein presentment, and in the plea of *Quare impedit* of churches vacant, the day shall be given from fifteen days to fifteen days, or from three weeks to three weeks, according as the place may be far or near.'[6]

One would have to turn to paraphrase, yet copious notes would still be required to explain the content. If I am following in the path of Stubbs, then so much the better. The current fashion lies in another direction, but I think it cannot be proved that free paraphrase gives any real sense of the style of the original. It merely lulls the student into the mistaken assumption that medieval history is easy. The Latin of the diplomas tends to be flatfooted, formulaic, and sometimes syntactically tortured, just as our own laws often are because of the need to cover all possible contingencies and loopholes. Hopefully the content will capture the imagination of the student even if the style does not. Most of the narrative sources are, by contrast, highly entertaining.

I wish to express my warmest thanks to the following scholars for their helpful suggestions: Professor Frederick Behrends, Dr Karl Brunner, Dr Kurt-Ulrich Jäschke, Professor Gerhart Ladner, Professor

---

[4] *Ibid.*, p. 159. Nida is not dogmatic about dynamic equivalence; he is merely enthusiastic. He points out that this is only one of several ways to execute acceptable translations. Another example of the type of idiomatic translation he favours is the following: 'The phrase "uncircumcised of heart" (Acts 7:51) must, of course, be radically altered in a number of receptor languages, as it has been in Cakchiquel, "with your hearts unprepared" ' (*ibid.*, p. 220).

[5] *Remains of Old Latin*, IV, *Archaic Inscriptions*, London, 1959.

[6] 'The Provisions of the Barons or of Westminster, October 1259', trans. William Stubbs, in *Select Documents of English Constitutional History*, ed. George Burton Adams and H. Morse Stephens, New York, 1910, p. 65.

Arthur J. Slavin, Professor Herwig Wolfram; and to the members of my seminar: Mr Charles Clark, Dr Lynn Hallgren, Professor C. E. Licka, Mr Louis Lumaghi, and Mr Gerald Snyder. I must also acknowledge with thanks the permission of Professor Mary Bernardine Bergman, O.S.B., to use extracts from her translation of the *Gesta Ottonis*; that of Columbia University Press for extracts from Harriet Pratt Lattin, *The Letters of Gerbert*; Theodor E. Mommsen and Karl F. Morrison, *Imperial Lives and Letters of The Eleventh Century;* Francis J. Tschan, *History of The Archbishops of Hamburg–Bremen* and *The Chronicle of The Slavs*; that of Routledge and Kegan Paul Ltd for extracts from F. A. Wright, *The Works of Liudprand of Cremona*. Detailed references appear at the appropriate places.

CONTENTS

INTRODUCTION
THE AGE OF THE SAXONS
AND SALIANS

The Reign of Henry I (919-936)

Everyone seems to agree as to who the German emperors were even when they are not so sure as to the nature of the empire which they sought to govern. Historians have been able to catalogue their deeds and accomplishments, but they have not always succeeded in telling why they did what they did. Although we shall mention some of these 'why' questions that have baffled historians, we do not pretend to answer them. Yet to exclude them altogether on the grounds that they cannot be answered would be to leave the intellectual mortar out of the historical edifice.[1] It is often the 'why' question that attracts the historian to a particular period or problem. Only the unusually detached reader of a mystery novel is content to know how the murderer carried out his crime without also asking why he did it. Likewise, in our courts the question of motive is taken into account in the judging of criminals: it is considered more heinous to premeditate a murder than to run down a man by mistake with an automobile, though the results are the same for the deceased. To be sure, we cannot know with certainty what was in the criminal's mind at the time of the murder, and still less can we know about the mind of a king who has been dead for a thousand years.

Even when the sources tell us why the king did something, we would be foolish to take the statement at face value. Perhaps the chronicler had an axe to grind. Maybe he was simply currying favour. Or perhaps (worst of all) the king himself did not really understand his own motives any more than we can always understand our own. Nevertheless, we shall repeat certain of the 'why' questions which historians have raised about the Saxons and Salians, because they are interesting even if unanswerable, and they are a part of the historiography of the tenth and eleventh centuries.

[1] Since David Hackett Fischer has so thoroughly and amusingly discredited the asking of 'why' questions, an apologia would seem to be in order. See *Historians' Fallacies: Toward a Logic of Historical Thought*, New York, 1970, pp. 14–15.

The first of these 'why' questions is: Why did Henry the Fowler refuse to be anointed? As the successful duke of Saxony, Henry had been recommended by his predecessor, Conrad I of Franconia, and he was designated king of the Germans in May 919 when the Frankish and Saxon nobles met at Fritzlar. Henry accepted the kingdom but declined to be anointed by a clerical official. This was in sharp contrast to his predecessor: Conrad's accession at Forchheim on 10 November 911 was legitimized with holy oil applied by clerical hands. In Walter Ullmann's opinion, 'Conrad's lack of blood charisma had to be compensated by the charisma of grace'.[2] Since Conrad's connection to the Carolingian dynasty which preceded him was a tenuous one, the necessary magic of the coronation ceremony was supplied by holy oil.

Henry, on the other hand, rejected the oil and thereby also rejected the clergy as the agent that made him a real king. Carl Erdmann has conjectured that this was deliberate, that Henry meant to contrast most sharply with the practices of Conrad, an unfortunate ruler who was heavily dependent upon his clerical advisers.[3] Henry also broke with tradition when he dispensed with a royal chapel. The chapel, which included the chancery, normally produced the documents which the king would have occasion to issue. Inasmuch as the royal chapel was a Carolingian invention and had been taken over by Conrad I, the lack of a chapel at Henry's court has been interpreted as another sign that he wished to inaugurate a purely secular reign.[4] Henry assumed Conrad's regalia but did not take over his archchaplain, Archbishop Pilgrim of Salzburg, nor his chancellor, Bishop Solomon of Constance. Pilgrim was excluded because his territory, Bavaria, lay outside the new king's jurisdiction. Solomon, however, seems to have been rejected on political grounds: he was the most powerful representative of the politics of Conrad, and that is what Henry wanted to break away from.[5] The only member of Conrad's chapel taken over by Henry was the notary Simon, and apparently the king added no new notaries for six years.[6] Henry did not issue a diploma for almost a year after taking office, and in that first diploma

[2] *The Carolingian Renaissance and the Idea of Kingship* (The Birkbeck Lectures, 1968–9), London, 1969, p. 127.

[3] 'Der ungesalbte König', *Deutches Archiv für die Erforschung des Mittelalters*, II (1938), 311–40.

[4] Josef Fleckenstein, *Die Hofkapelle der deutschen Könige*, II, *Die Hofkapelle im Rahmen der ottonisch-salischen Reichskirche*, Stuttgart, 1966, 3. Fleckenstein goes on to show that the break with tradition may not have been so radical after all. Similarly Geoffrey Barraclough argues that Henry's refusal of anointment has been over-emphasized: it was not necessarily an anticlerical declaration but merely showed his independence in general. See *Mediaeval Germany 911–1250, Essays by German Historians*, I, *Introduction*, Oxford, 1948, 36.

[5] Fleckenstein, *Hofkapelle*, II, 5.

[6] *Ibid.*, p. 6.

(Doc. 1) Simon the notary was named, but no archchaplain.[7] When Henry finally did get around to appointing an archchaplain (and by definition he thereby established a royal chapel), he chose the man from whom he had refused to receive holy oil, Archbishop Heriger of Mainz. Therefore, while Henry broke with tradition in refusing anointment, he later resumed the traditional practice of having a royal archchaplain, with the inevitable prestige for the Church that this office entailed. Although the archchaplain did not reside at court, one can assume that he was involved in the king's business.[8]

Although Henry refused anointment and delayed the establishment of a royal chapel, his reign was not entirely marked by eccentric behaviour. He was only too willing to receive the kingdom which Conrad had offered him, the kingdom of the East Franks. 'Henry I, on his elevation to the throne, ceases to be a Saxon and passes under Frankish law, adopts the traditions and takes over the powers of the Frankish kings, becomes a Frank.'[9] This Frankish kingdom, the *regnum Theutonicorum*, consisted of the eastern part of the old Carolingian empire, though Henry did not automatically obtain control over the whole territory. The act of succession conferred upon him the title of king but scarcely enlarged his realm beyond the confines of Saxony. The Frankish nobles were present and acquiesced in the choice of Henry as Conrad's successor, but their duke, Eberhard, remained virtually independent of the new king. The duchies of Bavaria and Swabia did not even send representatives to the royal ceremony.

The duchies had begun as administrative units under Charlemagne, and these units were based on tribal divisions. As Charles pushed out east in the wake of his predecessors, the old tribes were absorbed, and the duchies were immediately placed under the rule of men loyal to Charles, for the most part Frankish nobles attached to the court. Often the rulers of these duchies would come in time to identify with the people they led, a perfectly natural process, but this is not to say that the dukes inherited an organic relationship with their subjects through ancient blood ties.

The power of the duchies varied according to the personality of the duke and the amount of loyalty he could command from his local fighting nobles. In the tenth century the dukes were frequently embroiled in revolts against the monarch, yet they often belonged to the

---

[7] The name of the archchaplain, Archbishop Heriger of Mainz, was added later, but Heriger is not given the title of archchaplain in this document.

[8] It might be mentioned that the royal chaplains also had the duty of guarding the relics in the king's possession and of holding divine services at court. But we are more interested in the chancery, a subdivision of the chapel, which supervised the drafting of documents.

[9] Barraclough, *Mediaeval Germany*, I, 48.

royal family themselves. Hence the power to revolt depended on more than the mere possession of a territorial base. When a rebellion against the king is led by a man who is both the duke of Bavaria and the monarch's brother, it is difficult to say which of these relationships is the more important at a time when kinship ties and family feuds were often the springboard for acts that otherwise seem purely political.

In the thirteenth century the territorial princes did rise up and frustrate the German kings, but one of the reasons for their success is the fact that the rulers of the tenth and eleventh centuries had already solved the problem of the duchies and had moved on to the larger goals of imperial power. During the era of the Saxons and Salians the dukes schemed and often revolted, but they did not succeed in permanently appropriating regalian rights. Not until the time of Henry V, the last of the Salians (1106–25), did the ambition of the dukes begin systematically to weaken the monarch's hold upon Germany.

By skilful manœuvring Henry I was able to extract the acknowledgement of his sovereignty from Burchard, duke of Swabia and Duke Arnulf 'the Bad' of Bavaria. Then he turned to the acquisition of Lotharingia, which had been invaded by the French king Charles the Simple in 920. Henry was in no way entitled to Lotharingia, for by the Treaty of Verdun in 843 it had been accorded independent status. Nevertheless, he wanted to add it to his realm. Rather than fight the French king, he struck a bargain on 7 November 921 aboard a boat anchored in the Rhine. Henry did not acquire the territory of the Lotharingians, but he did extort recognition of himself as king of the East Franks, a significant accomplishment.

He followed it up with military and matrimonial pressure: in 923 and 924 Henry took his army into Lotharingia to fight Rudolf of Burgundy who was (like himself) encroaching upon the hapless duchy. The resident duke, Giselbert, who like a cat always landed on his feet, had come to terms with Rudolf, but when bottled up at Zülpich by Henry, he had no choice but to recognize the Saxon king. In 928 Giselbert cemented his ties with the Saxon dynasty by marrying Henry's daughter Gerberga.

Henry was equally concerned with Swabia because of its historical ties to Burgundy and Italy. Though he established his claim to royal lands in Swabia within a year after coming to power, he could not wrest control of the Swabian Church from Duke Burchard. When Burchard died in 926, Henry was at last in a position to influence Swabian affairs, and this he did by appointing as the new duke a Frank named Herman, a cousin of Duke Eberhard of Franconia.[10] By this appointment the duchy of Swabia lost its independence and came under

---

[10] Martin Lintzel, 'Heinrich I. und das Herzogtum Schwaben', *Ausgewählte Schriften*, II, Berlin, 1961, 77.

the control of the Saxon king. The new situation is revealed in the royal diplomas that began to be issued for the Swabian Church. In August of 926, Henry freed from serfdom a priest named Baldmunt who was resident at a Swabian monastery (Doc. 2). 'In the earliest times, the ministers in private churches were predominantly bondmen of the lord: anything they earned during their lifetime, therefore, went to swell the *peculium* – that is, the property invested in the domanial church – anything they left at the time of death was acquired wholly or partially by the lord.'[11] But unfree priests ceased to be the rule after the eighth century. However, once a free clergy was the rule, they came to inherit the movable property of the church which was not used for divine services. Since the lord did not wish to see any of his own private chapel property acquired by his clerk, he would sometimes have one of his serfs ordained priest, even though this practice was proscribed by the Church.

A few months later Henry granted a piece of property to the bishop of Chur (3 November 926), also in Swabia, and confirmed the rights of the abbey of St Gall (4 November 926). Three of the Swabian bishops attended the synod of Erfurt in 932, whereas only one of them had attended the synod which Henry had convened in Coblenz in 922 at a time when Burchard still controlled the Swabian clergy. The Bavarian prelates were totally absent from the synod of Erfurt, and this lack of participation reflects how Henry's influence was non-existent in Bavaria. Yet he was apparently on good terms with the Bavarian Duke Arnulf, for we find Arnulf's name as intercessor on behalf of the priest Baldmunt mentioned above. Martin Lintzel suggests that Arnulf may not have been averse to Henry's influence in Swabia, for that would prevent Henry from turning his attention to Italy where Arnulf had ambitions himself.[12]

Henry was not as lucky on the northern and eastern frontiers of his kingdom as he was on the west and south. The Danes, the Slavs, and the Hungarians were making almost continual raids across his borders. These bold and skilful barbarians required strong defensive measures if Henry was to maintain his kingdom intact. Two of his major accomplishments can be attributed to the threat of invaders – the building up of the army and the establishment of fortified towns.

In 924, according to the Saxon historian Widukind of Corvey, the Hungarians 'made such a slaughter in those days and burned so many monasteries that we have decided to pass over our calamities in silence

[11] Ulrich Stutz, 'The Proprietary Church as an Element of Mediaeval Germanic Ecclesiastical Law', in *Mediaeval Germany*, II, trans. Barraclough, Oxford, 1948, 52.

[12] Lintzel, 'Heinrich I.', p. 83.

rather than to enumerate them with words'.[13] But he did record the doleful fact that the king was forced to shut himself up in the fortress of Werla for protection, 'because he did not trust an army that was rude and unaccustomed to open war against so cruel a tribe'.[14] Luckily a Hungarian prince was taken captive by the Saxons, and in exchange for his return Henry demanded peace for nine years. In the interim he built up the army and fortified his towns so as to be prepared for future onslaughts from the east.

The fortress of Werla with its massive ramparts is an example of the structural plan that Henry was to adopt throughout Saxony.[15] However, the older view that he alone was responsible for the spread of fortified towns in Saxony has given way in the light of archaeological evidence to the conclusion that he merely adopted a style of architecture and town planning that was already in existence and put it to good advantage.[16] Henry may deserve the nickname of 'city-builder' which later writers awarded him, but only for his energy, not for his originality.

Widukind tells us how Henry organized the population during the truce with the Hungarians. He had eight out of nine men work the fields while the ninth stayed in the fortified area and managed the housing for the others. All councils and gatherings were to be held within the towns, and the citizens were disciplined to practice during peace time the skills they might need in time of war.

The result of Henry's spartan tactics was that the Saxons were so hardened to conditions of warfare that the king did not hesitate to turn his defensive policy to one of the offensive, and in the winter of 928 he invaded the territory of the Slavic Wends, capturing the town of Brandenburg. He went on to fight the Dalemintzi, a Slavic tribe on the lower Elbe, and established the fortress of Meissen as an eastern outpost. Finally, he attempted to subdue the Bohemians, who were allies of the Wends and therefore enemies of the Germans. With Duke Arnulf of Bavaria as his ally, Henry marched on Prague, ready to fight. But the reigning duke, Wenceslas, surrendered without a battle and received his

[13] *Rerum gestarum Saxonicarum Libri tres*, ed. G. Waitz *et al.*, 5th edn, Hanover, 1935, p. 45.

[14] *Ibid.*

[15] A great deal has been written about castle Werla, which is located near the Harz mountains on the bank of the river Oker, about 8 miles north-north-east of the town of Goslar. The best and most recent treatment of the remains of Werla from an archaeological point of view is that of Hermann Schroller, 'Die Ausgrabung der Pfalz Werla und ihre Probleme', in *Deutsche Königspfalzen*, II, Göttingen, 1965, 140–9, with a magnificent map (facing p. 148) and aerial photos of the site (facing p. 144).

[16] Herbert Jankuhn, ' "Heinrichsburgen" und Königspfalzen', *Deutsche Königspfalzen*, II, 67. Apparently such burgs were built from the end of the eighth to the beginning of the eleventh century and were not confined to Saxony.

country back as a fief of the German crown. Bohemia was now legally under Saxon control and had to pay a yearly tribute to Henry.

The Slavs, however, were no more inclined to remain subdued than were the Saxons when Charles the Great had attempted to crush them more than a century before. Henry, like Charles, insisted that the barbarians not only pay a yearly tribute but that they accept Christianity as well. It was the Hungarians, though, who were Henry's greatest rivals and enemies, for it was they who exacted tribute from the Saxon king, not the other way round, and in 933 the nine years' truce was up. Henry did not pay the expected tribute this time, and the Hungarians invaded his kingdom. A great battle took place near Merseburg on the river Unstrut on 15 March 933 (the location, which is named Riade by Widukind, has only been tentatively identified). After years of careful planning against these demons on horseback, Henry was ready to overwhelm them, and that is what he did. The Hungarians were beaten and fled back to their own territory. Henry kept the tribute that he had been accustomed to pay them and turned it over instead to the Church where it was to be doled out to the poor.

Widukind says that as a result of this victory Henry was hailed by the army as father of his country, lord, and *imperator*. The word *imperator* meant originally a successful general, but it later came to mean 'emperor'. It seems certain that in this context it meant only field commander, but the same word was used of Henry's son Otto the Great when he subdued the Hungarians at the even more important battle of Lechfeld in 955. Since Otto actually did bear the title of emperor after the year 962, it is tempting to read some of the majesty of the term back into the acclamation by the army in 955. But in the case of Henry in 933 such an attribution would be dubious. It must be remembered that although Henry accepted Conrad's crown and became king of the Germans, he refused both anointment and coronation. Still less does he seem to have had imperial ambitions. Though he was planning a trip to Rome at the time of his death in 936, there is no reason to suppose he meant to go there to receive the crown of the Roman Empire.

After the resounding defeat of the Hungarians at Riade, Henry deserved a rest, but the very next year, 934, the Danes attacked along the northern borders of his kingdom. This was nothing new: the Danes and Saxons were ancient enemies. Only when threatened by Charles the Great had they made common cause, for then they were defending their pagan religion as well as their traditional independence.[17] The Annals of Corvey tell us simply that in 934 Henry conquered the Danes. Widukind reports that since the king had subdued everyone else around him, he

[17] Georg Waitz, *Jahrbücher des deutschen Reichs unter König Heinrich I.*, 4th edn, Darmstadt, 1963, p. 159.

set out against the Danes, who were harassing the Frisian coast with acts of piracy; after imposing tribute on them, he compelled their king to receive baptism.

Adam of Bremen, whose chronicle of the archbishops of Hamburg–Bremen was composed in the 1070s, has a fuller and more colourful account of the Danish invasion. Though he was not an eye-witness, his story is worth repeating:

'Over the Danes there ruled at that time Harthacanute Gorm, a savage worm, I say, and not moderately hostile to the Christian people. He set about completely to destroy Christianity in Denmark, driving the priests of God from its bounds and also torturing very many of them to death.

'But then King Henry, who feared God even from his boyhood and placed all trust in His mercy, triumphed over the Hungarians in many and mighty battles. Likewise he struck down the Bohemians and the Sorbs [i.e. the Wends], who had been subdued by other kings, and the other Slavic peoples, with such force in one great encounter [Lenzen, 929] that the rest – and just a few were left – of their own accord promised the king that they would pay tribute, and God that they would be Christians.

'Then he invaded Denmark with an army and in the first battle so thoroughly terrified King Gorm that the latter pledged himself to obey his commands and, as a suppliant, sued for peace. The victorious Henry then set the bounds of the kingdom at Schleswig, which is now called Haddeby, appointed a margrave, and ordered a colony of Saxons to settle there. All these facts, related by a certain Danish bishop, a prudent man, we transmit to our Church as faithfully as we have truthfully received them.

'When our most blessed archbishop Unni saw that the door of the faith had been opened to the gentiles, he gave thanks to God for the salvation of the pagans, and more especially because the mission of the Church of Hamburg, long neglected on account of the adverse times, had with the help of God's mercy and through the valor of King Henry been given occasion and opportunity for its work.'[18]

Although Adam's version is impressionistic (for example, Haddeby and Schleswig are by no means identical), it reveals what the northern clerics thought Henry had done for the Church, and that was considerable. The Saxon king is praised over and over for his strong dynamic leadership in the face of powerful enemies. It was in the sealing of the borders and the extension of the frontiers that Henry built a sturdy foundation upon which his gifted son Otto could build.

[18] Adam of Bremen, *History of the Archbishops of Hamburg–Bremen*, trans. Francis J. Tschan, New York, 1959, pp. 49–50.

2

The Reign of Otto I (936-973)

Before Henry died he had designated his son Otto as his successor.[1] Though Otto lived scarcely longer than his father (Henry lived to the age of sixty, Otto to sixty-two), he had a much longer reign, coming to power at the age of twenty-four. Unlike his father, Otto arranged an impressive coronation at Aachen, the church built by Charles the Great, which Widukind calls 'the place of universal election' (Doc. 3). The ceremony was attended by four dukes and three archbishops, together with a large crowd of spectators.

As Widukind describes it, the great German nobles first gave their hands to Otto, promising him fealty, and thereby 'made him king according to their custom'. This preliminary ceremony took place in the portico of the church and was a purely secular affair. Then Otto proceeded into the church to receive the crown. As we see from the words of Archbishop Hildibert of Mainz, the election was already accomplished and involved only the princes. It was up to the audience within the church to approve or disapprove the choice. Of course, they noisily approved – unanimously, according to Widukind – and Archbishop Hildibert proceeded to confer the regalia upon the new king – sword, bracelets, cloak, sceptre and staff. Then Otto was anointed and crowned by Hildibert and Wikfried, archbishop of Cologne. After ascending the throne, the king heard mass, and the company adjourned to the palace, about a block away from the church, on the site of the present Aachen town-hall.

The coronation banquet that took place in the palace was arranged in such a way that Otto's major rivals in Germany symbolically served the new king: Duke Giselbert of Lotharingia was chamberlain; Duke

[1] Otto's elder half-brother Thankmar was excluded as illegitimate because his mother Hatheburg, a Wend, had vowed to take the veil upon the death of her first husband. The marriage was annulled and Henry then married Matilda. She would have preferred that her younger son, Henry, succeed to the throne, for he had been born after his father became king, but the elder son Otto was the choice of Henry himself.

Eberhard of Franconia, steward; Duke Herman of Swabia, cupbearer; and Duke Arnulf of Bavaria, marshal.[2] By their oaths of fealty in the portico and their waiting upon the new king at the banquet, the reign began auspiciously with every sign of unity and co-operation for a 'greater Germany'. As we shall see, these early hopes were later somewhat dampened.

Otto inherited his father's problems along with the crown. 'For in those days', reports Widukind, 'the Saxons were afflicted with many enemies, the Slavs to the east, the Franks to the south, the Lotharingians to the west, the Danes and also the Slavs to the north: on account of this the barbarians drew out the long struggle' (Doc. 4). Perhaps the most baffling of these enemies were the Slavs, for according to Widukind they preferred war to peace and discomfort to comfort: 'What seems to us a heavy burden the Slavs held as a kind of pleasure.'

Otto had planted enclaves of Saxons in the eastern marches to defend the borders, and the commanders of these units were Herman Billung to the north and Count Gero to the south. The importance of these marcher lords can hardly be overestimated.

'Herman and Gero were the two men who, throughout the reign of Otto, by their untiring efforts not only kept the Wends in check, but established German authority on a firm footing in the marches between the Elbe and the Oder; they relieved the king of a difficult task, enabling him thereby to turn his whole attention to his policy of centralizing the government, of extending the royal influence, and later of adding Italy to his dominions and of restoring the imperial title.'[3]

Gero has been called 'one of the greatest and bravest men of this iron era, a tireless warrior of Germany against the Slavs'.[4] In October 955, after years of service, Gero decisively defeated the Uchri, one of the Slavic tribes, and was rewarded by a grant of land from the king (Docs. 4 and 5). From the start Otto's promotion of Gero did not go down well with his own half-brother Thankmar. Thankmar, who had been excluded from the throne in 936, thought the eastern territory (later known as the Mark of Gero) should be awarded to himself. As a result of Gero's

[2] Similarly at the Carolingian court the service of the king included such offices as chamberlain, seneschal (or steward), and cupbearer, which were symbolically important. 'Since this empire consists of many lands,' says Hincmar of Reims, 'care was taken that the servants were chosen from various lands so that the individual territories might the more confidently appeal to the palace if they knew that their leading families and compatriots had a place at court.'

[3] Austin Lane Poole, *The Cambridge Medieval History*, III, *Germany and the Western Empire*, Cambridge, 1964, 187.

[4] Rudolf Köpke and Ernst Dümmler, *Kaiser Otto der Grosse*, Darmstadt, 1962, p. 386.

appointment, Thankmar joined the rebellion led by Duke Eberhard of Franconia in 938.[5]

Eberhard, like the other dukes, had pledged his loyalty to the young king and had served him at the coronation banquet, but it is unlikely that any of the dukes wished to transport ceremonial deference into real life. Henry the Fowler had been content to be titular head of the Germans, while his territory was actually confined to Saxony. Otto, however, was not going to leave the dukes their convenient independence.

Otto's younger brother Henry also threw in his lot with Eberhard. We learn of this defection from several sources, the most interesting being that of Hroswitha (Doc. 6), because she was at such pains to underplay it. She ascribes Henry's disloyal behaviour to the work of the devil and overlooks the fact that, with or without diabolic influence, it amounted to treason. Hroswitha was in an awkward position to write a history of Otto's reign, for her superior at the convent of Gandersheim was Abbess Gerberga, the daughter of the wayward Duke Henry.[6] In the opening lines of the *Gesta Ottonis*, Hroswitha tells us that it was Gerberga who imposed upon her the task of recounting the events of the reign of Otto, Gerberga's uncle. We can understand her dilemma, which she describes in Dantesque terms:

'I was like a stranger wandering without a guide through the depth of an unknown forest where every path was covered over and mantled with heavy snow. In vain he tries to follow the directions of those who are showing the way only by a nod. Now he wanders through pathless ways, now by chance he comes upon the trail of the right path, until at length, when he has traversed half of the thick-treed domain, he attains the peace of long-sought rest. There staying his step, he dares not proceed farther, until either he is led on by someone overtaking him or follows the footsteps of one who has preceded him. In like manner, I, bidden to undertake a complete chronicle of illustrious achievements, have gone on my way stumbling and hesitating, so great was the difficulty of finding a path in the forest of these royal deeds.'

Quite likely the abbess assigned this task to her talented pupil in order to smooth over the awkwardness of Duke Henry's revolt. The poem was to be submitted to Archbishop William of Mainz, primate of Germany and Gerberga's superior. William was the illegitimate half-brother of Otto, and was loyal to the throne. He could act as a suitable

[5] Another member of the rebellion was Wichmann, elder brother of Herman Billung, who administered the eastern mark north of Gero's territory.
[6] *Hroswitha of Gandersheim. Her Life, Times, and Works, and a Comprehensive Bibliography*, ed. Anne Lyon Haight, New York, 1965, p. 8.

intercessor for the abbess of Gandersheim and patch up whatever hard feelings might have existed between the emperor and his niece. The nunnery could only be the beneficiary. This motive explains the fulsome praise throughout the *Gesta Ottonis*, especially the astronomical metaphors: 'Otto . . . shone as the morning star, beaming with a radiance of goodness famed far and wide. . . . Upon him the King of Heaven bestowed gifts of such sweet grace that he, worthily distinguished in all respects, eclipsed by the renown of his achievements all the kings whom the ocean with its reciprocal waves enfolds.'

Otto's younger brother Bruno is called the wisest man alive, and Otto's first wife, Edith, daughter of Edward the Elder, is rated by the English as 'the best of all women who existed at the time'. That the disloyal brother Henry is not described in superlatives may therefore be interpreted as at least a mental reservation. He is merely 'illustrious', 'a brave leader', and 'a courageous fighter'. Similarly Liudulf, the child of Otto's first wife, is called modestly 'a son worthy of such parents'. Liudulf, like his uncle Henry, was a rebel, a trouble maker, and a trial to Otto, though Otto seems to have been reluctant to brand him a traitor.[7] If we cut in half what Hroswitha says about the dynasty, we can see that she does in fact make distinctions among the members of the family. Though at first glance the *Gesta Ottonis* would seem to consist of pure panegyric, in fact the author is somewhat discriminating within the limits of her difficult assignment.

The rebellions of Otto's kinsmen and rivals illustrate the difficulty he had in forcing the dukes to submit to the royal will. Arnulf of Bavaria died the year after the coronation, and his sons refused to honour their father's promise of fealty. Otto invaded Bavaria in 938 to put them down, banished one of the sons, Arnulf, leader of the revolt, but was later reconciled with him. He not only allowed Arnulf to return but made him Count Palatine with the responsibility of looking after royal interests in Bavaria. This was not the only time that Otto forgave and even rewarded his malcontent rivals. Whether it was a wise policy or not is arguable.

[7] Actually most of the section dealing with Liudulf's rebellion has been lost, but we know from other sources that it was not a casual defection. Hroswitha tells of the happy reunion between Otto and Liudulf, when all was forgiven, though she suppresses the fact that the duchy of Swabia was taken away from the delinquent son and was not restored. Hroswitha may have been trying to show that Henry was not the only one of Otto's relatives who was led astray by the devil and bad advisers. Then he alone would not bear the stigma of disloyalty. Conversely, since Henry's reputation was to be rehabilitated by the poem, Liudulf's revolt would also have to be whitewashed to make a plausible 'history' of the reign. Henry was actually more active against Otto than was Liudulf. Therefore unless Hroswitha wanted to distort the rebellions violently, she would perforce have to regard Liudulf with some tolerance.

During the same year Duke Eberhard of Franconia revolted and seized the city of Hellmern, burning the town and putting the citizens to death. Otto merely fined the offender 100 pounds of silver and insulted him: his companions had to carry dogs to the royal palace in Magdeburg.[8] Thereafter Eberhard escalated his rebellion and was joined by Otto's half-brother Thankmar. Together they took the king's brother Henry prisoner in the Saxon fortress of Eresburg. However, the townspeople remained loyal to the king and opened their gates. For kidnapping the king's brother, Thankmar was slain and Eberhard was imprisoned at Hildesheim. Before Henry was released, however, he had entered into a compact with Eberhard against Otto in which Henry was to become the new king.

In 939 Duke Giselbert of Lotharingia, though married to Otto's sister Gerberga, joined the rebellion, and the king was forced to fight a battle at Birthen on the Rhine. Otto won a stunning victory, probably because of clever tactics, though the success was attributed to his possession of the Holy Lance.[9] The fighting continued, and later in the same year the rebels were joined by the French king Louis d'Outremer, son of Charles the Simple. Louis hoped to regain Lotharingia for France but he had antagonized so many of his major vassals that they promised their support to Otto. Battles took place as far west as Laon, only 87 miles north-east of Paris.

At the height of the rebellion, Archbishop Frederick of Mainz joined the opposition against the king, and it looked as if Otto would have trouble controlling even Saxony. Fortunately for him Duke Eberhard was killed in battle, and Duke Giselbert was drowned, after which the wind quickly went out of the sails of the remaining rebels. Henry was pardoned but repaid his brother's largesse by conniving at a scheme to assassinate Otto in 941. Even after this outrage the king was able once again to forgive his errant brother.

With the death of the dukes of Lotharingia and Franconia, Otto was in a position to attach these duchies more closely to the royal interests, and this he did by governing Franconia himself and by marrying off his daughter Liutgard to the newly appointed duke of Lotharingia, Conrad the Red. More dynastic marriages followed: Otto's brother Henry married a daughter of Arnulf and thereby became duke of Bavaria; his son

---

[8] Köpke-Dümmler, *Kaiser Otto der Grosse*, p. 63. The fine was a stiff one, and it was to be paid in horses. The carrying of a dog through the street was an old Germanic punishment.

[9] The Lance – holy because it supposedly contained a nail from the Cross – was obtained by Henry the Fowler from Rudolf II of Burgundy. It also figures prominently in Otto's crucial victory over the Hungarians at Lechfeld in 955. See Percy Ernst Schramm, 'Die "Heilige Lanze" ', in *Herrschaftszeichen und Staatssymbolik*, II, Stuttgart, 1955, 492–537.

Liudulf acquired Swabia by marrying the daughter of Duke Herman.
These marriages, taking place between 947 and 949, mark a respite if
not an end to revolt.

Otto was beginning to get a grip on the duchies, to exercise the power
of a German king rather than a Saxon duke. This gradual extension of
influence can be seen in the royal diplomas of the period. Up to 942 they
were issued only from Saxony and Franconia; in that year Otto began
issuing them from Lotharingia; in 952 from Swabia; and finally from
Bavaria in 953.[10] Another sign of the early weakness of Otto's hold on
the monarchy is that the office of archchaplain was filled simultaneously
by the archbishops of Mainz, Trier, Cologne, and Salzburg, a senseless
and unprecedented division of the title that can only mean Otto was
unable to refuse the requests of his most powerful bishops.[11] Eventually
the royal chapel underwent a significant change: it was enlarged and
became a new institution, 'a headquarters of imperial policy and in a
certain sense the centre of the imperial church'.[12]

On 30 March 951, while celebrating Easter at Aachen, Otto made
the fateful decision to go to Italy. Again the question of 'why?' in-
evitably comes to mind, and has been variously answered. For one thing
he was now *able* to go, since the German duchies were not in a state of
rebellion, though Conrad the Red of Lotharingia and the king's son
Liudulf were to revolt a few years later. The confines of Germany were
more or less secure. In the east, under the protection of marcher lords,
the Slavs were being held at bay, while the king's brother Henry, now
the loyal duke of Bavaria, had beaten the Hungarians and added the
territory of Aquileia to the German crown. There was nothing spec-
tacular to be gained by pushing still farther east, and Otto's campaigns
in the west against the French in the 940s had been indecisive. To the
south lay Italy, the seat of ancient Rome and the papacy, with both
memories and wealth. Otto did not *have* to go to Italy; it was merely a
tempting possibility.[13]

The so-called 'Italian policy' has been the subject of much debate on
the part of scholars seeking to evaluate the accomplishments of the
German emperors. Modern historians have often pointed to the debacle
of 1268, with the following interregnum and the attendant breakdown
of central power in Germany, as one of the principal causes for the
failure of the German people to achieve statehood before the mid-
nineteenth century. Yet to judge the Italian policy on the basis of later

[10] Fleckenstein, *Hofkapelle*, II, 18.
[11] *Ibid.*, pp. 22–3.
[12] *Ibid.*, p. 18.
[13] This is the gist of Martin Lintzel, 'Die Kaiserpolitik Ottos des Grossen',
in *Ausgewählte Schriften*, II, Berlin, 1961, 142–208, partially translated in
Boyd H. Hill, Jr, *The Rise of the First Reich*, New York, 1969, pp. 85–96.

developments and the frustration of modern German nationalists does not help to elucidate the problems of the tenth and eleventh centuries.

Otto I's reign was modelled on that of Charlemagne. His coronation at Aachen, the seat of Carolingian power, was no accident. The influence of Charles can be exaggerated, but it was undeniably a powerful precedent towards Italian involvement. Moreover, the imperial crown was the traditional prerequisite for rule over the Middle Kingdom, including Burgundy and Lotharingia. In order to receive the crown from the hands of the pope, it was customary for the candidate to go to Rome. Before this step could be taken, it was usual to claim the title of king of Italy in the Lombard capital of Pavia. In order to descend upon Lombardy the German monarch needed only to accept one of the frequent appeals by various Italian magnates, the greatest of whom was the pope himself.

Just as each emperor tended to define his place in world history by his position as a local or a universal Christian monarch, so too each emperor had his own attitude towards Italy. Henry III's actions were often determined by his straightforward attempts to reform the Church. His riding roughshod over the disputing popes represents his concern for clerical reform more than any ambition to control the papacy *per se*. The fact that Henry's efforts paid off, that the papacy grew strong, and that a militant papacy was the principal cause of the failure of the later Hohenstaufen in the thirteenth century cannot be said to represent a miscalculation on the part of Henry III. Likewise the involvement of earlier German kings in Italy cannot be judged an unfortunate policy from the outset.

In short, one must distinguish as far as possible between events, motives, and ideals. The Italian policy of the emperors proved ultimately a disaster, but it is not necessary to brand the early deeds of the German monarchs as the cause of it. The most influential model of all for the emperors of the tenth and eleventh centuries was the Roman Empire. A successful nation-state was not an exciting prospect; an empire was. Given this fact, the policy of ambitious German rulers falls into place. Going to Italy was a journey towards empire.

The immediate pretext for the invasion of Italy by Otto I was the death of King Lothar in 950.[14] Lothar's widow Adelaide was deprived of her claim to the throne when Berengar, the marquess of Ivrea, had himself crowned king of Italy on 15 December 950 at Pavia, the Lombard capital. Adelaide was threatened by the ambitious Berengar, who put her in prison after she refused to marry his son Adalbert. Otto

---

[14] Lothar was called 'king of Italy', though his territory did not contain the whole peninsula but only the northern portion.

boldly entered Pavia, had himself crowned king of the Lombards, and married Adelaide (his first wife, Edith, had died in 946).

Charles the Great had also married a Lombard noblewoman for dynastic reasons, the daughter of King Desiderius, but he repudiated her and turned to warfare to implement his Italian policy. Charles besieged Pavia in 773, and when King Desiderius surrendered in 774, Lombardy passed under Frankish control. Otto's position was somewhat different from that of his great Frankish predecessor, for by marrying Adelaide he engendered rebellion at home, and this caused him to cut short his Pavian adventure and return to Germany. Liudulf in particular was unhappy, for he feared that the new marriage would produce children who would brush aside his own hereditary claim to the throne.

Liudulf, Conrad of Lotharingia, and Archbishop Frederick of Mainz joined in a conspiracy against the king with the result that in 953–4 all the duchies were in revolt. Otto's strongest and most successful ally during this rebellion was his brother Bruno, archbishop of Cologne, and the latter part of Otto's reign is marked by a greater reliance upon the clergy for support.

'Under both the Ottonian and the Salian dynasties, right down to the beginning of the Investiture Contest, Germany was ruled through the Church alone.' These fundamental words of Paul Joachimsen should perhaps be memorized: nowhere do the prejudices of modern life work so much havoc for the student as in the area of what we today call Church–State relations. It is as difficult for us to comprehend this fact as it is to bear in mind that the Ptolemaic earth-centred universe was really accepted by scientists and theologians alike in the Middle Ages.

One might even tell students that Church and State simply did not exist as separate entities, and although this would be an exaggeration, it might be justified as a pedagogical device. The Church can neither be defined as a department of government (since there was no central administration comparable to Byzantium or to the twelfth- and thirteenth-century bureaucracies of England and France), nor can it be described as an institution independent of the monarchy.

Thus for the period covered in this work, the role of the king was as grand advocate; the bishops served him, and he utilized their resources without being accused of despoiling with secular hands the things of the Lord. On the contrary, the close-knit relation between clergy and monarch which the Ottonians inherited from their Carolingian predecessors made the interdependence between king and Church a traditional one. The bond between throne and altar persisted as the principal tool for giving men peace on earth and salvation after death, until the reforms of the Gregorians in the late eleventh century.

When the uprising of 953–4 failed, Otto deprived both Conrad and Liudulf of their duchies. One of the reasons for the unpopularity of the revolt was that the conspirators had openly courted the help of the Hungarians, who had readily entered Bavaria with great expectations. As soon as the rebellion had been crushed, Otto was compelled to drive out the tenacious Hungarians, and a famous battle was fought at Lechfeld near Augsburg on 10 August 955.[15]

By the end of the decade Otto had consolidated the duchies under the king, secured the frontiers against invading barbarians, and attracted the bishops into his service. In 960 when Pope John XII called upon Otto to journey to Italy in order to rescue the papacy from the threat of Berengar, he was then in a position to accept the challenge (Doc. 7).

Charles the Great had gone to Rome almost two centuries earlier under similar circumstances. Summoned by Pope Hadrian I to expel the invading Lombard king Desiderius, Charles entered Rome at Eastertime 774. The *Liber Pontificalis* tells us that he renewed certain charters for the papacy which had been drawn up by his father Pippin around 754. The land donated to St Peter included vast areas of Italy over which Charles did not have control. For this reason the diploma was for a time suspected of being a forgery.

As we shall see, Otto's dealings with the papacy in 962 bear an astonishing resemblance to those of Charles in 774, even to the charge of forgery in connection with the document that resulted. This diploma, known as the *Ottonianum* (Doc. 8), has occasioned a great deal of speculation in print, the basic treatment being that of Theodor Sickel.[16] Sickel, who edited the diplomas of Otto for the *Monumenta*, gained access to the papal archives as soon as they were opened to the public and declared, after painstaking analysis, that the document was genuine. However, the problems raised by the text still await a definitive solution.[17] Otto, like Charles, did not control the Italian lands that he guaranteed to the pope, even though he had been crowned emperor in St Peter's on 2 February 962 (Doc. 7). The crux of the argument appears in paragraphs 15–19 of the *Ottonianum*, in which the new emperor extracts a sworn promise from the populace of Rome that they would not

---

[15] Widukind's account of the battle of Lechfeld is available in English translation in Brian Pullan, *Sources for the History of Medieval Europe from the mid-eighth to the mid-thirteenth century*, Oxford, 1966, pp. 116–17, and in a longer excerpt in Oliver J. Thatcher and Edgar Holmes McNeal, *A Source Book for Mediaeval History*, New York, 1905, pp. 75–7, and Hill, *Rise of the First Reich*, pp. 15–18.

[16] *Das Privilegium Otto I. für die römische Kirche*, Innsbruck, 1883.

[17] Sickel's monograph on the *Ottonianum* does not duplicate the clarity and order of the edited diplomas, though it undoubtedly contained the last word on the subject at the time of its publication.

C

elect a pope until he had been notified by his legates and that the papal candidate must also swear an oath to the emperor's son or legates. The force of this so-called *sacramentum* is that the emperor would henceforth have ultimate control over papal elections. How could Otto be in a position to stipulate such a condition when he himself had to take an oath to Pope John in December 961, before the pope invited him into the city of Rome ?[18] The question has been variously and voluminously answered since Sickel's day, one of the more ingenious conjectures being that the paragraphs which contain the oath must have been interpolated later when the emperor had indeed secured control of the papacy.[19]

John XII's debauchery was notorious (see Liudprand's scurrilous attack in Doc. 7), though it was his insubordination that led to his downfall. Otto, now the anointed emperor of the Roman Empire, was not about to be deprived of the ancient capital by a scheming pope. In the autumn of 963, after invading Rome with an army, he deposed John at a synod which Liudprand describes in detail (Doc. 7). On the same day (4 December 963) a layman was elected Pope Leo VIII. This man, formerly chief notary (*protoscriniarius*) of the papal chancery, was more compliant than John, and readily accepted the papacy on the tacit assumption that the office would be subordinate to that of the emperor. Otto had no legal right to depose John, but once accomplished, the deed had important consequences for papal–imperial relations. 'The Emperor's new right to confirm the papal election reduced the Bishop of Rome to a momentous dependence.'[20]

[18] The oath which Otto took (actually his representative took it) is the following: 'I, Otto, king, cause my representative to promise and swear to you, Pope John, in my name, by the Father, Son, and Holy Spirit, and by this piece of life-giving cross and by these relics of the saints, that, if I shall come to Rome with the consent of God, I will exalt the holy Roman church and you, her ruler, to the best of my ability. And you shall never by my wish, advice, consent, or instigation, suffer any loss in life or in limb, or in the honor which you now have or which you shall have obtained from me. I will never make laws or rules in regard to the things which are under your jurisdiction or the jurisdiction of the Romans without your consent. I will restore to you all the lands of St Peter that shall have come into my hands; and I will cause the one to whom I shall have committed Italy to rule in my absence to swear to you that he will always aid you according to his ability in defending the lands of St Peter' (Thatcher and McNeal, *Source Book*, pp. 114–15).
[19] Walter Ullmann, 'The Origins of the *Ottonianum*', *Cambridge Historical Journal*, XI (1953), 114–28. Not everyone agrees with Ullmann's thesis (e.g. Friedrich Kempf *et al.*, *The Church in the Age of Feudalism*, trans. Anselm Biggs, New York, 1969, p. 209, n. 8), but unanimous approval has not been granted to any scholar since Sickel, whose monograph can more easily be praised than read.
[20] Kempf, *The Church in the Age of Feudalism*, p. 209.

In fact, it was not until the time of Otto's grandson, Otto III, that the German emperor could designate a pope at his pleasure and have some assurance that the Romans would not repudiate him. Meanwhile John XII would not stay deposed, but bided his time outside the ancient capital until the fickle Romans turned against the foreign monarch. While Otto was absent in Spoleto, Pope Leo was deposed by a synod of the very prelates who had selected him, and John was reinstated. But he lived only a few months, and upon his death the Romans (against the stipulations of the *Ottonianum*) wished to elect the Cardinal Deacon Benedict. A delegation was despatched to intercept Otto, who was on the road to Rome with his army, to obtain his permission. He refused, according to the *Liber Pontificalis*, and is reported to have replied: 'When I lay down my sword, then I will also give permission that Lord Pope Leo never again ascend the chair of St Peter.'[21]

Undaunted, the Romans proceeded to elect Benedict V (a learned man, nicknamed 'the grammarian') and swore never to abandon him but to defend him against the imperial might.[22] On account of this defiance Otto blockaded Rome until, starved into submission, the city capitulated on 23 June 964, and Leo VIII was restored to the papal chair. Otto returned to Germany in 965. In March of that year upon the death of Leo, the Romans, chastened by the siege of the preceding year, waited for instructions from the emperor before electing a new pope. Otto sent two legates to Rome (one of them being Liudprand), and a new pope was canonically chosen – John XIII.

Very early in John's reign, however, a new anti-imperial faction began to form under the leadership of the urban prefect Peter. The pope was seized and imprisoned in the Castel Sant'Angelo (the ancient tomb of Hadrian), and then banished. Consequently Otto arranged a second trip to Italy and crossed the Alps by the Septimer pass in late August of 966. On 10 November, Otto restored John to the papacy after some ten months of exile. Peter, the head of the conspiracy, was captured while trying to escape and was turned over to Pope John, who showed him no mercy. First his beard was cut off, and he was suspended by his own hair from the equestrian statue of Marcus Aurelius; then he was taken down, stripped of his clothing, and set backwards upon a donkey, after which he was led in disgrace around the city; at long last he was banished beyond the Alps.[23] A dozen or so of the conspirators were hanged, some were blinded, and two dead rebels were exhumed and their bones destroyed. The pre-eminence of the emperor had been re-established, but at a terrible price which the Romans were not soon to forget.

The claims of universality on the part of the German emperor could

[21] Köpke-Dümmler, *Kaiser Otto der Grosse*, p. 361.
[22] *Ibid.*, p. 362.   [23] *Ibid.*, p. 412.

not be maintained if Rome were independent of his control. Precisely how universal was Otto's idea of empire can be disputed. Certainly the regalia, the ceremonies, the official diplomatic forms all point to a kind of revival of Roman imperial affectations, but whether these symbols reflect the realities of German ambitions is another story. Did Otto and his successors understand the *imperium* as a broad claim to rule over many peoples with different habits and customs, who were united by the person of the ruler and by the ideology of empire and Christianity ? The emperors themselves, busy with everyday affairs, were seldom explicit, but the sense of empire did exist quite early and was articulated by writers like Hroswitha and Gerbert.

When the empire was first revived on Christmas Day 800, the pope considered that he was creating an ally in Charlemagne and that the Frankish emperor would help the papacy to realize its claim to universal rule over all Christians. Instead, the renewed empire accreted much of the authority in western Europe that theoretically was to be lodged in the see of St Peter. As the empire gained new vitality under the Saxons in the tenth century, the fortunes of the papacy suffered another eclipse, and for a century it seemed as if the pope were to play servant to the emperor rather than the reverse.

One of the ways in which Otto demonstrated his imperial authority was to adjudicate legal problems and to grant deeds and other diplomas. In Ravenna, in time for Easter (31 March 967), he spent over a month in this ancient town dispensing imperial justice. One case concerned Peter, archbishop of Ravenna, who charged that a deacon named Rainerius had invaded his diocese, put him in chains, and plundered his church (Doc. 9). Otto and Pope John XIII presided in court when the case was heard, and since the defendant, Rainerius, did not appear when summoned for the third time, his property was awarded to the archbishop. At the beginning of the document which contains the proceedings Otto styles himself 'most pious enduring august Lord Otto, great pacific emperor crowned by God', a somewhat high-flown intitulation when compared with the simple designation of his first diploma in 936, 'Otto king by divine clemency'.[24] After the names of the emperor and pope come the other members of the court – bishops, dukes, counts, and various clerical and lay officials, altogether an impressive assembly. Peter's case is stated by his attorney, Lord Ursus. No discussion is presented, merely the fact that Rainerius by refusing to appear has forfeited his property. To insure that Peter keeps it, a fine of 2,000 gold

[24] Intitulation is the technical diplomatic term for the name and title of the donor or person issuing the document. See Herwig Wolfram, *Intitulatio*, I, *Lateinische Königs- und Fürstentitel bis zum Ende des 8. Jahrhunderts*, Vienna, 1967.

mancusi is levied against anyone who should presume to take it away from him, half to go to the imperial fisc and half to Archbishop Peter.[25]

In the autumn of 967 at Verona, Otto was reunited with his son and namesake, a boy of twelve who had already been crowned king. On 29 October an imperial diet for Italy took place in the suburb of S. Zeno to settle some questions of perennial dispute, for example, whether a simple oath on the Gospels would suffice to establish the right of property. If one of the parties accused the other's title of being forged, the matter was now to be decided through trial by combat. Another conclusion of the diet was that sons of bishops, priests, and deacons were forbidden from ever becoming notaries, mayors, counts, or judges.

After celebrating All Soul's Day in Verona, the emperor and his son went to Mantua, but before leaving, Otto gave a sum of money to Rather, bishop of Verona, to reimburse him for the visit of the royal court to his city, the gift to be applied to the building of the church of S. Zeno.[26] Rather also received a comprehensive privilege for his bishopric (Doc. 10). At the request of his son, Otto added to the possessions of the church the tolls of town gate and river bank as well as market rights. He also gave the church the right to try the offences of tenants living on its lands.

Rather was a man of great literary ability and small diplomatic skill. Born in Liége (Lotharingia) and raised for the monastery, he became a virtual exile because of the political vicissitudes of the times. First consecrated bishop of Verona in 931, he became so disillusioned that when Duke Arnulf the Bad of Bavaria invaded Italy in 934, Rather welcomed him with open arms. Arnulf was defeated by King Hugh, and Rather was imprisoned at Walbert Tower in Pavia. Eventually he was able to return to Lotharingia. In 946 he again functioned as bishop of Verona, but his authority was always questioned by the unruly Italians, and in 948 he was deprived of his see once more.[27] In 952 he tutored Otto's brother Bruno, chancellor of the royal chapel and eventually archbishop of Cologne. At court he was rated among the palace philoso-

---

[25] The *mancusus* was a gold coin of either Arab or Italo-Byzantine origin. See Philip Grierson, 'Carolingian Europe and the Arabs: the Myth of the Mancus', *Revue belge de philologie et d'histoire*, XXXII (1954), 1059–74.

[26] Rather, who was not noted for subtle flattery, said that the presence of the king had consumed all he possessed. See Georg Waitz, *Deutsche Verfassungsgeschichte*, 2nd edn, VIII, Graz, 1955, 229. It required 30 pounds of silver to support Otto's court for a day, or 10,000 pounds for a year; in 968 his retinue is said to have consumed 1000 swine and sheep, 10 *Fuder* (= 2,700 gallons) of wine and an equal amount of beer, and 1,000 measures of grain, among other commodities. See James Westfall Thompson, *Feudal Germany*, I, New York, 1962, 339.

[27] Eleanor Duckett, *Death and Life in the Tenth Century*, Ann Arbor, 1967, pp. 309–10.

phers (*inter palatinos philosophos primus*) though his position seems to have been that of a teacher.[28]

In 953, Rather was appointed bishop of Liége, but he had to give it up in 955 when the local count replaced him with his own nephew. This time he found employment with Otto's natural son William, archbishop of Mainz. When Otto went to Italy in 961, he succeeded in having Rather reinstalled as bishop of Verona for the third time, in which post he remained until 968. During all this misfortune and displacement Rather turned to writing for solace and expression of his pent-up feelings. His *Praeloquia* are a veritable little world of tenth-century people of all classes, with especially biting comments about the derelict Italian clergy.[29]

On 2 December 967, Otto renewed the treaty with the Venetians, which had been ratified in 814 by Charles the Great and the Byzantine emperor Leo V. Venice had become a bone of contention between the Eastern and Western empires. Though the Venetians spoke a dialect of Latin and acknowledged the pope in Rome as head of the Church, they had been politically subordinate to Byzantium for centuries. The prestige of the Eastern empire among western Europeans was enormous, for the citizens of Byzantium held the traditional title of 'Romans' (*Romaioi*), which they acquired when Constantine moved his capital from Rome to Constantinople. The inhabitants of Charlemagne's empire, on the other hand, had no common name, and their emperor could not claim to be the legitimate successor of Constantine or Justinian. At first under Byzantine rule, Venice had gradually attained *de facto* independence, and in 805 the Venetian doge paid homage to Charles, which was interpreted as an act of defiance in Constantinople.[30] A Greek fleet was dispatched to the upper Adriatic, provoking the Venetians to defend their semi-independent status and creating more tension between East and West. In 810 Charlemagne's eldest son Pippin, who was king of Lombardy, answered the call of the Venetian doges to enter the province in order to put down both internal and external enemies.[31]

The expedition was a fiasco, since the Venetians fought for their liberty against the Franks. At this time Byzantium found it convenient to come to some agreement over the contested province. A Byzantine legate was sent all the way to Aachen to offer Charles an imperial peace

[28] Fleckenstein, *Hofkapelle*, II, 46, quoting the history of the abbots of Lobbes, the Lotharingian monastery in which Rather was educated.

[29] A small excerpt in translation appears in Robert Sabatino Lopez, *The Tenth Century: How Dark the Dark Ages?* (Source Problems in World Civilization), New York, 1959, p. 34.

[30] *The Cambridge Medieval History*, IV, *The Byzantine Empire*, Cambridge, 1966, 257–8.

[31] *Ibid.*, p. 259.

– that is, recognition that he was emperor of the Western empire. A treaty was then drawn up resolving problems of travel, tolls, and extradition. The independence of Venetia was guaranteed, though it was still nominally under Byzantine control. An important chapter in European history was closed: Venice never suffered from the meddling of the East again.

The renewal pact of 967 (one of many such) was requested by the Venetian doge Peter Candiano IV (Doc. 11). The question of regulations between Venice and her neighbours was still very much alive, even though the threat of Byzantine interference was a dead issue. Questions about refugees, captives, and wergild remained controversial and had to be negotiated. 'Even when she was obliged to surrender the extra-territoriality of her citizens within the Western empire to Otto the Great, she obtained in return the perpetuity of her treaty with him.'[32]

Certain conclusions can be drawn from this document. Like the vast number of similar renewals, whether about land or about privileges governing trade, transport, and the treatment of felons, the stipulations duplicate to a great extent the work of the Carolingians. This fact is a strong point in the argument that Otto was unoriginal and that he merely continued the traditions and ambitions of his great predecessor Charles the Great, that Charles was in fact a model and guide for Otto throughout his career. On the other hand, it would be surprising if Otto had thrown out all previous legislation and inaugurated a totally new system of imperial dispensation. This sort of innovation would have been unthinkable. The diplomas granted to counts and bishops, abbots and popes, were retained all over medieval Europe by the successors of the grantees, who not only wanted them reconfirmed by any new and powerful monarch but if possible extended in scope at every reissue. The property-holders of the tenth century were no different from those of the twentieth in their unwillingness to yield an inch of ground or a 'tax break' or a special immunity. Otto could scarcely be expected to expropriate lands and revoke privileges at will in a wholesale fashion; nor could Charles the Great. The changes in the diplomas from reign to reign are more subtle than that. Perhaps the emperor allows a given abbey the right to elect its own abbot but retains the ultimate veto power in the choice (we see this under Henry II). Or perhaps the lands of an abbey, guaranteed in an ancient deed, are reassigned to a bishopric, thus amounting to a political favour for the bishop but doing no literal violation to the terms of the diploma (this was also a favourite ploy of Henry II).

The proper study of diplomas requires minute attention to details. Not only must the content – the 'disposition' – be scrutinized, but also

[32] C. W. Previté-Orton, *Cambridge Medieval History*, III, 170.

the time and place of issue, the intitulation of the monarch or other grantor, the changing of stipulations by the insertion of new clauses, the names of notaries and chaplains – those who 'authenticated' the act. From all these minutiae we can tell whether the territory of the kingdom is being expanded or whittled away: the ruler does not ordinarily issue documents from lands in which he has no power. The name of the 'recognoscent', the man who guarantees that the document is valid because he has seen it (either personally or through a representative), tells us who is important at court among the clergy. If there are four archchaplains, as in the early days of Otto's reign, we assume that they are influential with the king; if the position devolves upon the king's brother alone (as it did on Bruno in 951 even before he had become bishop), it is a sign that the king has now asserted his authority over the royal chapel.[33]

The study of diplomas must be a comparative one, for a deed cannot be meaningfully studied in isolation. The more information we have about the subject of the document, the better. A case in point is Otto's project of creating an archbishopric in Magdeburg as an eastern outpost of missionary activity among the pagan Slavs. We know that he formed this plan as early as 954, but he did not carry it out until 968. Why? The document of donation alone does not give us the answer (Doc. 12). To be sure, he needed papal permission, but this he received from Pope John XII shortly after the imperial coronation in 962. The chief impediment was Archbishop William of Mainz, in whose jurisdiction Magdeburg lay. Although a natural son of the king, he did not want to surrender the claims of Mainz to the Magdeburg church just to please his father. When he died in 968, Otto replaced him with Hatto, Abbot of Fulda, a nephew and strong supporter of the royal house. When we investigate the background of the diploma concerning Magdeburg, we can see that Otto did not have absolute control of his bishops, that it proved easier to acquire a privilege from the pope than to gain the support of the archbishop of Mainz. It is easy to see why: the pope was not a rival of the archbishop of Mainz. He had everything to gain from allowing the German monarch to Christianize the Slavs. From the point of view of the archbishop of Mainz, however, the position was quite the reverse: he had nothing to gain from the erection of this new archbishopric; he would merely be forfeiting revenue and prestige.

When Otto was finally able to realize his dream by appointing an archbishop, he chose the remarkable Adalbert from the monastery of St Maximin at Trier (Lotharingia), who had functioned as a notary in the royal chancery and then as missionary to the Russians. Sent to Kiev in answer to the request in 959 of Olga, widow of Duke Igor of

[33] Fleckenstein, *Hofkapelle*, II, 31.

Kiev, he found upon his arrival that the pious duchess had been succeeded by her son, who was not interested in the missionizing of Russia,
and so he returned to Germany.[34] In Adalbert, Otto had a distinguished
archbishop for Magdeburg; it was he who continued the chronicle of
Regino of Prüm, covering the years 907–67.[35]

It will be noted in the diploma that the emperor does not allow the
choice of archbishop to be made by anyone but himself. However, he
does allow some leeway in the appointment of bishops to the three sees
that would be subordinate to Adalbert's – Meissen, Merseburg, and
Zeitz.[36] The venerable Boso, missionary to the Slavs, is to have either
Merseburg or Zeitz, whichever he prefers, and the other is to be assigned
by Archbishop Adalbert with the approval of the emperor.[37]

Otto's control over the German prelates in 968 was not complete, but
it was more effective than at the time of his coronation. Some of the
bishops, like the secular magnates, fell away in revolt during the first
half of his reign. The primate of Germany, Frederick of Mainz (d. 954),
figures prominently: '. . . wherever so much as one person appeared as
an enemy of the king,' says Adalbert in his chronicle, 'he [Frederick]
immediately joined him as a second.' Though the author of this unflattering comment was Frederick's rival, he hardly seems to have
exaggerated the facts. The great churchmen, like the great laymen, had
economic interests to defend against the encroachment of the monarchy.
They were exposed to politics and diplomacy as members of the royal
chapel. They were also expected to be loyal to Rome, no matter how
despicable the reigning pope might be. For these reasons, Otto did not
obtain immediate or total control of the Church in Germany. It was a
delicate task to manipulate the bishops towards the advancement of
imperial goals. The German episcopate was composed of nobles; they
were not obscure men who had worked their way up from humble
beginnings and who would be grateful to the monarch for their appointment.

During the reign of Otto I all the major themes of the later Saxons
and Salians are sketched out: rebellion from the German nobles,

[34] Wilhelm von Giesebrecht, *Geschichte der deutschen Kaiserzeit*, I, Merseburg,
1929, 421.

[35] Giesebrecht was the first to suggest that Adalbert of St Maximin's might be
the continuator of Regino, basing his conjecture partly on the fact that the annal
stops at 967, the year before Adalbert was appointed archbishop of Magdeburg.
See *Geschichte der deutschen Kaiserzeit*, 5th edn, I, Leipzig, 1881, 778.

[36] Otto had vowed to found a bishopric at Merseburg before the battle of
Lechfeld: the new see was to be dedicated to St Lawrence, whose day it was.

[37] Boso, a monk of St Emmeram's in Regensburg, chose Merseburg; Zeitz
was filled by Hugh I (968–79); and Meissen by Burchard (968–9). See Edgar
Nathaniel Johnson, *The Secular Activities of the German Episcopate, 919–1024*,
The University of Nebraska Studies, XXX–XXXI (1932), 173 and 255.

reliance on the Church to further the imperial policy, attempted control of the papacy and the attendant 'protection' of Italy. Another topic, mentioned in connection with the Venetian pact, is that of the Eastern empire. In this particular instance (Doc. 11) the question had been settled in the time of Charles the Great – Venice remained independent of dominance from either the East or the West.

In the time of Otto the Great, however, the Greeks still had control in southern Italy, and they were condescending about the claims of the Western emperor. In 968 Otto sent Liudprand to Constantinople to sue for the hand of a Greek princess as a bride for Otto II. He was laughed to scorn. The Emperor Nicephorus Phocas questioned Liudprand about Otto's power, his dominions, and his army. Liudprand says that he replied soberly and truthfully, but he was branded a liar by his host. 'Your master's soldiers cannot ride and they do not know how to fight on foot. The size of their shields, the weight of their cuirasses, the length of their swords, and the heaviness of their helmets, does not allow them to fight either way.' And adding insult to injury, Nicephorus continued: 'Their gluttony also prevents them. Their God is their belly, their courage but wind, their bravery drunkenness. Fasting for them means dissolution; sobriety, panic.'[38] This is only a small sample of what Liudprand was obliged to swallow from the Eastern emperor. It is hard to see how, after his own diatribe, Nicephorus could accuse the Germans of being uncouth. And if the Germans were so bad, why would the emperor even allow their envoy to broach the subject of a dynastic marriage between the Greeks and Germans ? In any case an agreement was not reached until after the death of Nicephorus, when in 972 Otto II was wed to Princess Theophano.

[38] 'The Embassy to Constantinople', *The Works of Liudprand of Cremona*, trans. F. A. Wright, London, 1930, pp. 241–2.

3

The Reign of Otto II (973-983)

Otto II, known as 'the Red', was already co-regent with his father, having received the imperial crown from Pope John XIII on Christmas Day 967. Therefore he was easily able to take over the government upon his father's death in 973. His reign was a short one, only ten years long, and not notably successful. Perhaps the most important deed of Otto II was his marriage to a Byzantine princess. This union implied acceptance of the Saxon dynasty as emperors of the West, and one might think that Constantinople would now relinquish its tenuous hold on Italy. It was an auspicious time for such a hope, since the new emperor in Constantinople, John Tzimisces, was preoccupied with consolidating Byzantine claims on the eastern frontier.[1] Tzimisces was threatened both by the Caliph of Baghdad and the Fatimid Caliph of Egypt.

Theophano was to bring the Byzantine lands in Italy as her dowry.[2] Since Otto I already claimed northern and central Italy, this donation would theoretically give his son the whole peninsula.[3] In return Otto gave Theophano lands within the Western empire as a marriage present (Doc. 13). The diploma which reports the transaction was issued in Rome on 14 April 972, the day of the wedding. Like the *Ottonianum* (Doc. 8) it is a calligraphic copy done in gold letters on purple parchment. In content it is even more ornate, for it contains an elaborate *arenga* or preamble on the sanctity of marriage. Otto declares that he has decided to pledge himself to 'the bond of legitimate matrimony and the

---

[1] Tzimisces was uncle to Theophano. It was he who consented to the marriage that his predecessor, Nicephorus Phocas, would not condone. On Theophano's identity see G. Ostrogorsky, *History of the Byzantine State*, trans. Joan Hussey, New Brunswick, New Jersey, p. 263, n. 1. She is clearly called 'niece of John' in Doc. 13.

[2] At least this is what Otto I had in mind when he sent Liudprand to Constantinople in 968.

[3] As it turned out, Otto merely got Capua-Benevento and gave up a claim to Apulia and Calabria. See Karl Uhlirz, *Jahrbücher des Deutschen Reiches unter Otto II. und Otto III.*, I, Berlin, 1967, 24–5.

joint control of the empire'. One might conclude that he and Theophano would govern both the Eastern and Western empires, but in fact they 'jointly controlled' only the Western. Theoretically there was still only one Roman Empire even though a Western emperor had been recognized as early as 814 when Charles the Great and Emperor Leo V agreed to settle the status of the province of Venetia (Doc. 11). The later Carolingians were not granted such acknowledgement of their position by the East. In 972 Otto insists upon his imperial title though he does not specify which empire he controls.

Otto awarded his bride a province in northern Italy (Istria) and certain properties beyond the Alps, one of which (Nordhausen) had belonged to his grandmother Matilda, wife of Henry the Fowler. Otto II, like the other Saxon kings, has been accused of reckless spending and of unnecessarily depleting the fisc, that is, the royal lands. James Westfall Thompson says that he gave away seventy-one royal manors during his short reign.[4] Yet it might be argued that both Otto I and his son needed the loyalty of the bishops and were willing to pay for it. Moreover, both of them exacted tributes from conquered lands, which helps explain why they did so much fighting. The attempt to annex Italy can be seen as a desire to increase the royal treasury as much as to renew the Roman Empire. Otto I had managed to extort tribute from the Greeks in Calabria and Apulia, but his son was denied tribute from Calabria even though married to a Byzantine princess.[5] Young Otto's trouble was that his generalship did not equal his ambitions. Never reconciled to the renunciation of southern Italy, he died while fighting the Greeks and Saracens there in 983.

In the interim he had problems at home. For seven years he was obliged to contend with open revolt in Lotharingia and Bavaria. The rebellion of the Bavarians was made more serious by their alliance with the Polish Duke Mesco and the Bohemian Duke Boleslav. Otto imprisoned the leader of the revolt, Duke Henry 'the Wrangler', and turned his attention to fighting the Danes. He finally accepted their offer of tribute, and concluded a truce with Harold Bluetooth in 975. In 976 he took Bavaria away from Duke Henry and in the same year fought an inconclusive campaign against Boleslav of Bohemia. Finally in 978 Otto overcame Boleslav at Magdeburg where he received homage from the Bohemian duke.

Otto was also engaged on the western front. He made a foray into Lotharingia in 977 to put down a revolt and to protect the duchy from the French king Lothair. Otto and Theophano were forced to abandon Aachen when Lothair appeared at the gates of the town with a large

[4] *Feudal Germany*, I, 343.
[5] Waitz, *Deutsche Verfassungsgeschichte*, VIII, 376.

army. After Lothair had ransacked the royal palace of the old Carolingian capital, he withdrew westward, and Otto started after him in revenge. Arriving as far west as the hill of Montmartre overlooking Paris, the king ordered the clerics in his company to sing a halleluja in triumph over the hostile town. Finally in 980 Lothair abandoned his claims to Lotharingia.

Otto II had to fight as many enemies as his father, and for a while he did so energetically and with a great deal of success. In 980 he was in a position to do what his father had done in 951 – to go to Italy. But his three years of fighting there proved disastrous. As soon as he was out of Germany, fresh revolts broke out along the Slavic and Danish borders.

Otto went to Italy ostensibly to drive out the Muslims from Calabria and Apulia, but also if possible to put an end to the Byzantine control of these provinces. The Italians, however, were not united behind the German emperor and were contesting among themselves for various pieces of real estate. It was an impossible situation. Nevertheless, the monarch issued documents along the way just as if it had been peace-time.

From Rome in 981 he granted the monks at Regensburg a farm which they had bought from a Jew by the name of Samuel (Doc. 14). This diploma, though by no means as earthshaking as the *Ottonianum* or the marriage present to Theophano, raises a number of interesting questions of economic and social importance. What was the status of the Jews at this time with respect to owning property? What did it mean to 'own property' anyway? And if Samuel had sold this property to the monks at Regensburg, why did the emperor subsequently have to 'grant' it to them?

The Jews were not persecuted under the Frankish or Saxon kings. Although prevented from holding land by feudal contract because of the necessary oaths, they acquired property in both France and Germany.[6]

[6] H. Graetz, *History of the Jews*, III, Philedphia, 1894, 143–4. See also Irving A. Agus, *The Heroic Age of Franco–German Jewry*, New York, 1969, Chap. VII, 'Real Property', pp. 170–84. Most of the examples are taken from Agus's earlier work *Urban Civilization in Pre-Crusade Europe*, 2 vols, New York, 1965. Moreover, the Jews involved in these cases are largely vintners from southern France. Though *Urban Civilization* has a misleading title and *The Heroic Age* seems innocent of all proof-reading, Agus's material is fascinating. For a more rigorous presentation see Salo Wittmayer Baron, *A Social and Religious History of the Jews*, 2nd edn, IV, *Meeting of East and West*, New York, 1957, 64–75. Persecution of the Jews in Germany begins with Henry II (1002–24), a more zealous Christian than any of the Ottos. Henry issued a decree expelling the Jews of Mainz in 1012, though Baron makes the observation that this did not necessarily mean that they left or converted wholesale: '. . . here as elsewhere this decree, even if issued, need not have been the cause of the departure or conversion of more than a handful of Jews, the majority quietly persisting until the decree was either formally revoked or informally allowed to sink into oblivion' (*ibid.*, p. 66). The decree was revoked in 1013, yet Baron adds, '. . . we sense in

If Samuel 'sold' the farm to the monks of St Emmeram, he must have 'owned' it in some sense but probably did not hold it as a fief.[7] That the emperor would formalize the sale with a diploma is not surprising: in that way he took credit for the donation as if the Jew's estate really belonged to him. It was traditional for the German emperors, as successors of Titus, to take the Jews under their protection as a special class.

Otto issued this diploma for the monastery of St Emmeram's in April of 981 when he was in Rome. Now he planned to conquer southern Italy as if it were the 'manifest destiny' of the German emperor to control the entire peninsula. There were not only Greeks and Saracens to battle, but local Italian princelings. One of these, Pandulf Ironhead, who ruled central Italy, died in March of 981. His son Landulf inherited Capua-Benevento (supposedly a territory which Otto II had acquired in 972 by his marriage to Theophano); a second son, Pandulf, controlled Salerno, which was nominally under Byzantine suzerainty. The Salernitans, however, ejected Pandulf and brought in a certain Duke Manso III of Amalfi. This was provocation for Otto since Manso was an ally of the Byzantines. He therefore besieged Salerno but did not really conquer the town, for they would only yield if he recognized their duke. Little was gained by this move.

In December 981, Otto presided in royal court over a dispute involving the abbot of the cloister of St Vincent near Benevento and Count Landulf, grandson of Pandulf Ironhead (Doc. 15). The document (actually a *placitum* rather than a diploma) was dictated by the abbot rather than by the emperor and was written down by John, imperial chancellor in Italy. The bishops of Pavia and Bergamo were in attendance, as were the counts of Teatino. Abbot John, speaking in the first person, recounts how he and his advocate Audoald produced the monastery's deeds in court, which stipulated a penalty of 1,000 gold pieces from anyone who harmed the cloister. Count Landulf had claimed that the monastery property was crown land and belonged to the county of Iserniense, which was under his control. Moreover, he alleged that the monastery charters were forgeries, but when he heard the testimony of Abbot John and saw the documents in court, he

these events the first rumblings of the future Crusades and sharp popular outbreaks against the Jews' (*ibid.*, p. 272).

[7] The French word 'fief' appeared for the first time between 1008 and 1016 in a Latinized form *feodum* and designated a blacksmith's tenement in the Rhineland. At that time the word was far more comprehensive than it later became. See Marc Bloch, *Feudal Society*, trans. L. A. Manyon, London, 1961, p. 168. For the various other Latin words for fief see Bloch, pp. 164–8. The German word *Lehen* (cognate with English 'loan') best indicates the essential nature of feudal property: it was lent rather than sold outright to the tenant.

relented and gave up his claim. He was to be fined 100 gold pounds unless within three days he issued charters of his own to the monastery guaranteeing their lands.

Otto's untenable position in southern Italy can be seen in the account by the historian Thietmar of Merseburg (Doc. 16). He reports that Otto fought the Greeks in Tarento and then took on the Saracens, who massacred some 4,000 of Otto's troops including many nobles. After this disastrous defeat, the emperor escaped by being taken aboard a Greek vessel. They headed for Rossano where Theophano was waiting, but not trusting the captain to carry Theophano and her treasure, Otto jumped overboard and swam to shore. Perhaps he was afraid of being held for ransom or even of being killed. Thietmar does not say.

The emperor gave up fighting after his defeat at the hands of the Saracens. He fell ill in Pavia, died in Rome on 7 December 983, and was buried in St Peter's. Thietmar sums up his short reign with a telling comment: 'Twice five solar years had he ruled after his father, as protector of kingdom and empire, a terror to all enemies and an unshakable bulwark for the flocks entrusted to him. Probably the opinion of the people wavered frightfully in such important questions, but the compassion of the divine majesty bolstered it rapidly.' The implication of mutiny on the part of Otto's subjects is clear, and there was good reason for it.

Thietmar adds an even more critical comment about Otto II: 'Mindful of human fate and as one myself greatly in need of mercy, I implore the Lord of heaven and earth that whatever sin this Otto did against my church, He of His grace will forgive.' Otto had offended the Church in 981 by appointing Bishop Gisler of Merseburg as archbishop of Magdeburg even though the clergy had elected a man named Otrich, head of the cathedral school of Magdeburg. Otto had guaranteed them the right of election in a diploma issued in 979. According to Thietmar, an envoy from Magdeburg was dispatched to Rome to obtain the emperor's confirmation of their choice. He asked Gisler to convey the information to Otto, but Gisler begged for the archbishopric for himself. He obtained his request, and the see of Merseburg was then dismantled since it was contrary to canon law for a bishop to be transferred. Merseburg was Thietmar's own church, and he resented this action on the part of the crafty Gisler, who was 'no shepherd, but a hireling'. Thietmar also accuses Dietrich, bishop of Metz, of having had a hand in the deal. Dietrich and Gisler arrived together in Magdeburg on 30 November. 'Dietrich was a friend of the emperor, very dear to him, and corrupt in his morals. He gained one thousand talents of gold and silver from Archbishop Gisler for casting a shadow over the truth. To this same Dietrich someone said one day: "May God satisfy you in the future, since all of us cannot do so here with gold!" [8] In 1004 the see of Merseburg was restored and in 1009 Thietmar became its bishop, remaining in that position until his death in 1018.

[8] Duckett, *Death and Life in the Tenth Century*, p. 150.

4

The Reign of Otto III (983-1002)

When Otto II died at the age of twenty-eight, his son Otto III was only three years old. News of his father's death in Rome reached the heir in Aachen, where he was spending Christmas in order to receive the royal crown. Henry the Wrangler, duke of Bavaria, immediately set out for Cologne where the child king was staying in the custody of Archbishop Willigis of Mainz.[1] Henry apparently wanted to seize the crown by first acting as regent for his cousin. The archbishops of Cologne, Metz, Magdeburg, and Trier gave him their support, but he failed to win over the bishop of Verdun or the archbishop of Reims. Nor did he convince Gerbert of Aurillac who was a resident scholar at the cathedral school of Reims. Gerbert was one of the cleverest men of the tenth century and was to become a staunch supporter of the young Otto.

Henry the Wrangler had himself proclaimed king at Eastertime 984, in Quedlinburg, but though he received fealty from some of the Slavic tribes, he failed to win the support of the Saxon nobles. In June of the same year Gerbert wrote to Archbishop Willigis of Mainz on behalf of Archbishop Adalbero of Reims, just a few days before it was learned that Henry had capitulated and turned over Otto III to his mother Theophano (Doc. 17). Gerbert asks Willigis to support Theophano as regent rather than the predatory Henry: 'It was proper that the lamb be entrusted to his mother, not to the wolf.' The tone of the letter is sombre and troubled. There are allusions to Otto's minority as a time of grief and turmoil, both on a national and a personal level. Gerbert couples his suggestion to support Theophano with a request that Willigis urge her to recall Gerbert to the German court. He mentions the 'weariness of my journeying among the Gauls', a somewhat ironical remark inasmuch as he himself was born in France. Perhaps the most

[1] Henry, son of Otto I's brother Henry, had been deposed at a diet held at Regensburg in July 976 for having led a revolt against Otto II. Rebelling again, he was tried at Easter 978 in Magdeburg and this time sentenced to banishment.

revealing aspect of the letter is the fact that Gerbert and his superior, Archbishop Adalbero, felt it necessary to prop up Willigis on the side of the young Otto. Gerbert refers to an earlier letter written to Willigis which was apparently answered either in a noncommittal way or not at all. Yet Willigis is considered a staunch supporter of the Saxon dynasty and one of the few who could be counted on in this dark hour.

Gerbert's own respect for the Saxons can be seen in his lament for Otto II, whose conversation is described as 'Socratic'. Even allowing for deliberate flattery, one gets an unexpectedly intellectual impression of the young emperor, who passed much of his reign in battle. Gerbert had spent the years 970–2 at the German court and was more contented there than as abbot of Bobbio in Lombardy (an appointment given him by Otto II in 982) or as scholar in residence at Reims. He eventually obtained his wish in 997 when he became tutor to Otto III, but in the meantime he was an invaluable ally in Lotharingia.

Henry the Wrangler did not have a base of operations in Swabia or Lotharingia, nor even in his own former duchy of Bavaria, and rather than fight for the crown with so little support, he requested of the German princes at a diet near Worms that his claim be considered. But they unanimously decided in favour of Otto III. Finally in 985 Henry agreed to withdraw his claim in exchange for the duchy of Bavaria. The regency passed jointly to Theophano, Otto's mother, and to his grandmother, Adelaide.

These two redoubtable ladies, both bearing the title of Augusta, were equally ambitious to be regents for young Otto. Note that Gerbert mentions Theophano as the one to support in his letter to Willigis of Mainz. The elderly Adelaide, though thrust aside by her daughter-in-law, outlived Theophano, and in 991 she took over the regency alone. We find a respectful letter to her from her grandson in which he thanks her for her prayers in his behalf and hints that his accession as emperor could not have come about without her approval (Doc. 18).

Otto III took over the reins of government in 994 just before he turned fifteen, the age of majority in Germany. The young king had been under the influence of two remarkable women, one of them a Greek with a strong will. When Theophano was joint regent, she issued two diplomas in her own name, calling herself *imperatrix augusta* and *Theophanius . . . imperator augustus*![2] It was customary in the Eastern empire for a woman to rule in her own right, the first one to do so being Irene (797–802). One wonders what other Byzantine conventions would have been taken over by Otto III if his mother had not died so soon.

[2] *Monumenta Germaniae historica, Diplomatum regum et imperatorum*, II, Pt II, *Ottonis III. diplomata*, ed. Theodor Sickel, 2nd unaltered edn, Berlin, 1957, 876–7.

As it was, she made a lasting impression on the German court, for Otto was an enthusiast for Greek ways, for example, his use of the office of *protosphatarius* (see Doc. 25). In 995 he sent an envoy to Constantinople to find an Eastern princess for a bride after the tradition of his mother.

In May 996, Otto was crowned emperor by Pope Gregory V, the first German pope and a relative of Otto himself.[3] His pre-coronation title can be seen in Doc. 19, 'Otto king', and at the end of the diploma, 'most glorious king'. This diploma renews the immunity of the cloister of Hornbach, allowing the abbot to be compensated from the royal treasury for slain churchmen. The form and style of the deed seem wholly in keeping with those of Otto's predecessors.

In 997, after the imperial coronation, we find Otto using the title 'emperor augustus of the Romans'. This intitulation had already been used by Otto II in his later years, but Otto III seems to have taken it literally. After all, he was half Greek. He had inherited from Theophano a reverence for the Eastern empire, whose ruler always claimed to be the true heir of Rome.

The influence of Charles the Great upon Otto was also enormous – for example, when he founded three monasteries in the neighbourhood of Aachen and endowed them with land and art works.[4] In his plan to 'renew' the empire as Charles had done, he was powerfully aided by Gerbert, who was invited to visit the court as a teacher-in-residence in the spring of 997. Gerbert's position as archbishop of Reims had proved untenable, for the see was a pawn in the struggle between the Carolingians and Capetians for the French crown and also in the dispute between France and the papacy.[5]

When Archbishop Adalbero died in 989, Gerbert felt confident that he would succeed him in Reims.[6] But Hugh Capet installed Arnulf, an illegitimate son of the Carolingian Lothair (d. 986). Arnulf surprised his benefactor Hugh, however, by siding with his rival Charles, duke of Lower Lorraine. Arnulf opened the gates of Reims, and Charles and his soldiers sacked the city. Gerbert was virtually a prisoner for eight months until he escaped to Senlis where he gave testimony at a synod of bishops convoked by King Hugh. In 991 Arnulf was forced to step down from the archiepiscopal chair, and Gerbert was named his successor.[7] However, his right to the see of Reims was contested. In June 995, Pope John XV sent a legate to investigate the matter. In two councils Gerbert was condemned, but he continued to function as archbishop.

[3] He was Chaplain Bruno of Carinthia, a great-grandson of Otto the Great. Otto III nominated him to the papacy upon the death of John XV.
[4] Percy Ernst Schramm, *Kaiser, Rom, und Renovatio*, Darmstadt, 1962, p. 93.
[5] *Ibid.*, p. 96.
[6] *The Letters of Gerbert*, trans. Harriet Pratt Lattin, New York, 1961, p. 10.
[7] *Ibid.*, p. 12.

In 996, feeling that his authority had been thoroughly undermined, he journeyed to Rome to seek the recognition of the new pope, Gregory V. Though a cousin and appointee of Otto III, Gregory would not recognize Gerbert's claim over those of his deposed rival Arnulf. It was upon the return trip from this unsuccessful interview that Gerbert met Otto, the newly crowned emperor. Otto put Gerbert to work drafting letters for him, having been impressed by the man's erudition and urbanity. The foundation was laid for the future relationship between the two, for Gerbert's position as adviser and tutor at court, and ultimately for his appointment as pope.

However, the intrigue over the see of Reims continued. In 997 Otto wrote Gerbert a letter, telling him that his rival Arnulf had gone to see the pope (Doc. 21). Otto had heard about it from the papal legate. Though Gerbert fought hard to maintain his position as archbishop of Reims, he concluded that it was useless. In April of 997 he left France for good and went to Germany.

Even before Gerbert officially joined Otto's chapel, we can see his influence. When the two met in Pavia in 996, the young emperor had Gerbert draft a letter to Pope Gregory about certain counties in Italy that were under dispute (Doc. 22). These counties had formed part of the disposition of the *Ottonianum* in 962 (Doc. 8), and it was advantageous for both emperor and pope to have control of them since they extended along the Adriatic in such a way as to form a buffer zone or corridor that facilitated travel between Ravenna and Rome. In the letter Otto informs Gregory that he is leaving the eight disputed counties under the control of the margraves of Tuscany and Spoleto-Camerino, without either claiming or relinquishing ultimate imperial authority over the territory.

In January 1001, when Gerbert had been made Pope Sylvester II by Otto, a diploma was issued by the emperor which fixed the status of the eight counties south of Ravenna (Doc. 23).[8] This deed, in the words of Percy Schramm, is 'one of the most unusual documents of the Middle Ages and for that reason was for a long time regarded as a forgery.'[9] He conjectures that Otto may have claimed imperial rights in the disputed territory on his way to Rome to collect the imperial crown in 996. His letter to Pope Gregory (Doc. 22) shows that 'a balance had to be struck which would not encroach upon the rights of either party'.[10] By 1001

[8] That these are the same eight counties as those mentioned (but left unnamed) in Doc. 22 is established by Schramm, *Kaiser, Rom, und Renovatio*, p. 162, n. 4.

[9] *Ibid.*, p. 161. Schramm's chapter 'Otto III and the Roman Church according to the Donation Document of January, 1001' can be found translated in Hill, *Rise of the First Reich*, pp. 133–45.

[10] Scramm, *Kaiser, Rom, und Renovatio*, p. 162.

the positions of pope and emperor were unchanged even though Gregory had been succeeded by Gerbert. Yet the express claims of the emperor are dramatically stated, for Otto alleges that the documentary foundation of the papal claims is fallacious. Specifically, Otto exposes the Donation of Constantine as a forgery.[11] This discovery by Otto's chancery was subsequently ignored, not to be revived until the fifteenth century.

Moreover, Otto also discredits the renewal pact of Charles the Bald (d. 877) because Charles had supposedly been driven from Italy by his cousin Carloman (d. 880), called 'the better Charles' in the diploma. Charles the Bald's authority in Italy was therefore nil when he reissued the charter for the pope. It was awkward for Otto III, however, that his grandfather had similarly renewed the old pacts. Otto could not allege that the *Ottonianum* was a forgery or an illegal renewal, so he bypassed it rather than renewing it. He issued a new diploma laying claim to eight counties that should have belonged to the pope.[12]

Then he generously donates them to Pope Sylvester II after having made it quite clear that the property did not automatically belong to the pope.[13] '. . . having disdained these forged deeds and false writings, we give to St Peter out of our largesse what is ours, not what is his, just as if we were conferring our own property.' Moreover he only donates the eight counties for the pope to 'administer . . . for the success of his apostolate and our empire', not for absolute ownership or alienation. As Schramm says, 'it is not a question of a donation in the usual sense, but a gift whereby the donor does not give away all rights. That this is really the case is proven if one examines who actually received the gift: not the Roman Church, which is not mentioned in the dispositive part of the deed at all, not the Pope and his successors on the papal chair, who are discussed only in the conclusion, nor Sylvester II either, but St Peter alone!'[14] This is in sharp contrast to the name of the recipient

[11] For a thorough discussion of the relation of DO.III.389 to the Donation of Constantine, see Horst Fuhrmann, 'Konstantinische Schenkung und abendländisches Kaisertum', *Deutsches Archiv*, XXII (1966), 63–178, especially pp. 128–54.
[12] Schramm points out that Otto III could not have renewed the *Ottonianum* or there would be some mention of it in the renewal of Henry II in 1020 (*Kaiser, Rom, und Renovatio*, p. 166).
[13] Sylvester I was pope under Constantine, and it appears that Gerbert took the name Sylvester II to emphasize Otto's claim to what Constantine had fictitiously donated to the papacy. Harriet Lattin sees it as 'a declaration that emperor and pope agreed on a policy of strengthening and pushing the bounds of the Christian Roman empire' (*Letters of Gerbert*, p. 16). It seems strange that Gerbert would take the name of a pope whose credentials were now being called into question by Otto III. Either Gerbert styled himself Sylvester in 999 without knowing the Donation was a forgery, or he was being ironical, which is hardly likely.   [14] *Kaiser, Rom, und Renovatio*, pp. 171–2.

in the *Ottonianum* where the disposition reads 'to you, blessed Apostle Peter, and your vicar, Pope John, and his successors'.

Moreover, there is a curious new intitulation at the head of the document where Otto refers to himself not only as 'emperor augustus of the Romans' but also as 'servant of the Apostles'. The significance of this latter title is, according to Schramm, that the emperor had reached a new relationship with the pope and that all rights not specified to the pope remained with the emperor.[15] As 'servant of the Apostles' Otto could give away eight counties and yet retain the property for himself. He 'merely transferred it from the property of the empire to that of a saint whose worldly arm was no one other than himself'.

It is remarkable that Otto III should so shrewdly construe the possibilities of empire *vis-a-vis* the papacy when the man who occupied the chair of St Peter was Sylvester II, a trusted adviser and one of the most capable men of his time. C. W. Previté-Orton's picture of the young emperor is one of a dreamer, a visionary, and a boy who was humoured in his wild plans by his tutor Gerbert.[16] But when Gerbert became Sylvester II, practical statesman, he could not afford to share in Otto's dreams wholeheartedly: 'Otto's schemes were far stranger [than those of Otto I], the offspring of his wayward and perfervid nature.' The donation of 1001 is viewed not as a brilliant counterstroke to the *Ottonianum*, which had given the pope too much control over Italy, but as 'a strange, scolding, argumentative diploma' denouncing the Donation of Constantine as a forgery.[17]

Quite a different evaluation of Otto III is given by Frances Dvornik:

'Although Otto III (983–1002) put an end to the rule of the pro-Byzantine Crescentius in Rome, and although he himself appointed a German and then a French pope, and proclaimed a renovation of the Roman Empire, there was quite a chance, that had he lived longer, Constantinople and Rome would have been able to reach a new and enduring understanding. He was the son of a Byzantine princess, introduced Byzantine ceremonial at his court, and his second request for a Byzantine bride was received very favourably in Constantinople. The so-called Ottonian renaissance gave a foretaste of the advantages to western Europe had friendly contact with the cultured Byzantines been maintained'.[18]

Otto was fortunate in having a learned and loyal man like Gerbert in

[15] *Kaiser, Rom, und Renovatio*, p. 174.
[16] *Cambridge Medieval History*, III, 173.
[17] *Ibid.*, p. 174. Since the Donation *is* a forgery, one wonders why Previté-Orton did not consider it a piece of scholarship on Otto's part and that of his chancery to call it one.
[18] *Ibid.*, IV, 458.

the office of pope, but it is not to be imagined that the papacy was thereby reduced to the status of a lackey. Gerbert had a record of vigorous administration as abbot of Bobbio and archbishop of Reims. He was similarly active in the office of archbishop of Ravenna to which he was appointed in 998, though his career there was cut short by his elevation to the papacy less than a year later.

In December of 999, Gerbert, now Sylvester II, issued a papal privilege to the monastery of Fulda (Doc. 24). It is instructive to compare this document with Henry the Fowler's diploma of immunity to Fulda issued in 920 (Doc. 1). We observe that royal and papal jurisdictions would appear to overlap. Henry exempts the abbot from the incursions of royal officials who might want to hear lawsuits, levy taxes, exact duties of lodging and victualling, and raise oath-helpers. Moreover, he returns the tithe to them from the royal fisc to be used for maintenance of the buildings and hospitality to travellers and paupers. And as long as the monks can find suitable candidates, they have the right of electing their own abbot. None of these stipulations would *necessarily* conflict with the authority of the pope, except for the statement that the monastery was 'divinely granted to us within the kingdom'. The king is therefore in a sense claiming that he is the proprietor of Fulda, and this gives him the legal basis upon which to issue a diploma of immunity. Louis the Pious and Conrad I had taken the same position, for the diploma is largely a reiteration of their charters.

This royal proprietorship runs directly counter to the papal claims of Sylvester II (Doc. 24): '. . . we confirm to you and to your successors in perpetuity everything which your predecessors legally and reasonably requested from our predecessors . . . we grant and confirm to you the monastery of Fulda . . . with all cells, churches, manors, and all their appurtenances. . . .' The wording is similar to the royal charter of 920 and those that preceded it. Hence there is a documentary record of donation and reconfirmation from both the secular and ecclesiastical establishments, and unless both bodies continued in their generous policy of exemption and immunity plus local control over the property and its personnel, there could be a conflict of interests. Sylvester's privilege warns the prince not to subject the possessions of Fulda to any mortal nor to give them away in the form of a benefice, 'but let the church of Fulda, always free and secure, zealously serve the Roman see alone'. The pope declares the allegiance of the monks to be entirely directed towards Rome, as if he were their sole proprietor. The punishment for infringement of the papal diploma is excommunication.

If the king should decide to revoke any of the tax exemptions granted to Fulda, he would undergo the risk of papal censure. Or if the abbot should commit some crime that had consequences for the secular ruler (like treason) and the ruler wanted to try him in royal court, he would also run into opposition from the pope, whose diploma specifies that the abbot must be examined only by the Apostolic See. Likewise the pope reserves the exclusive right to consecrate all abbots, and he does not make explicit the right of the monks to choose their own candidate. If the pope were to appoint an abbot directly, he would be violating the terms of the royal deed for Fulda, and they might have recourse to the king if they were suffering from the indignities of a tyrannical pope.

In practice, however, papal and royal documents of protection did not begin to exclude each other until the advent of the Investiture Contest.[19] The monasteries were part of the proprietary church system much as the bishoprics and parishes.[20] The king took only formal cognizance of the monks' right to elect their own abbot and often inserted his own candidate, while also requiring the performance of services for the state. The houses sought exemptions from these burdens, whence the issuance of royal diplomas of immunity. At the same time there was a tendency for the regular clergy to free themselves from the control of local bishops, supported in this endeavour by the papal curia. The idea of papal protection apparently developed on the model of royal diplomas of immunity and property rights.[21] Hence, it is not surprising that Sylvester II's privilege for Fulda in 999 should resemble the deed of Henry I in 920.

A notable adjudication by the emperor between secular and ecclesiastical rights to property is found in the record of a hearing which took place in Pavia in the year 1001 (Doc. 25). The palace official Lanfranc begins:

'I come from the emperor and hold for him and his realm a monastery with the area that surrounds it, located within the city of Pavia dedicated to the Lord Saviour and St Felix and called Regine, with all the cottages, camps, chapels, mills, and fisheries and all things located everywhere between the city of Pavia and outside together with all serfs and bondmaids, and emancipated serfs, male and female, pertaining and belonging to the same monastery, completely and fully.'

In other words, the emperor is acting as patron and protector of the monastery much as we might expect the pope to do, and specifically against the incursions of a noblewoman and her son, who is deacon of the church at Pavia. Lanfranc is not actually prosecuting Countess

[19] Gerhart Ladner, *Theologie und Politik vor dem Investiturstreit*, Leipzig, 1936, p. 69.
[20] Edmund E. Stengel, 'Die Kirchenverfassung Westeuropas im Mittelalter', *Abhandlungen und Untersuchungen zur mittelalterlichen Geschichte*, Cologne, 1960, p. 12.
[21] *Ibid.*, pp. 12–14.

Rotlind and her son Hubert; rather, he is challenging them to dispute the claim of the house to the properties which he has enumerated. They do not accept the challenge but acknowledge that the monastery's properties do not belong to themselves, 'nor ought they to belong to us legally since we do not have any diploma or deed, nor can we have, by which we can contradict or take away from the law of the lord emperor or of his realm, as they are of his realm and ought to be by law'.

This settlement guaranteed the rights of the monastery under imperial authority and against the ambitions of local nobility. It was an acknowledgement both of the integrity of the house's property and of the jurisdiction of the German emperor over legal questions in northern Italy. But the 'hearing' is a bit of a sham, an imperial *fait accompli*, for all the ecclesiastical magnates named in the document had been appointed by the emperor. Only Otto's partisans were represented.[22]

Certain Greek affectations are evident in Doc. 25, for instance, the title of *protospatharius* borne by Count Palatine Otto, and the use of Greek characters in the names of two witnesses. C. W. Previté-Orton took a dim view of such symptoms. They were a 'gaudy imitation' of the outward form of the Eastern empire; they were 'rudely borrowed'; and the German Augustus is accused of puerility and 'semibarbarism'.[23] This harsh verdict does not seem to be justified. The addition of a few Greek titles and characters to the diploma in question do not invalidate it or confuse its content. Another criticism by Previté-Orton is that Otto fused the German and Italian chanceries, 'to the muddling of their formal and perhaps of their practical business'. Yet he does not level the same charge at Charlemagne who also had a single chancery for Italy and the Frankish domains.

In fact, Otto retained a separate chancery for Italy until 998 when, upon the death of Hildibald of Worms, he bestowed the position of chancellor for the whole empire upon Heribert, archbishop of Cologne.[24] The fusing of the two chanceries corresponded to the young emperor's concept of government. 'One can characterize it as imperial centralization which resulted from setting the *imperium* above the *regna*. This fusion offered at the same time the advantage of the greatest clarity.'[25]

Most detractors of Otto III stress his Greek mother's influence and his adulation of Eastern forms, but the model of Charles the Great was equally powerful for him and does not seem to have prejudiced opinion against him. The most obvious proof of Otto's reverence for his great

[22] Mathilde Uhlirz, *Jahrbücher des Deustchen Reiches unter Otto II. und Otto III.*, II, Berlin, 1954, 381.
[23] *Cambridge Medieval History*, III, 174.
[24] Fleckenstein, *Hofkapelle*, II, 166 and n. 63.
[25] *Ibid.*

Frankish predecessor is the famous incident of his opening Charlemagne's tomb in the cathedral of Aachen, as recounted in the chronicle
of the Lombard monastery of Novalesa. The emperor was accompanied
into the sepulchre by the Count Palatine of Lomello, the *protospatharius*
who chaired the judicial proceedings against Countess Rotlind (Doc.
25). Charles was entombed in a seated position. His finger-nails had
pierced his gloves, and the tip of his nose was missing, so Otto cut his
nails, changed his clothes, and replaced the nose tip with gold. After
taking one of Charles's teeth as a momento, he left and sealed up the
tomb once more. This somewhat grisly account has the ring of truth
about it because of the selection of details. Whether it is altogether
accurate is disputed, but it is not questioned that Otto III practically
worshipped Charles and wanted to follow his example in renovating the
Roman Empire, a motto that is found on the seals of both monarchs.

The *renovatio* theme has ordinarily drawn in its wake the view of the
Saxon emperors as priest-kings, the so-called *Rex-Sacerdos* interpretation. According to its most enthusiastic followers, Otto III functioned
not only as emperor but also as pope, the empire of the Saxons becoming
coterminous with the *imperium Christianum*. The implications of the
sacerdotal king thesis have now been called into question by Karl Morrison, who strikes a healthy balance between what the liturgy says (and
the coronation ceremonies are admittedly sacral in character) and what
we can reasonably attribute to the monarchs in the way of concrete
plans and policies.[26] In Morrison's view the relationship between pope
and emperor in the tenth century has been idealized and universalized,
and the reason may be said to lie in an overly literal reading of imperial
slogans and intitulations. In short, 'There was no imperial constitution
and thus there could be no imperial constitutional theory.'[27]

It might be added that a sceptical attitude toward the diplomas is
needed if one is not to go astray by taking them at face value. Their
traditional formulaic nature gives them a more solemn character than
may in fact be consistent with the views of any particular monarch. A
counter-dose of contemporary narrative sources often reveals just how
insecure the emperor was both at home and abroad. Over-reliance on
the diplomas might lead one to the conclusion that imperial programmes
were far more 'Roman', more sacral, and more effective than they in
fact were.

According to Schramm, Otto's renewal plans comprehended both
Church and State, and they were neither absurd nor barbaric. 'Not his
own fame nor the honour of Rome, not the prestige of his house nor any

[26] 'Saxon Germany and the Myth of the Sacerdotal King', Appendix B, *Tradition and Authority in the Western Church, 300–1140*, Princeton, 1969, pp.
373–89.   [27] *Ibid.*, p. 380.

other goal attached to this world impelled . . . the emperor in his attempt to restore the *Respublica*; the real goal was a justification before God. Here on earth it amounted to living "honourably" and to putting all of his strength into the service of his task so as to prepare a way to heaven by means of good works.'[28] The religious side of the renewal was as important as the secular. As part of his overall plans, Otto made a famous trip to Poland in the year 1000 to visit the tomb of St Adalbert of Prague in Gnesen.[29] The Hungarians had become Christianized, and the Russians had received an embassy from Rome in 1000. Papal legates were also active in Dalmatia. The Polish trip can therefore be seen as 'nothing less than the unlocking of the whole non-Byzantine east to the Christian Church as far as it was within the purview of Central Europe . . .'.[30] In Poland, Otto set up a bishopric, thereby giving the land an ecclesiastical organization. The gift of part of Adalbert's relics he divided characteristically between Rome and Aachen, the 'second Rome'.

Otto III died in the year 1002 at the age of twenty-two before his dreams of a revived Roman Empire were fully realized. Although a great connoisseur of things Roman, he had made plans to be buried not in St Peter's beside his father but in the palace chapel at Aachen, the burial place of Charles the Great.[31] It can be endlessly argued whether Otto III did more harm than good for Germany, depending upon one's definition of a well-run state. On the ideological, cultural and intellectual side Otto was well educated and highly sophisticated as well as ambitious. Two of his advisers, Leo of Vercelli and Gerbert of Aurillac, were among the most learned men of the age, and their understanding of classical literature was profound. Otto himself, unlike his grandfather, knew both Greek and Latin. The self-awareness revealed in his diplomatic correspondence proves how seriously he took his commitment to renewing the empire.

Geoffrey Barraclough makes a convincing case for the legitimacy of Ottonian claims and aspirations to empire, showing that the imperial policy was nothing new and that if Otto I had not gravitated to Italy, the dukes of Bavaria and Swabia would have filled the vacuum.[32] Moreover,

[28] Schramm, *Kaiser, Rom, und Renovatio*, pp. 129–30.
[29] See Francis Dvornik, *The Slavs, Their Early History and Civilization*, Boston, 1956, p. 262: 'In order to stress before all Europe the importance of the fact that Poland was the first country to join the Roman Empire in its revived form as a federation of Christian princes under two leaders – the Emperor and the Pope – Otto III went in person to Gniezno.'
[30] Schramm, *Kaiser, Rom, und Renovatio*, p. 138.
[31] The tomb is now marked by a plaque in the floor of the fifteenth-century addition on the eastern side of the ninth-century octagonal church built by Charles.   [32] *The Origins of Modern Germany*, Oxford, 1957, p. 66.

the intervention in Italy, far from conflicting with interests at home, was made to serve German ambitions, for example, the expansion to the east; nor can the Italian policy be blamed for the hostility of the dukes back home, who revolted for a variety of other reasons.[33] Much of the criticism levelled at the Saxon emperors derives from a misapprehension of the kind of empire they ruled: it was 'limited and concrete' and did not imply 'universal dominion or overlordship throughout the west'.[34] Finally, the Ottos cannot be held responsible for the catastrophe that befell the Italian policy under the Hohenstaufen.

On the economic, social, and military side Otto III was less successful. Much of the land which he bestowed on ambitious prelates is thought to have been needlessly expended. The royal fisc was not inexhaustible, though Otto sometimes acted as if it had been. As for social legislation, he is credited with the dubious distinction of binding every serf of the Church forever to bondage. The decree was drafted by that notable scholar Leo of Vercelli. It is understandable that Leo might find such servitude among the tenants of the Church convenient, but it does not add to the lustre of the emperor since the trend away from bondage had been established for some time.

Otto died without heirs. He had obtained the hand of a Byzantine princess to strengthen the ties between East and West. The drive toward rapport with Byzantium and renewal of the Roman Empire on a grand scale came to an abrupt halt in 1002 with the death of the young emperor.

[33] *The Origin of Modern Germany*, Oxford, 1957, p. 67.

[34] *Ibid.*, pp. 67–8. Cf. the view of A. J. P. Taylor that 'universalism' was one of the permanent features of the German Empire (*The Course of German History*, p. 16).

5

The Reign of Henry II (1002-1024)

Since there were no direct descendants on the death of Otto III, the succession passed to the collateral line in Bavaria. There the ruling duke was Henry, son of Henry the Wrangler, grandson of Henry the younger brother of Otto the Great. After putting down various competitors, Duke Henry was crowned at Mainz on 7 June 1002. A ceremonial coronation at Aachen followed in September, and Henry was now accepted both inside and outside Germany as the new king.

Because of his father's rebellion against Otto II, which deprived him temporarily of his duchy, young Henry had been educated for a career in the Church. This early training had its effect on the king's policy. He was far more diligent than his predecessor in exercising control over the Church, and he used ecclesiastical donation as a way of building up his own power base instead of merely depleting the fisc.

Henry's authority in Church affairs is evident in a diploma of confirmation to the abbey of St Gall issued in 1004 (Doc. 26). Since this diploma was drawn up early in his reign, Henry styles himself simply 'king of the Franks and Lombards', but he does not hesitate to meddle in the affairs of the house, for although he grants the monks the right to elect their own abbot, he demands a part in the choice. This stipulation does not appear in Henry the Fowler's charter for Fulda in the year 920 (Doc. 1). The first Henry gave the monks at Fulda total control of the choice of abbot, at least on paper. We need not assume that Henry the Fowler had no interest in the appointment of abbots nor that Henry II exercised tyrannical control in all cases, but the presence of such a stipulation in the charter is suggestive and fits in with what we know of his later career.

Henry II sought to influence the selection of abbots, but also of bishops, a policy which had been followed by Otto the Great. When the see of Magdeburg fell vacant in 1004, Henry filled it with his own appointee, Tagino of Bavaria, even though the local clergy had selected one of their own men. 'To Henry . . . the right of election was useful for giving canonical sanction to a choice made by himself, and the utmost allowed to electors was to name a candidate; thus in course of time most of the German bishoprics were filled by his nominees.'[1]

On All Saints' Day in the year 1007 Henry convoked a synod of bishops at Frankfurt in order to establish a new see – that of Bamberg (Doc. 27). The preamble explains that

'. . . the great and peaceable king Henry, trusting in God and conscientious towards men, pondering again and again with magnanimous deliberation of mind how he might be most pleasing to God, determined in the course of his cogitation with the highest inspiration of the divinity that he would choose God as his heir and bestow by deed and set up out of all his hereditary property a bishopric in honour of St Peter, prince of the Apostles, in a certain place named Bamberg where he had hereditary property from his father, so that the paganism of the Slavs would be destroyed and the memory of the name of Christ would always be remembered there.'

The naming of God as his heir shows the sacerdotal character of Henry's concept of the monarchy. (It also shows, of course, that he had no offspring!) He even wore a gown reminiscent of the figured robes of biblical high priests.[2] According to Walter Ullmann, 'Henry's empire was a priest-state: the "populus Christianus" as he understood the term, was entrusted to him, and being a Christian people they had to be given suitable ecclesiastical officers. The *sacerdotium* was to be regenerated because it was vital to the governmental machinery of Henry II.'[3]

Henry appointed his chancellor Eberhard as the first bishop of Bamberg and made numerous grants to the new see: diplomas 144–171 (all in the year 1007) record gifts of property. This richly endowed bishopric became not only a missionary outpost to the Slavs but a cultural centre as well. Eberhard was one of Henry's three chancellors. He first

[1] Edwin H. Holthouse, *Cambridge Medieval History*, III, 232. Henry continued to interfere in the appointment of subsequent archbishops at Magdeburg. When the clergy there persisted in electing a local candidate in 1012, Henry removed him from office by making him a royal chaplain, and then forced the election of his own man. Thus the right of free election was one that could be circumvented even though solemnized by royal charter.

[2] The figures were from the zodiac and the apocalypse. See Walter Ullmann, *The Growth of Papal Government in the Middle Ages*, 2nd edn, London, 1962, p. 248 and notes 3 and 4.

[3] *Ibid.*, p. 248. Ullmann says that the emphasis on *sacerdotium* in the reign of Henry II as compared with Otto III can be seen in portraits of the monarch showing him being crowned by Christ, the hand of God, and the Holy Ghost, whereas Otto III is crowned by Saints Peter and Paul (*ibid.*, pp. 246 and 247, n. 1). However, Otto II is depicted in the frontispiece to the Aachen Gospels as being crowned by the hand of God. See Ernst Kantorowicz, *The King's Two Bodies*, Princeton, 1957, pp. 61–78 and fig. 5.

appears in the documents as both chancellor and intercessor, that is, the person whose intervention is said to have prompted the king to draft the document, and he is called *familiarissimus nobis cancellarius*.[4] He retained his position as chancellor when named to the see of Bamberg in 1007, but after 12 March 1009, he countersigns only those documents destined for Italian recipients, that is, he becomes chancellor for Italy.[5]

Next to Bamberg, Henry's favourite religious establishment was the abbey of Gandersheim, which had been founded by his ancestor Liudulf of Saxony in 842. It was also the burial place of his father, Duke Henry the Wrangler. The nunnery was well endowed with land and privileges. We have seen how the influential Abbess Gerberga, daughter of Duke Henry of Bavaria, commissioned Hroswitha to write a flattering history of Otto the Great (Doc. 6). Under Otto II the abbey continued to flourish, for Otto's daughter Sophia became a member of the religious community. In 990 Sophia's brother, Otto III, granted market and toll rights to Gandersheim, and most significant the privilege of coining money. In short, Gandersheim was becoming a cultural and commercial rival of Hildesheim.

A quarrel developed as to whether Hildesheim or Mainz should have jurisdiction of Gandersheim. It began in 987 when Princess Sophia was supposed to take the veil. She did not consider Bishop Osdag of Hildesheim distinguished enough to carry out this task and requested that Archbishop Willigis of Mainz officiate.[6] Osdag protested that he did not wish to act as a mere aide, but Willigis claimed that Gandersheim was within the archdiocese of Mainz and that he would therefore preside. On the day of the ceremony, attended by the eight-year-old Otto III and the Empress-mother Theophano, Osdag complained publicly that his rights were being infringed, and Willigis strenuously insisted on his own pre-eminence. Osdag was permitted to assist the archbishop in the veiling of Sophia, but Willigis had the honour of officiating at the main altar.

During the first six years of the pontificate of Bishop Bernward (993-1022), Hildesheim and Mainz seem to have worked out a mutual agreement regarding Gandersheim, but this amicable relationship did not last, because Sophia and Willigis conspired to have the nunnery fall to the juridiction of Mainz.[7] The historian Thancmar says that they even produced charters supposedly proving their contention, but he

[4] Fleckenstein, *Hofkapelle*, II, 167.

[5] *Ibid.*, p. 168. Fleckenstein says, however, that there were not really two chanceries at this time but rather one chancery with an Italian section and a German section, for the personnel (particularly the notaries) seem to have overlapped.

[6] Francis J. Tschan, *Saint Bernward of Hildesheim*, I, Notre Dame, 1942, 163.

[7] *Ibid.*, pp. 164-5.

accords them no validity since he was an avid supporter of Bernward. Actually the geographical situation of Gandersheim was ambiguous enough for Willigis easily to make a case for Mainz.

His protégée Sophia managed to turn all the nuns against Bernward, with the result that he received a chilly reception when he set foot in Gandersheim.[8] When the new church at Gandersheim was ready to be consecrated in the year 1000, the ageing abbess Gerberga summoned Bernward to do the honours, while Sophia, wishing to have Willigis officiate, assembled her armed retainers. But as she was not present to give them orders, Bernward was able to enter the church and celebrate mass. Then he forbade anyone to consecrate the church without his permission. The nuns replied by cursing and throwing their oblations at his feet.[9] Moreover, Archbishop Willigis came to Gandersheim on 20 September, intent upon consecrating the church and sent a message to Bernward ordering his presence. Bernward refused to appear, and Willigis did not dare to consecrate the church in his absence. It looked as if the situation had reached an impasse, so Bernward, anxious to retain his richest monastery, set out for Rome on 2 November to consult the pope, reaching his destination in January of 1001.

Both Pope Sylvester II and Emperor Otto III agreed with the bishop of Hildesheim against Willigis, and so did the duke of Bavaria, the future Henry II, who like Bernward was a vigorous reformer. Duke Henry had the added incentive of helping his aunt Gerberga, abbess of Gandersheim, whose wishes for the nunnery had been flouted by the bold Princess Sophia.

A synod was convoked to decide the case, and Willigis, who had uncanonically convoked a synod of his own at Gandersheim during Bernward's absence, was declared to have had no authority to do so. The pope reconfirmed Gandersheim to the bishop of Hildesheim, a total victory for Bernward.[10] Moreover, he sent his legate to present a letter of reprimand to Archbishop Willigis in a synod convened in June 1001 at Pöhlde, a royal fortress in the diocese of Mainz. But Willigis, after disrupting the meeting with his own unruly armed

[8] Tschan, *Bernward of Hildesheim*, I, 170. Sophia was personally annoyed when the zealous Bernward admonished her on her way of life. She had gone off to live at court from 994 to 997 and attended her brother's imperial coronation in Rome in 996. Apparently Bernward disliked the relaxation of conventual rules and strict obedience which was the trend among the younger noble ladies at the nunnery, among whom Sophia was the most eminent.

[9] *Ibid.*, p. 173.

[10] Uhlirz, *Jahrbücher*, II, 350. The resolution of the council was issued in the name of *duo principes*, the pope and the emperor, whose joint authority was apparently necessary to make any impression on the powerful primate of Germany.

retainers, slipped out of town during a recess and thwarted the plans of pope and emperor. The fact that the archbishop could exhibit such contempt for his sovereign shows where Otto's III's Italian policy had brought affairs in Germany.

When Otto died in 1002, the case was still unsettled, for the pope had not been able to force his authority on the German primate. It might be thought that the new king, Henry II, would immediately espouse Bernward's cause, as he had already done when duke of Bavaria, but this was not the case. Archbishop Willigis had given Henry strong support in his bid for the crown while Bernward for a time backed a rival. Moreover, the hostile Sophia, a cousin of the new king, had now become abbess of Gandersheim. Bernward was not in a position to press his claims. On the other hand, the church at Gandersheim did remain unconsecrated, so that the bishop of Hildesheim could still fancy that he retained his old spiritual authority over the nuns there. In the meantime he made himself useful to the new monarch and endeavoured to prove his loyalty, even going with him to battle against Count Baldwin of Flanders.

Finally at Pöhlde on Christmas Day 1006, Willigis capitulated. It has been conjectured that in lieu of Gandersheim he accepted Würzburg: though already under his archdiocese there was a threat of it being raised to an archdiocese in its own right, and it would thereby be lost to Mainz. The bishop of Würzburg, Henry, had promised the king to push forward the foundation of Bamberg in exchange for his own elevation to archbishop. However, the king, after receiving Bishop Henry's support, reneged, and that is why we find Henry of Würzburg mentioned but not present at the Frankfurt synod of 1007 which established Bamberg (Doc. 27). He was apparently too annoyed to attend.

At last, on Sunday 5 January 1007, Bernward was given the honour of consecrating the church of Gandersheim.[11] Willigis attended but did not preside, and even the headstrong Sophia made no public show of displeasure. When the interior of the church had been blessed, Willigis, Bernward, and King Henry told the crowd assembled outside that the dispute belonged to the bishops of Hildesheim, whereupon Willigis renounced his erroneous claims.

The results of this public acknowledgement are embodied in a document that Henry issued in 1013 (Doc. 28). He probably issued an earlier one soon after the ceremony at Gandersheim in 1007, but this is thought to have been destroyed in the fire which burned the cathedral of Hildesheim in the year 1013. It is an indication of Henry's diplomatic skill in managing Church affairs that the powerful archbishop of Mainz backed down gracefully and, as far as we know, did not again question

[11] Tschan, *Bernward of Hildesheim*, I, 195.

E

the authority of the bishops of Hildesheim over Gandersheim, even though the abbess wished to come under the control of Mainz. This diplomatic coup contrasts sharply with the ineffectual synod in Rome of Otto III and Pope Sylvester II, who while enthusiastically supporting Bernward's claim had insufficient authority in German ecclesiastical affairs to see that their orders were actually carried out. Henry seems to have commanded so much respect from the great primate that Willigis found it convenient to back down from his long-standing claim.

One of the ways that Henry chose to increase the loyalty of the bishops was by awarding smaller abbeys to episcopal sees. One such donation, made in 1017, transferred the Benedictine monastery of Helmarshausen to the bishopric of Paderborn (Doc. 29). The reason for the donation as set forth in the diploma is that bishops have the duty of visiting religious houses, 'and if they find anything there outside the rule they are to put a stop to it and correct the situation'. We have no reason to doubt the king's desire to reform the monasteries, for he was an enthusiastic supporter of the Cluniac ideals. 'Filled with ecclesiastical spirit, he set himself to regulate Church affairs as seemed to him best in the Church's interest; and the instinct for order which urged him from the first to promote its efficiency developed at last into a passionate zeal for its reformation.'[12]

If his primary purpose was to reform the Church by controlling the bishops, the method chosen was nevertheless calculated to produce episcopal enthusiasm for the crown. By turning over abbey lands to the bishops, Henry cleverly enriched a powerful class of prelates without dipping into the fisc. This was both sound politics and sound economic policy. It also made it easier for him to appoint bishops at will. Otto the Great had done the same with marked success, even where the diocese had been guaranteed the right of free election by royal charter. The old Frankish custom had been to allow the members of the Church, both lay and clerical, to elect new bishops, but this practice sometimes resulted in the appointment of a local man for political reasons alone. When the king intervened in episcopal appointments, the choice was also political but with a difference: the royal candidate was free of local control and could exercise his authority without undue interference on the part of the nearest count or duke.

Paderborn was a bishopric from which Henry had withheld the right of free election altogether. The incumbent, Meinwerk, was a royal appointee and was no doubt delighted at the addition to the wealth of his church.[13] When he came to Paderborn as bishop, he destroyed the

[12] Holthouse, *Cambridge Medieval History*, III, 231.
[13] Though the clergy of Paderborn were guaranteed by Rome the free selection of their own bishop, they sent envoys to Henry upon the death of Bishop Rethari

liturgical books in use there because of their poor quality and obtained better ones. He was also a patron of the plastic arts and ordered a valuable goblet given him by Henry II to be made into a fine chalice. So the effect of this particular appointment was to raise local standards, and though Paderborn never rivalled Hildesheim as a cultural centre, it was certainly well advanced by Bishop Meinwerk, a wealthy and cultivated man.

In awarding monastic property to bishoprics, Henry was exploiting an ancient rivalry between the secular and regular clergy. The abbots were violently opposed to becoming, as it were, the poor cousins of the bishops, but it suited Henry's concept of their respective functions. In accordance with Cluniac ideals, he believed: 'Monks were intended for prayer and spiritual contemplation apart. Bishops were meant for service in the outside world.'[14] It was only natural that the abbots whose property was being stripped away were bitter, particularly those whose property was not awarded to a bishop but was reannexed to the fisc, which sometimes happened. When alienation of property was accompanied by demands for strict observance of monastic rule, the results were predictably unstable. In 1005 Henry interfered in the affairs of the rich abbey of Hersfeld by appointing as abbot the reformer Godehard, who gave the monks the choice of either a strictly regular life-style or immediate expulsion. Nearly all the members of the abbey left forthwith, and the land formerly reserved for their use was transferred by the king to the possession of the abbot. In this way Henry was assured of continued reform at Hersfeld.

Godehard succeeded in reviving Hersfeld under strict rule, and most of the monks gradually drifted back. However, this did not prevent the monarch from further supervision of abbey affairs. There was trouble between Hersfeld and the near-by monastery of Fulda among the dependants, or what was called the 'family', those tenants who lived and worked on the cloister grounds. The long-standing feud between the two foundations gave rise to fights, thefts, and murders. Henry's solution was ruthless: he issued a diploma in 1024 ordering that old grievances be redressed (Doc. 30). Any servant caught breaking into the courtyard of either monastery with a force of armed men for the purpose

on 6 March 1009, asking the monarch to select a new man. Henry called Meinwerk to fill the empty post and with the ceremonial handing over of a glove, together with the word *accipe*, entrusted the bishopric to his care. When Meinwerk, who was a rich man, asked what he was expected to do with Paderborn since he obviously might have qualified for a more important church, the king replied: 'because I truly consider this, therefore I desire that you mercifully remedy this lack of riches'. See Hanns Leo Mikoletzky, *Kaiser Heinrich II. und die Kirche*, Vienna, 1946, p. 33, quoting the *Vita Meinwerci*.

[14] Thompson, *Feudal Germany*, I, 65.

of murder or robbery was to be punished by having his skin and hair removed and having a white-hot sword applied to his cheeks. His henchmen would also lose skin and hair. Moreover, a suitable wergild for any murder victim was to be paid to the appropriate church. The advocates of the monasteries were charged with the duty of seeing that the sentence was carried out, and they were expressly warned against circumventing the terms of the charter either because of pity or bribery.

Henry's ecclesiastical policy, severe at times, was an effective one. He received the enthusiastic support of the bishops while enforcing needed reforms on the monasteries. The fisc was replenished, and the German Church once again became a solid base for royal policy. The only drawback was that the bishops became secularized in the acquisition of so much power and wealth. It was predictable that they should begin to act independently when the chance came. They had neither motive nor opportunity to revolt under Henry II, a capable efficient ruler, but the possibility of later strife was introduced. Yet it is hard to see how Henry could have done better. The throne he inherited was coveted by two powerful rivals: Margrave Eckhard of Meissen and Duke Herman II of Swabia. Henry had to fight for support all over the kingdom. Germany had been virtually abandoned in favour of Italy by Henry's predecessor, Otto III, and consequently there were notable defections on almost every frontier: Lombardy, Bohemia, and Lotharingia, revolted from German overlordship. The powerful Polish Duke Boleslav the Mighty invaded the Mark of Gero up to the Elbe and then occupied the Mark of Meissen. Boleslav ruthlessly seized Bohemia, had the duke blinded, and then got himself accepted as duke of the Bohemians in Prague. Henry was obliged to fight Boleslav in three separate wars. In 1004 he invaded Italy in order to retrieve the traditional crown of Lombardy for the German king, and in 1005 the Frisians revolted. In the following year Count Baldwin IV of Flanders crossed the Scheldt and took the town of Valenciennes. Henry replied by laying waste the surrounding territory, but it was not until 1007 that Baldwin took an oath of fealty to Henry.

Henry's most important military ventures were in the East, for they were coupled with a desire to Christianize the area as well as to conquer it. Although he was a devout ruler, Henry did not wage a crusade in the technical sense. By Carl Erdmann's definition a crusade involves the detachment of the ethic of war from the person of the ruler and the transfer of the Christian tasks to the army.[15] Henry even allied himself with the heathen Slavic tribe of Liutizi against the Christian Poles at one point. For this reason Erdmann calls the campaigns against the

[15] *Die Entstehung des Kreuzzugsgedankens*, Stuttgart, 1955, p. 95.

Slavs a 'heathen war' coupled with a 'heathen mission' rather than a crusade.[16]

Henry was no crusader though he was a great reformer. It was his good fortune that during the latter part of his reign the see of St Peter was occupied by a congenial pope, Benedict VIII. In 1020 Benedict honoured the emperor by personally coming to Bamberg to consecrate the new basilica of St Stephen. In the same year the so-called *Heinricianum* was issued for the pope, the reconfirmation of the donation document of Otto the Great in 962. Hanns Leo Mikoletzky calls it a 'frequently overrated document', and says that Henry would not have been overly concerned with the problem of its many binding stipulations.

'For the content of these privileges had taken on a rigid form, whose confirmation was perhaps a question of prestige for the papacy but no longer an exalted obligation of the German king. The recognition of the Church's property and rights which found expression there would surely have been advanced by the Curia in case of emergency on the ground of earlier confirmations without this gesture of Henry's. . . . '[17]

This interpretation of the whole tradition of the *Ottonianum* assumes that it was a prestigious advantage for the papacy, whereas Percy Schramm takes the position that it was a political triumph for the emperor.

[16] *Ibid.* A. J. P. Taylor would simply call it extermination (*The Course of German History*, p. 14).
[17] *Heinrich II. und die Kirche*, pp. 68–9.

6

The Reign of Conrad II (1024-1039)

Henry II, surnamed 'the Saint', having made God his heir, died without offspring at Castle Grona on 13 July 1024, and was buried at Bamberg. The male line of the Saxon kings had come to an end, but there were suitable candidates stemming from Otto the Great's daughter Liutgard, who had married Conrad the Red, duke of Lotharingia. The choice devolved upon two cousins by the name of Conrad. The elder had the reputation of good character alone, whereas the younger had vast estates in Franconia and a reforming attitude in ecclesiastical affairs similar to that of the late emperor. Yet it was the penurious elder Conrad who was elected in the end, precisely because he was known to oppose the Cluniac reforms; for the bishops, most of whom were also opposed to Cluny, considered him a safer candidate from their point of view.

The story of the election of Conrad II is told by the historian Wipo, who was chaplain to the king (Doc. 31). The situation was desperate, for there was no automatically acceptable candidate for the first time in almost a hundred years. 'In a short time after the death of the Emperor,' says Wipo in his *Deeds of Conrad II*, 'the commonwealth, so to speak, desolate through the loss of its father, began to stagger. From this happening all the best men had fear and anxiety that the empire was in danger, but the worst prayed that this were so.' The secular and ecclesiastical princes of the realm gathered on the Rhine at a place called Kamba, between Mainz and Worms, to elect a successor to Henry. Wipo puts into the mouth of the elder Conrad a somewhat florid speech, whose main point is that whichever Conrad gets the throne, the other will be equally honoured, though he does not say he will be equally powerful. Archbishop Aribo of Mainz led off the voting, and he 'acclaimed and elected the elder Cuono [i.e. Conrad] as his lord and king, and rector and defender of the fatherland'.[1] The other magnates fol-

---

[1] Aribo was rewarded for his good judgement when in 1025 Conrad deprived Bishop Eberhard of Bamberg of the archchancellorship of Italy and gave it to Aribo, who was already archchancellor of Germany. Thus the archbishop of

lowed suit, including the younger Conrad. Then Henry's widow, the Empress Kunigunda, handed over her husband's regalia to the new king. The election over, they repaired to Mainz for the consecration.

Though Wipo characterizes Conrad as 'a man of great humility, provident in counsel, truthful in statements, vigorous in deeds, not at all greedy, the most liberal of all kings in giving', it was none of these virtues that got him elected, but principally as we have said, his lack of reforming zeal. Since Aribo of Mainz, primate of Germany, did not favour a meddling monarch, Conrad the elder won out over his reform-minded cousin. Consequently, those members of the electoral party who were enthusiastic for Cluny went away disappointed from the consecration in Mainz. This was especially true of the lay and ecclesiastical magnates of Lotharingia, where Cluniac reforms were popular. In fact, the dukes of Upper and Lower Lorraine together with the Count of Hainault refused to recognize the new king when their own candidate was defeated.

The day after the consecration on 9 September 1024, Conrad issued his first charter at Mainz for Odilo, abbot of Cluny, and as a result of this gesture, the pro-Cluniac group in Lotharingia was persuaded to acknowledge the new monarch (Doc. 32). Conrad awarded two estates and a hide of land to the cloister of Peterlingen (or Payerne), a Cluniac establishment. The diploma states that Odilo and his congregation brought charters to Conrad which had been confirmed by Emperors Otto I, Otto II, Otto III, and the late Henry, granting the said lands and the right of appointing their own advocate. It is noteworthy that the charter reads as if Odilo were abbot of St Mary's of Peterlingen, whereas he resided at Cluny, the mother establishment. The peremptory handling of daughter monasteries by the abbot of Cluny is a mark of the tenure of Odilo (994–1049), who sought to bring all the Cluniac organizations under the closest possible supervision. '. . . whereas in the tenth and eleventh centuries the abbots of Cluny had been content to reform by imposing Cluniac uses and by temporary supervision, the tendency grew to deprive monasteries of their autonomy, and even to draw back into the system houses previously reformed, but left independent.'[2] As a consequence of Conrad's corroboration of the charters

Mainz became head of both major divisions of the imperial chancery. Aribo's church also received the gift of a county, which Conrad took away from the unlucky Meinwerk of Paderborn. Despite these favours, Aribo was by no means a tool in the hands of the new monarch: he stubbornly refused to crown Conrad's wife Gisela at the royal coronation in Mainz because she was considered to be too closely related to her husband. Archbishop Pilgrim of Cologne did not scruple to do the honours, and Gisela was crowned on 21 September 1024, not many days after Conrad's coronation at Mainz.

[2] Dom David Knowles, *The Monastic Order in England*, Cambridge, 1950, p. 146.

of his predecessors for Abbot Odilo, the antagonism of the reforming party among the German magnates was diminished, and the new king was able to travel through Lotharingia receiving the customary submission.

Conrad could now make his *Königsritt* through the provinces of the kingdom or, as Wipo called it, *iter regis per regna*.[3] His first destination was the palace at Aachen, where he sat upon Charlemagne's throne dispensing justice to those bringing complaints before him. In October we find him in Liége; then proceeding along the Maas he visited Nimwegen. Throughout Lotharingia the new king was peaceably accepted, despite his earlier unpopularity with the local bishops. In November he headed for Saxony and spent the Christmas holidays at Minden, joined by a great number of lay and clerical princes, including many of those who had been absent from the election of the new king. A similar gathering in honour of Henry II had taken place at Merseburg in June 1002, but in Conrad's case it was even more significant, for the crown had passed not merely from one individual to another but also from one dynasty to another, from the Saxons to the Salians.[4] According to Wipo the assembled magnates would not tender homage to the new king until he guaranteed the recognition of Saxon tribal law.[5]

At Eastertime of the following year Conrad had his first opportunity to dabble in Italian affairs. A certain Abbot Ambrose from a monastery near Lucca visited the king at Augsburg, asking for documentary confirmation of his property together with royal protection for the abbey.[6] This shows that there was still some feeling that the German king could exercise his overlordship in northern Italy, even though Conrad had not yet made the customary visit to obtain the Lombard crown and to assert his authority in the manner of his predecessors.

In fact, upon the death of Henry II a general uprising took place among those who were unwilling subjects of the German crown. During Henry's reign in 1004 the city of Pavia had been reduced to ashes as a result of the battle between the German army and the rebellious townspeople. Henry's warriors had taken refuge in the royal palace, the site of coronation of the Lombard king, and the Pavese, in an effort to drive them out, set fire to the building. The ancient fortress, symbolizing the foreign tyrants and going back reputedly to the myth-laden days of Theodoric, was burned to the ground.[7]

---

[3] Harry Bresslau, *Jahrbücher des Deutschen Reichs unter Konrad II.*, I, *1024–1031*, Berlin, 1967, 37 and n. 4.

[4] The etymology of the word 'Salian' has not been determined, though it seems to refer to a noble Frankish house. The chronicler Otto of Freising (b. 1146) calls the Salians 'the noblest of the Franks' (*nobilissimi Francorum, qui Salici dicuntur*). See Bresslau, *Jahrbücher*, II, 519–20.

[5] *Ibid.*, I, 42.   [6] *Ibid.*, p. 57.   [7] *Ibid.*, pp. 65–7.

The castle had been rebuilt, but in 1024 upon receiving news of the death of Henry, the excited inhabitants of Pavia assaulted the unprotected building and demolished it, and, according to Wipo, swore never to allow the construction of another within the town. But though the inhabitants of the Lombard communes were glad to throw off the German yoke, they were not joined in their xenophobia by the major nobles and prelates. Archbishop Aribert of Milan, Bishop Leo of Vercelli, together with the bishops of Como, Parma, Novara, Verona, and Modena remained loyal to the emperor's successor. The anti-German party was strong enough to engineer an offer of the Lombard crown to Robert of France, who refused it, and then to Duke William V of Aquitaine. However, these attempts to extricate Lombardy from under the German thumb were abortive.

Conrad met with Italian envoys at Constance in 1025, and there were even representatives from Pavia who tried to assuage the feelings of the angry king. Conrad announced that he would cross the Alps with an army, and Archbishop Aribert of Milan, making an example for the other Lombard prelates, swore to receive him, elect him king, and carry out the coronation.[8] Wipo tells us what the envoys from Pavia said in defence of the destruction of the palace: the citizens had not injured anyone, and they had remained true to Henry till the end of his life. It was inaccurate to say that they had destroyed the king's residence, for at the time they had had no king, which was technically true. The king is said to have replied: 'I know you did not destroy your king's palace, for you had no king at that time. But you cannot deny that you tore down a royal palace. When the king dies, the kingdom remains, just as the ship remains even when the helmsman has fallen. The buildings were public, not private.'[9] It is noteworthy that Conrad made a distinction between the property of the State and that of the monarch; they are often identical in the literature of the period.

In the next year, 1026, Conrad fulfilled his promise to enter Italy with a large army. He was accompanied by some of the most eminent prelates – Archbishops Aribo of Mainz and Pilgrim of Cologne, and Bishops Meinwerk of Paderborn and Adalbold of Utrecht. After crossing the Alps by way of the Brenner Pass, the king stopped at Verona where he issued a number of documents. From there he went to Milan where he received the Lombard crown from the hands of Archbishop Aribert. This was a departure from custom in that the ceremony usually took place in St Michael's Church in Pavia. The Pavese had not yet submitted to the new German king, and for that reason the place of coronation was the cathedral of Milan. For this service Aribert was rewarded

[8] *Ibid.*, p. 80.   *Ibid.*, p. 81.

with the rich abbey of Nonantola not far from Modena and the personal right to select and invest the abbot.[10]

Fom Milan, Conrad went to Vercelli where he celebrated Easter with the loyal Bishop Leo, who more than any other man was responsible for the fact that the king's opponents in Italy had not been more successful. Unfortunately Leo died on Easter day, 10 April, a great loss to the German crown and the Italian Church. The political repercussions were far-reaching, since the pro-German bishops among the Italian clergy would now pass under the control of Archbishop Aribert, a man of a different stripe from Leo. Leo, probably a German by birth, had belonged to the palace chapel of Otto III and was intimately acquainted and sympathetic with imperial plans. Aribert, by contrast, came from a prominent Lombard family and was inclined to favour imperial policies only when they coincided with his own ambitions for the Italian Church.

Since Pavia remained defiant, Conrad began a systematic campaign of destruction all around the city. Then he proceeded on a south-eastern course towards Rome. In Ravenna the inhabitants, like those of Pavia, were violently anti-German and rose in revolt, storming the city gate and overrunning the unsuspecting troops quartered on the outside. The Bavarian Count Eppo, who carried the banner of the king, attempted to make his way out of the city, probably to rally the soldiers before the gates. On a bridge over the river Montone he was surrounded by a contingent of armed men, but he managed to cut a path through them and dumped some of the bodies in the river below. Meanwhile the German troops within the city had regrouped and hacked down those citizens who did not flee for safety to the church or other places of refuge. 'When daylight broke, the penitent townspeople who had escaped the bloodbath appeared before Conrad dressed in hairshirts, barefoot, with unsheathed swords hanging round their necks, to beg for mercy and to take upon themselves whatever punishment the king would mete out.'[11]

Not until springtime of 1027 did he arrive in Rome. The imperial coronation, which took place in St Peter's on Easter Day, was perhaps the most splendid ever seen there. Two kings were in attendance, Rudolf III of Burgundy and Knut the Great of Scandinavia and England. The two German archbishops, Aribo of Mainz and Pilgrim of Cologne, were there besides most of the bishops. Abbot Odilo of Cluny attended, and so did the abbot of Reichenau. Among the Italian clergy were the Patriarch Poppo of Aquileia, the archbishops of Ravenna and Milan, forty bishops, and sixteen abbots. Pope John XIX, brother of the deceased Benedict VIII, with the clergy and people of Rome,

[10] Bresslau, *Jahrbücher*, II, p. 122.   [11] *Ibid.*, p. 131.

received Conrad, and the festivities were officially begun. It was customary for the king, before he entered St Peter's, to give his hand to one of the higher clergy who would lead him to the altar. Archbishop Aribert of Milan was supposed to have the honour, but the envious Archbishop Heribert of Ravenna grabbed Conrad's hand instead and led the king into the church, leaving Archbishop Aribert outside. Conrad could not afford to snub Aribert so he dropped the hand of Heribert and sent word via some of the prelates to bring Aribert inside. However, Aribert had departed from the scene, and the crowd out front was too thick to penetrate speedily. In order not to delay the ceremony any longer or to insult the archbishop of Milan, the king chose Bishop Arderich of Vercelli, the first among the suffragans of Milan, and had him act as a stand-in for Aribert. After the coronation the adherents of the archbishops of Milan and Ravenna exchanged words and then blows, the Milanese chasing their opponents to their quarters, which they ransacked and broke up.

This altercation was bad enough, but an even worse tumult erupted over the quarrel between a German and a Roman as to who should have possession of a steer's hide. The Romans had traditionally disliked the German overlord, and any small dispute might trigger their feelings to explosion. Soon the imperial army and the whole population of the city were involved. The Romans put up a good fight, but the Germans killed and wounded enough of them to quell the riot. As in Ravenna the beaten townspeople appeared contrite next day before the emperor, the freemen with unsheathed swords around their necks, the serfs with willow switches in symbolic acceptance of whatever punishment should be given them.

On 19 May the emperor and his son, the future Henry III, presided over a synod in a cloister near Verona (Doc. 33). In addition to the many German and Italian bishops in the audience was an important secular magnate, Count Hugo, an illegitimate member of the powerful Otbertine family of Lombardy.[12] The Otbertines had rebelled against Conrad's overlordship only a year before, and this is the first mention of any family member in the entourage of the emperor. The plaintiff was Duke Adalbero of Carinthia, in the company of his advocate Wecellinus.

Adalbero of Eppenstein had been appointed duke of Carinthia by Henry II in 1011, by-passing Conrad the elder and Conrad the younger, who were grandsons of the former duke. Conrad the younger at least inherited lands in Franconia, which helped him in his bid for the crown in 1024. It need hardly be said that Conrad the elder, the current German emperor, would scarcely be well disposed to Duke Adalbero in

[12] *Ibid.*, p. 182.

this lawsuit. Adalbero was claiming from the towns and villages under Patriarch Poppo of Aquileia the right of *fodrum*, the supplying of food for his men-at-arms. Poppo denied the claims of the duke and 'proved' his assertions by having his advocate and four oath-helpers swear that he owed no services to any man, neither dukes nor counts nor other officials. Duke Adalbero was condemned to give up his claim on pain of an indemnity of 100 pounds of gold. However, before the assembled princes would concur in the deprivation of Adalbero, they insisted that the emperor's son, young Henry, give his opinion in the matter. He was to pass judgement only as a prince, not as a judge for his father (an unusual constitutional detail, according to Waitz), and he refused to agree with Conrad. The emperor begged and threatened to no avail until at length, beside himself with anger, he fell down upon the floor in a stupour. Henry then admitted that he had sworn to the bishop of Freising, his old tutor, that he would not condemn Adalbero, but finally changed his mind, allowing Conrad to pronounce the sentence.[13] The grudge that Adalbero carried away from this court case was to be felt throughout Conrad's reign until in 1035, at the Diet of Bamberg, the duke was charged with treasonable intent, deposed, and deprived of his fiefs.

Conrad was suspicious not only of counts and dukes like Adalbero but equally so of ecclesiastical princes. His policy towards the Church, though different from that of Henry II, was none the less effective in its way. He made far fewer outright grants of land and cut down on waste in the administrative costs of ten major abbeys in Germany by putting them all under the control of one man, Poppo of Stablo.[14] Though frugal in granting land, he was generous in the matter of coinage and market rights.

One churchman who benefited from Conrad's liberality in this respect was Kadeloh, bishop of Naumburg, who was appointed in 1030. In that year he was granted the privilege of planting trees in a near-by area and the exclusive right to hunt there. In 1033 he himself issued a diploma, with the emperor's permission, which had important commercial consequences for the city of Naumburg (Doc. 34). This charter, unlike the imperial diplomas which we have seen up to now, is in the first person: 'Be it known . . . that I Kadeloh, bishop of Naumburg . . .

[13] Waitz, *Verfassungsgeschichte*, VIII, 37–8.

[14] Thompson, *Feudal Germany*, I, 71. Thompson gives very high marks to Conrad for his economic policy, which he characterizes as 'sound and constructive' (*ibid.*, p. 348). By contrast his son, Henry III, is guilty of 'exaggerated piety'; he 'wasted again what his father had recovered and conserved of the fisc' (*ibid.*, p. 349). Since Henry is often considered to be the ideal monarch of the Middle Ages it would seem that Thompson's emphasis on economics is here a bit wide of the mark.

have granted . . .' etc. He notifies the merchants of the town of Gena (modern Grossjena) that if they move to Naumburg, they will be exempt from property taxes and will have the right to carry on trade. The charter rights are corroborated at the end of the document by the imperial seal. We do not know how many businessmen took advantage of his offer, but we do know that the famous Peter and Paul's Fair of Naumburg goes back to this era.[15] In 1036 the successful Kadeloh, who had obtained for the merchants of Naumburg the same rights as the businessmen of royal cities, was appointed chancellor of Italy.

Kadeloh's promotion coincided with Conrad's second trip to Italy, and the new chancellor went along. There were two principal reasons for the campaign. For one thing Archbishop Aribert of Milan, the mighty prelate who at the imperial coronation in 1027 was cheated out of the honour of escorting the German king to the altar of St Peter's, had not proved to be a loyal pillar of imperial policy. Conrad was seeking to increase his control over the Italian Church by appointing German bishops; for example, Gebhard of Eichstätt was named archbishop of Ravenna. This policy did not allow Aribert sufficient authority in what he considered his own sphere of influence.

More significant, Aribert was directly involved in a dispute concerning the secular magnates, which gave the immediate impetus to Conrad's trip to Italy in 1036. The archbishop had deprived a lesser feudal vassal, or *valvassor*, of a fief in Milan, and this insult led to an open fight between the *valvassores* and their supporters, the *capitanei*, assisted by a force of city inhabitants. The annalist Saxo and the Swabian chronicle both report simply that 'Italy laboured under civil discord'. Wipo says, 'All the *valvassores* of Italy and common soldiers conspired against their lords and all lesser vassals against the greater so that they would not allow anything to go unpunished that had been done to them by their lords if it was against their own will. . . .' In the annals of St Gall the reason for the rebellion of the knights is given as excessive oppression by the unjust lords, and this same source reports that serfs also took part.[16]

The Milanese *valvassores*, who were joined in battle by knights from the countryside, defeated their rivals in a place named Campo Malo near Motta, between Lodi and Milan. At this point both sides agreed to call upon the emperor for a ruling. In fact, the *valvassores* said that if he did not come, they themselves would issue laws. Upon receiving the invitation Conrad is said to have remarked, 'If Italy hungers for law, I will satisfy her well, God willing'.[17] Bresslau interprets this statement as an

---

[15] Bresslau, *Jahrbücher*, I, 264.   [16] *Ibid.*, II, 212, and notes 1–3.
[17] *Ibid.*, p. 215. The source is Wipo: *si Italia modo esurit legem, concedente Deo bene legibus hanc satiabo.*

expression of 'the proud self-consciousness of the ruler, who alone had the obligation and the capacity to restore peace and order. So strong and relentless was the harsh nature of this emperor that he had to punish other insurrections against the constituted authority, yet in this case he could not do otherwise but to sympathize with the rebels.'[18]

Conrad's passion for justice was his most outstanding characteristic. Though the number of his diplomas is not greater than those of his predecessors, their content represents an improvement. '. . . much of the energetic legislation of the Saxons got nowhere, for it was all of a special, particular nature. It lacked co-ordination and the organic quality of real law. With the accession of the Salian emperors this defect began to be remedied. Conrad II's legislation, though not large in volume, is singularly constructive in quality. . . .'[19]

The emperor set out for Italy in December 1036, and spent Christmas in Verona.[20] He was received in Milan with the greatest respect from both the citizens and the archbishop, who met him in St Ambrose's Cathedral with splendid courtesy. But according to Wipo the peace lasted less than twenty-four hours. The crowd began to berate the emperor with accusations, specifically that he had wrongly appointed a bishop for Lodi over the head of their archbishop, and thereby harmed the population of Milan. Conrad thought Aribert had deliberately stirred up the crowd against him, though this has never been proved, but instead of resorting to arms right away, he called for a synod in Pavia where all grievances would be heard.

The imperial court convened in late March, and at once it was clear that the tables had been turned, for this time the audience directed its complaints against the archbishop.[21] Many of the spectators were *valvassores*, but there were also a significant number of the higher nobility who did not like Aribert, for example, Count Hugo of Milan, a member of the powerful Otbertine family. Conrad ordered the archbishop to come before the judicial chair and defend himself against the accusations, but he refused. After conferring with his friends for a while, Aribert offered up this haughty explanation: whatever he had found in the possession of the church of St Ambrose upon his assumption of office and whatever he had added to it, he meant to keep, nor would he give up a bit of it on anyone's request or command. He would not recognize the emperor's right, as highest judge in the realm, to give orders.

[18] Bresslau, *Jahrbücher*, I, p. 215.

[19] Thompson, *Feudal Germany*, I, 317. Yet the Ottonians were far more successful than the contemporary French. Thompson points to the 'lassitude' of Hugh Capet, who issued only twelve diplomas in nine years, as against 425 of Otto III.

[20] Bresslau, *Jahrbücher*, II, 227.   [21] *Ibid.*, p. 231.

Bresslau calls Aribert's behaviour nothing less than high treason, and in this he fully agrees with Conrad, who declared Aribert an enemy of the realm and a traitor.[22] Moreover, he condemned him to pay back what he had illegally usurped, and put him under arrest. This punishment was bound to cause a stir. Not since Otto I arrested Archbishop Frederick of Mainz had a German emperor proceeded so harshly against a prince of the Church.[23] Rumours flew thick and fast. In Bavaria it was even said that Aribert had made an attempt upon Conrad's life at a dinner party, but that the would-be murderer had been apprehended in time.

The emperor had put an end to the insubordinate behaviour of the Italian prelates. Henry II had not been able to accomplish this. Archbishop Arnulf of Milan, Aribert's predecessor, had similarly rebuffed the orders of the emperor in the most contemptuous way by refusing to recognize the new bishop of Asti, an imperial appointee, and humiliating him by force of arms. Henry pardoned Arnulf because he was not in a position to make an enemy of him, but Conrad was in a stronger position.

The emperor retreated to Piacenza to reconnoitre, and brought with him the closely guarded archbishop. But Aribert worked out a plan of escape with a monk named Albizo, who lay on Aribert's bed with the covers over his head in order to fool the guard. The archbishop in the clothes of an ordinary monk was then able to leave the camp without difficulty. Aribert was greeted with a most enthusiastic reception by the citizens of Milan, and the monk Albizo was later rewarded with the office of abbot at the S. Salvador cloister in Piacenza.[24]

Upon being informed of the escape of his prize captive, the emperor sent word to his son Henry to bring an army down from Germany to help him against Aribert. At the same time he summoned the Italian princes to bring their armies to Milan prepared to help the imperial troops besiege the city. While waiting for the armies to assemble, Conrad travelled around with his chancellor Kadeloh of Naumburg drafting deeds of confirmation for loyal bishops and abbots.

Now the emperor was ready to fight, but so was Aribert, whose loyal citizens had worked in the interim to secure the city against attack. Conrad had the first success when his troops demolished the fortress of Landriano near Lodi, a strong outwork of Milan. On 19 May a major battle took place outside the city walls. Though there were great losses

[22] *Ibid.*, pp. 232–3.
[23] Frederick was arrested in 939 for complicity in the early rebellion against Otto I. It is not certain exactly what part he played, except to break with the king and take the bishops with him, after which he was imprisoned somewhere in Saxony. See Johnson, *Secular Activities of the German Episcopate*, p. 29, n. 20.
[24] Bresslau, *Jahrbücher*, II, 236.

on both sides, the Milanese were more effective; they kept the imperial forces from entering the town and finally drove them into retreat to their camp some three miles away.[25] From then on Conrad contented himself with keeping the city surrounded and cut off; assault was out of the question.

The most important event of the month was the publication of a diploma on 28 May regulating feudal relations between the *capitanei* and the *valvassores* (Doc. 35). This edict, known as the *Constitutio de feudis*, was designed to prevent the kind of dispute which had brought Conrad to Italy in the first place. Its importance can hardly be over-estimated and it strengthens Conrad's claim to being considered a law-giver of distinction.

The notification section of the diploma alludes to the historical situation with these words: 'To all of our faithful of the holy Church of God, present as well as future, we wish it to be known that in order to reconcile the minds of the lords [*seniorum*] and knights [*militum*] so that they may always be mutually harmonious and may faithfully and steadfastly serve us and devotedly serve their lords. . . .' Two major conclusions emerge from the text: first, that the property of a vassal, whether lay or clerical, is to be secure against arbitrary and illegal usurpation, and second, that all fiefs are guaranteed hereditary. A tenant may not lose his lands unless a fault has been proved before the emperor himself in the case of a great lord, before the great lords or an imperial *missus* in the case of a lesser vassal. The greater vassals are forbidden from exchanging any holding of their knights without their consent. The penalty is 100 pounds of gold, one-half to be paid to the imperial fisc and one-half to the plaintiff. The diploma is countersigned by the Italian chancellor Kadeloh.

The economic and social significance of the *Constitutio de feudis* is that it 'extended the right of hereditary succession to sub-vassals and transformed them into free proprietors, quit of all but the largely formal ties which bound them to the sovereign'.[26] As a result they turned their attention away from their overlords towards the city, 'where the urban market offered them means of profitably employing their revenues, where artisan production was increasing, and where they enjoyed the advantage of solidarity with their peers'.[27] Towards the end of the eleventh century these liberated middle-class landowners elected their own representatives, who became the nucleus of the early Italian commune.

[25] Bresslau, *Jahrbücher*, II, p. 242.
[26] Gino Luzzatto, *An Economic History of Italy*, trans. Philip Jones, London, 1961, p. 70.
[27] *Ibid.*, p. 71.

Inasmuch as the imperial army had suffered heavy losses and the hot season was approaching, the emperor decided to raise the siege of Milan and quarter his troops in secure districts. But this did not mark the end of the struggle with Archbishop Aribert. Conrad determined to depose him and to replace him with his own candidate without even calling a synod to approve the action. The new archbishop, Ambrose, was a canon of the cathedral at Milan and had been a member of the imperial chapel. It was one thing to appoint Ambrose and another to get the population of Milan to accept him. As one would expect, they clung even more tenaciously to Aribert. Though Ambrose made great promises to both laymen and clerics in order to win support, he gained little but hostility. Nor did the forced recognition of the new archbishop by his suffragans succeed in getting him into the cathedral of St Ambrose.

While Conrad was thus engaged in trying to impose his will upon the recalcitrant Milanese, Count Odo of Champagne took advantage of his German rival's absence in Italy to invade Lotharingia, where he first plundered the bishopric of Toul and then reduced the town of Commercy to smouldering ruins.[28] At this moment word was brought to Odo that an envoy from Archbishop Aribert had arrived in Champagne to seek an alliance. Aribert, with the help of a number of dissident Lombard bishops, meant to wrest the crown away from Conrad. Not only were Aribert's old associates among the conspirators but also Bishop Hubald of Cremona, who had always been true to Conrad, and with good reason.

When Hubald was named to fill the post in 1030 and went to Milan for consecration, Archbishop Aribert delayed the ceremony until Hubald gave up claims to a piece of property belonging to the church of Cremona, in favour of Aribert's nephew and heir apparent, Gariard. Early in 1031 when Hubald was in Germany, he complained to Conrad, who issued orders to Gariard to give up his illegal hold on the property. Not only did Gariard not obey, he began a systematic campaign of harassment against Hubald by occupying other properties of the church of Cremona. On 27 February 1031, the emperor presented Hubald with a diploma guaranteeing him total authority over the city and claim to certain rights and properties that were in dispute. In March of 1037 at the synod of Pavia where Archbishop Aribert was declared guilty of high treason, his nephew was outlawed and deprived of the property which he had seized from Hubald.

Finally, in an undated charter that must have been issued before Hubald changed sides, Conrad granted the property of a certain Adam to the church of Cremona because Adam had murdered a canon who was under the emperor's protection (Doc. 36). Adam, says the emperor,

[28] Bresslau, *Jahrbücher*, II, 254–5.

F

was 'puffed up by the spirit of pride and spurred on by diabolic boldness', and by killing the cardinal deacon Henry 'destructively depre-
ciated the reverence of our majesty'. The movable and immovable
property of the said Adam was to be conveyed to the church of Cremona
'on condition that our faithful beloved Hubald, venerable bishop of the
same church . . . may perpetually do whatever seems right' to him and
his successors. The punishment for violation is a fine of 200 pounds of
gold, half to the imperial fisc and half to the church and its rector.

It is puzzling that after such support from the emperor, Hubald
should join Aribert's cause, yet that is what happened shortly after
this diploma was released. Bresslau conjectures that it was probably
the *Constitutio de feudis* which brought about Hubald's defection and
that his uncharacteristic behaviour shows how decisively the edict affected
feudal relations in Italy.[29]

[29] Bresslau, *Jahrbücher*, II, p. 256. This is the kind of statement that has
brought documentary history under attack, for the sources are too skimpy to
support the author's conclusions. Using David Hackett Fischer's apparatus,
one can say that the question of 'why' Hubald defected is unanswerable: the
historian can legitimately ask only 'how?' But, in defence of Bresslau, we can
say that it would be very unsatisfactory for the reader to learn that the loyal
Hubald between one week and the next changed his allegiance from the
emperor, who had been his patron for seven years, to that of the archbishop,
whose nephew had been stealing his church's property during the same period.
To gloss over the feeling of dismay on the part of the reader is to ignore the fact
that people have certain expectations while reading history. When a character
has been presented as consistently loyal, and for the most logical reasons, his
sudden defection arouses one's curiosity, the historian's perhaps most of all.
In the absence of documentary evidence, the researcher either can say that
he is unable to explain this apparent aberration, or he can offer what seems to
him a plausible explanation. If he does neither, he merely bewilders the reader,
who expects the author to function as a kind of touchstone when the evidence is
contradictory or baffling. Bresslau often makes a conjecture as to the motivation
of his characters, and this is usually most helpful. What is weak about his statement concerning Hubald is that there is no evidence whatsoever as to why he
defected. Thereupon Bresslau uses his conjecture about Hubald's motivation as
evidence for the powerful effect of the *Constitutio de feudis*. There are any number
of possible reasons for Hubald's defection. Perhaps he thought Conrad's
authority in Italy was waning and that his patron would leave him in the lurch.
Conrad had not succeeded in taking Milan. He had not gotten his own candidate
acknowledged as archbishop of St Ambrose. He had apparently not even been
able to make his documentary decisions stick in the case of Hubald's own church
of Cremona, for Gariard seems to have harassed him brazenly for years. In such
circumstances Hubald might have thrown in his lot with Aribert if he thought it
meant his retention of the see of Cremona. There is no necessary connection
between Hubald's defection and the *Constitutio de feudis* at all, and there are
other possible explanations. Without data we cannot jump to a conclusion that
will supply us with convenient evidence on another point. This is where the
argument begins to look rigged: convincing evidence cannot be deduced from
conjecture.

When Conrad learned about the conspiracy between Aribert and Odo of Champagne, he acted swiftly, first declaring traitors the three bishops who had acted as accomplices – Hubald of Cremona and the bishops of Vercelli and Piacenza. After putting them under the ban, he imprisoned them, though Hubald was later pardoned by Henry III. Not until Easter of 1038 did Conrad take revenge on Aribert. The emperor was making an extended visit at the castle of Spello in the duchy of Spoleto, and he summoned Pope Benedict IX, who had made more than one trip out of Rome to oblige the imperious Conrad. At this meeting the pope agreed to excommunicate Archbishop Aribert, thus forcing the recognition of Ambrose, the imperial candidate.[30] Though Aribert could ignore the ban of the pope as he had ignored that of the emperor, his ecclesiastical supporters would not, and thus it was an important victory for Conrad.

Bresslau remarks upon the fact that once again Conrad summoned the pope rather than going himself to Rome.[31] Why did Conrad avoid Rome once he had received the imperial crown? Are we to think that the emperor was not in control of the city, that he could not risk a visit to the pope? Bresslau says no, citing as evidence a diploma which Conrad issued at about the same time (Doc. 37). It prescribes that cases involving a Lombard as plaintiff or defendant are to be tried according to Roman law if the trial takes place in Rome or its environs. From this edict Bresslau concludes that Conrad did indeed have control of Rome.[32] Yet he adduces no evidence to prove that the communiqué had any effect on the Roman judges to whom it was addressed, as if whatever the emperor documented is assumed to have been automatically obeyed.[33]

Karl Hampe says that the Salians, far more than the Ottonians or the average Staufen, were inclined toward blunt, inconsiderate action and that Conrad had perhaps the most determined, forceful will of any

---

[30] *Ibid.*, pp. 286–7.　　　　[31] *Ibid.*, p. 285.　　　　[32] *Ibid.*, pp. 285–6.

[33] This is an example of Fischer's 'reversible reference', which is a sub-species of the 'pseudo fact'. 'The problem of the reversible reference rises whenever a historian tries to draw an inference directly from law to life. A law against X can be interpreted as evidence for the existence of X or for its nonexistence' (*Historians' Fallacies*, p. 45). Fischer's example is that an anti-litter law of 1657 in New Amsterdam and its subsequent enforcement tell nothing about the cleanliness of the inhabitants: they could have been spotless or they could have been slovenly. In the same way, Bresslau concludes that Conrad had power in Rome because he issued a directive to all Roman judges. The edict may show Conrad's *desire* to regulate legal matters in and around Rome, but it tells us nothing about his *power* to regulate or his success in effecting his will. For that we need other evidence. The document is silent about the emperor's hold on Rome, though it may reveal his pique towards the Lombards, who in the person of the archbishop of Milan and his suffragans had conspired to overthrow him. This illustrates one of the pitfalls of documentary history: one tends to identify the document with a necessary result.

monarch in the German Middle Ages.[34] His treatment of Aribert
certainly showed tenacity of purpose against formidable odds.[35] Walter
Ullmann sees Conrad as 'an upright and stern, though coldly calculating
monarch, to whom the *sacerdotium* was a mere machine. . . . There can
have been few medieval monarchs who acted so faithfully in the spirit of
the Roman Caesars as Conrad did. . . .'[36] His seal was inscribed 'Rome,
the head of the world, holds the reins of the round earth'.

[34] *Deutsche Kaisergeschichte in der Zeit der Salier und Staufen*, 11th edn,
Heidelberg, 1963, p. 7.

[35] Two other especially ruthless acts are attributed to Conrad. In 1036 he
imprisoned Archbishop Burchard of Lyons and put him in chains. Admittedly
Burchard had a terrible reputation as tyrant, adulterer, and thief of church
treasure, but the real reason that Conrad deposed him was that he was very much
anti-German. The second 'atrocity' occurred during a raid against the heathen
Slavic tribe of Liutizi, also in 1036. The Liutizi mutilated a crucifixion figure of
Christ, and Conrad gave Old Testament punishment, mutilating the perpetrators by putting out their eyes, cutting off their hands and feet, and leaving them
to die.

[36] *The Growth of Papal Government in the Middle Ages*, 2nd edn, London,
1962, pp. 249–50.

7

The Reign of Henry III (1039-1056)

Conrad had Archbishop Pilgrim of Cologne crown his son Henry king in Aachen on Easter Day 1028, when the boy was only eleven years old. By the time Conrad died in 1039 Henry had served an excellent political apprenticeship. He accompanied his father into battle against the Poles in 1031. In 1032 Henry is mentioned as being present for the issuing of certain imperial diplomas. He was sent to fight the Slavs to the northeast and the Bohemians, and he acquitted himself with distinction. When his father was recognized as king of Burgundy in 1034, Henry was also recognized. And in 1035 when Duke Adalbero of Carinthia was deposed by Conrad for treason, Henry (as we have seen) refused to give his consent to the proceedings. Though he eventually gave in, it was obvious that Henry had a mind of his own and certain scruples which his father did not possess.

Upon Conrad's death there was no trouble about the succession. After his father had been buried in the crypt of the cathedral of Speyer, Henry began his royal progress through the realm, starting with Aachen. He travelled through Lotharingia, Saxony, Bavaria, and Swabia, the tour lasting until Easter of 1041, when it was officially concluded in the castle at Ingelheim on the Rhine. Here he received an envoy from the old enemy of his father, Archbishop Aribert of Milan. Henry accepted the homage of the archbishop and thereby set the stage for successful domination of north Italy. But before he could go there in person, he had to put down Duke Bratislav of Bohemia, who had invaded Poland.

In July of 1040 Henry met with his allies at Goslar, a town near the Harz mountains that became the king's favourite residence. The campaign, which began in August, was a notable failure, and Henry had to retreat, leaving Bratislav in control. Exactly one year later, after conferences with his magnates and much careful planning, he invaded again. This time Henry was successful, and Bratislav did public homage to the German king in Regensburg.

In the winter of 1041–2 Henry dispensed justice in Burgundy. Unlike his father, he was pro-Cluniac and approved of the reforms that had issued from the famed Burgundian abbey. Henry's monastic policy can also be distinguished from that of Henry II, who had enriched the bishops at the expense of the abbots (Doc. 29). Henry III tried to undo this damage by revoking such grants and giving the alienated property back to the monasteries. Gerhart Ladner interprets this innovation as a sign of Henry's desire to have direct control of religious houses (*Reichsunmittelbarkeit*).[1] The policy of sponsoring imperial monasteries, which had been pursued by Otto the Great, was thus revived by Henry III. He issued an interesting diploma early in 1043 (Doc. 38), telling how his father took away a fief (*beneficium*) from the abbey at Hersfeld and awarded it to Count Otto of Hammerstein. Now that both Otto and his wife are dead, Henry restores the property, together with full rights of disposal, to the abbot of Hersfeld.

It was characteristic of Henry II that he should enrich the bishops at the expense of the abbots; and it was likewise characteristic of the less pious Conrad II that he would give away monastery property to a secular noble. Under Henry III both of these practices were stopped, and the grievances of at least some of the houses were redressed. The direct control of monasteries by Henry III typifies his desire to exert authority in every way – in the appointment of foreign dukes in Bavaria, Swabia, and Lotharingia (that is, dukes who were not residents of those duchies), the later transfer of Bavaria to his sons and then to his wife, the strengthening of control in the eastern marches, and the strong dynastic tendency illustrated in the numerous documentary 'interventions' on the part of Empress Agnes and Henry IV.[2]

Another sign of direct control was Henry's adaptation of the *Treuga Dei*, the truce of God, which he had witnessed in operation during his royal progress through Burgundy. This regulation of the Church forbade the use of arms on all high holidays, as well as every weekend from Wednesday evening to Monday morning, in remembrance of the Lord's Passion. Though this ordinance did not effectively keep down violence as specified, Henry was obviously impressed with its intent. At a synod in Constance in October 1043, he made his own contribution to peace, which came to be known as the 'Day of Pardon' or 'Day of Indulgence'. From the pulpit he offered forgiveness for all past offences in an effort to reduce the number of destructive private feuds going on.

After this important meeting Henry travelled north to Besançon to celebrate his wedding with Agnes of Poitou, daughter of Duke William

---

[1] *Theologie und Politik vor dem Investiturstreit*, Leipzig, 1936, p. 63. See pp. 64–8 where Ladner lists the cases in which Henry restored abbatial property that had been alienated to bishops.   [2] *Ibid.*, p. 70.

of Aquitaine.[3] Twenty-eight bishops were present for the splendid ceremony. At the reception held in Ingelheim, Henry sent the jesters and jugglers away, for he was a serious king and wanted to keep the festivities on a solemn note. Within a few weeks after the wedding, on 29 November, Queen Agnes was given the honour of 'intervening' officially. She is listed as intercessor in a diploma reconfirming certain properties to the Italian monastery of Leno near Brescia.[4] The union with Agnes was designed to secure Henry's control over Burgundy, for the bride was a grand-daughter of Otto-William of Burgundy. A peaceful Burgundy to the south-west would facilitate the king's access to Italy. It is significant that Henry set up a separate chancery for Burgundy in 1045 and named Archbishop Hugo of Besançon as chancellor. This important territory was to function as a separate realm with its own laws.

By 1046 the borders were sufficiently secure for Henry to contemplate his first official visit to Italy as king of the Germans. He was on good terms with the pardoned Archbishop Aribert of Milan as well as with the pope. The serviceable Benedict IX had sanctioned Henry's marriage even though the bride and groom were both descendants of Henry the Fowler. Many churchmen in Germany had not been so undestanding of an uncanonical marriage. The Roman reform party revolted against Pope Benedict in 1044 and put in his place Sylvester III, bishop of S. Sabina, but he lasted only seven weeks. He was followed by a canon who took the name Gregory VI and generously reimbursed Benedict with a large sum of money for the privilege of being pope. Henry did not care for office-buyers, and he therefore called a synod in Pavia on 24 October 1046, to forbid simony. On 20 December at Sutri he took the more drastic step of deposing both Pope Gregory and Pope Sylvester. This edict was issued again in Rome three days later, and after Archbishop Adalbert of Bremen refused the offer of the papacy Henry conferred the honour upon Bishop Suidger of Bamberg, an excellent man, who reigned as Clement II.[5] This is the beginning of the

[3] Henry's first wife, Gunnhild, was the daughter of King Knut of England and Scandinavia. By this match Knut obtained the Kiel district of Schleswig, and the border remained unchanged for 800 years. Henry's father gained peace of mind in that the Norsemen would not attack his northern frontier. Unfortunately the marriage lasted only two years, for Gunnhild died of a fever when she accompanied her husband to Italy in 1038, where he had gone to help his father against Archbishop Aribert and the *capitanei*.

[4] Ernst Steindorff, *Jahrbücher des Deutschen Reichs unter Heinrich III.*, I, Darmstadt, 1963, 195.

[5] Adalbert was so powerful and so arrogant that he did not need to be pope in order to expand his authority. See the story of his downfall told by Adam of Bremen (Doc. 47). 'Adalbert dreamed of erecting his see into a huge patriarchate of northern Europe; almost, one might say, to make himself pope of all Baltic and Northern Atlantic Christendom.' See Thompson, *Feudal Germany*, I, 131.

line of reform popes which culminated with Gregory VII. It was the
keystone of Henry's policy that to reform the Church the head would
have to be a reformer.

'As supreme protector of Christendom . . . he could not but be resolved
to take matters into his own hands. The papacy being the chief pro-
tectorate of the empire . . . had to be purged of the unsuitable and useless individuals . . . Sutri signifies the consummation of the monarch's
supreme protective functions: Christendom had to be protected against
these unworthy individuals.'[6]

On the same day as the consecration of the new pope – Christmas
1046 – Henry and Agnes were crowned emperor and empress. The
Romans not only greeted the new imperial pair on their way to the
Lateran Palace, they also yielded to Henry the right to be 'patrician', an
office of great importance for Church affairs since it facilitated control
of papal elections.[7] Peter Damiani, prior of the Hermits of Fonte-
Avellana and an eyewitness of Henry's coronation, wrote that the patriciate conferred upon the emperor the right to have not only the first
but the decisive vote in choosing the pope. This power was not new.
It had been assumed by Otto the Great in 962 in his *Ottonianum*, whereby the Roman people swore that they would never elect or ordain a
pope without the consent of the emperor and his son (Doc. 8). What is
new is the close connection between the primacy in papal elections and
the office of patrician, and still more the assumption of the title of
patrician by the emperor.[8] Formerly the patriciate had been a stepping-
stone to the office of emperor.

To the papacy Henry's policy signified the tyranny of German customs over Roman, for in Germany the lord owned his chapel outright
and appointed a priest for it. This proprietary system had gradually
engulfed the bishops, so that the monarch eventually felt that they were
his to appoint and direct. Only in the reign of Henry III did the same
idea of proprietary control expand to include the Holy See as well.
'. . . a few more emperors like Henry III, and the mother-church in
Western Christendon would have bcome the private church of the
German ruler.'[9]

From Rome, Henry travelled to southern Italy with the pope in his
company. In the spring of 1047 we find him once again in the north
issuing diplomas for a variety of reasons. At S. Marotto in the county

[6] Ullmann, *Growth of Papal Government*, p. 251.
[7] Steindorff, *Jahrbücher*, I, 316.
[8] *Ibid.*, pp. 316–17.
[9] Ulrich Stutz, 'The Proprietary Church as an Element of Mediaeval Germanic Ecclesiastical Law', in *Mediaeval Germany*, II, trans. Geoffrey Barraclough, 64.

of Fermo he held a *placitum* for Bishop Bernard II of Ascoli in nothern Apulia, who claimed that a farm and a castle belonging to him had been appropriated by a certain lady named Albasia (Doc. 39). Albasia maintained that her husband had acquired the property through exchange with a certain Atto. The emperor then asked her if she could produce either the donor of the land or any witnesses who had seen the transaction. Albasia said that they were unwilling to appear in court. Henry then inquired of one of the judges, Bonusfilius by name, what the law was, and Bonusfilius replied, 'Lord, the law is that you cause her to renounce her possession in the aforesaid matter to the aforesaid bishop, that you have the aforesaid bishop patch up his quarrel with the aforesaid Albasia, and that you ought to make a perpetual grant to the aforesaid bishop and his advocate.'

And that is what the emperor did. He also put the bishop under his protective ban and set a penalty of 100 pounds of gold, half to go to the imperial fisc and half to the bishop. After the *placitum* had ended, a document recording the action was drawn up by Folcho, a palace notary.

It is astonishing that the emperor took time to sit in judgement on such relatively minor cases.[10] On the other hand, by dispensing justice throughout the realm he was asserting his right to make law and to arbitrate disputes between citizens of the empire. In this particular case Henry made a loyal vassal of the bishop of Ascoli as well. In 1055 the emperor issued a politically significant diploma for Bishop Bernard: he not only reconfirmed all the possessions of the church of Ascoli, he turned over all the rights which he had formerly granted to the county of Ascoli to the church, thus making the bishop a count. Steindorff sees this in principle as 'the very same trend toward secularization of the Church or the spiritualization of the State which the emperor observed in his relations with the higher clergy including the papacy'.[11]

Shortly after Henry decided the case between Albasia and Bishop Bernard, he issued an important diploma in Rimini (Doc. 40). It settles a conflict between the ecclesiastical rule that no cleric should swear an oath and the custom of taking an oath when involved in a lawsuit. Henry attributes to Theodosius the original law preventing clergy from taking an oath, and though the attribution is erroneous, it is interesting that the emperor went so far back for a diplomatic precedent. Furthermore, he alludes to Justinian as an authority for the statement that some canons of the fathers have the force of law; hence the canon forbidding clergy from oath-swearing should be observed. Bishops, priests, and all

[10] The entire diplomatic output of Henry III amounts to 335 diplomas, and though many of these are reconfirmations of earlier documents, the activity represented by such a number is undeniable.

[11] *Jahrbücher*, II, 308.

other secular clergy, together with abbots, monks, and nuns are guaranteed the right of refusing to take an oath before any criminal or civil court. They may fulfil their obligations by having their advocates take the oath for them.

The overall import of the decree, in Steindorff's opinion, is that the points of contact between the clergy and the secular community are being diminished, and this trend is vigorously supported by Henry III.[12] Yet it conflicts with Steindorff's earlier statement that Henry secularized the Church and spiritualized the State. The narrowing of contacts between clergy and secular society would seem to be in the opposite direction. Local customs obviously played a part in the decision: in Romagna clerics had always had an advocate swear the oath, whereas in Lombardy they took it themselves. At the *placitum* concerning Albasia there were jurists from Romagna present, but also the eminent Bonus-filius from Pavia, and it is the latter, a Lombard, who tells the emperor what the law is. In this case, however, the emperor favours the custom of Romagna over that of Lombardy, deciding that neither secular nor regular clergy should take an oath except through the agency of an advocate. To be sure, the diploma was issued at Rimini, which is in Romagna, but the decree affects the clerics of all churches, not just the surrounding locale. Whatever Henry's motives in prohibiting religious persons from swearing an oath, the decree cannot easily be reconciled with his general policy of secularizing the Church. This would seem to be a case where the documents do not support the generalizations made about them.

During this same spring of 1047 Henry drew up an interesting charter for the inhabitants of Val Scalve in the province of Como, guaranteeing them the right to carry on trade in iron and other wares throughout the empire (Doc. 41). For this privilege they must pay 1,000 pounds of iron to the royal court at Darfo (modern Dervio) in Val Camonica, but they are exempted from all other obligations such as toll and *fodrum*, nor can any local magnate exact duties from them. The fine is 100 pounds of gold, half to the fisc and half to the inhabitants of Val Scalve. Possibly there were metal workshops at Darfo which processed the ore, but the delivery of 1,000 pounds would not begin to cover the needs of the court and the army for a year.[13] The payment was a token. It is probable that the annual iron output was delivered to various estates and castles in the empire, the remainder being sold in Italy, 'the land of an advanced money economy'.[14]

---

[12] *Jahrbücher*, I, 331–2.

[13] Carlrichard Brühl, *Fodrum, Gistum, Servitium Regis*, I, Cologne, 1968, 521–2.

[14] *Ibid.*, p. 522.

Very little is known about the organization of trade before the twelfth century, except that merchants did not form a constituent part of the feudal system.[15] Canon law discouraged buying and selling, for it was not easy to tell ill-gotten gain from honest.[16] Yet the Saxon and Salian emperors seem to have been generous in their granting of market, mint, and toll rights, even to bishoprics and abbeys, and trade does not seem to have been frowned upon – quite the contrary.

We know much more of the emperor's dealings with the papacy than of his trade policies. When Clement II died in 1047, only nine months after his appointment, Henry installed Bishop Bruno of Toul, who took the name of Leo IX.[17] Bruno was a reformer, and he brought with him a number of French and German prelates who were to help him reorganize the papacy. He founded the college of cardinals in the modern sense of the term. 'Up to then a body of purely spiritual character, whose functions were limited to supporting the pope in the observation of his duties in the divine service, it now began to assume the role of a senate of Roman Church government.'[18] Another significant change made by Leo was to model the papal chancery upon the imperial: diplomas were henceforth distinguished from epistles.

For more than a century the popes had been largely political appointees of great Italian families like the Crescentii. Undoubtedly they would have continued to function as mere tools of the Roman aristocracy had not the impetus to reform been thrust upon them from the north. Leo brought to the office of pope a conception of his role as leader of all Christians, and his appointment had the effect of strengthening the authority of the Church, for it was only when the papacy was freed from its subservience to the Italian aristocracy that the office could be powerfully exercised north of the Alps.

In retrospect the popes of the tenth century, though devoted to keeping themselves in office and living like secular princes, had less weight than the popes after 1049, who were ambitious for reform and for the redirection of ecclesiastical energies. The pope now became known to northern Europeans by holding synods in France and Germany and by refusing to spend any more time in Rome than necessary. Consequently Leo obtained the loyal support of the reformers of Cluny, who had hitherto considered the papacy an object of ridicule. With well-organized monastic assistance and new international recognition from Church

[15] R. de Roover, 'The Organization of Trade', in *The Cambridge Economic History of Europe*, ed. M. M. Postan *et al.*, III, Cambridge, 1963, 46.
[16] *Ibid.*, pp. 46–7.
[17] Actually Benedict IX was back on the papal throne for the third time immediately after the death of Clement, but he lasted only three weeks. He was followed by Damasus II in 1048.
[18] Hampe, *Deutsche Kaisergeschichte*, p. 26.

members, the pope was in a strong position to influence European politics as well as morals. In time the moderate reforms of the efficient Leo were supplanted by the overweening demands of Gregory VII, whose concept of his role as spiritual leader brooked no shrinking from worldly power.

In October 1049, Leo and Henry together presided over a reform synod in Mainz, the biggest Church gathering on German soil since the Easter meeting of 1020 held at Bamberg by Henry II and Pope Benedict VIII. Forty bishops were present, including the powerful Adalbert, who had moved his diocesan residence from Bremen to Hamburg. Many distinguished abbots were also there, among the most prominent being those of Hersfeld and Fulda. In the retinue of the emperor were his chancellors for Germany and Italy, the duke of Saxony, and several Hessian counts. Most striking is the presence of an ambassador from the Greek emperor Constantine IX.[19]

The two major conclusions of the synod were to forbid simony and to outlaw clerical marriages. Adalbert of Hamburg-Bremen held that clergy might marry if the union would prevent debauchery and fornication. Under such circumstances marriage could even be said to possess a kind of sanctity. But the ideal was abstinence and celibacy, as exemplified by his own blameless conduct, a fairly typical comment from the vain Adalbert.

The deliberation over simony was equally important. A Burgundian cleric named Bertald accused Archbishop Hugh of Besançon of usurpation, claiming the office of archbishop for himself.[20] Bertald's case was represented by the archbishop of Cologne, who set the beginning of the dispute back in 1010 when Archbishop Hector of Besançon had died. Bertald claimed that he had been selected as the successor by King Rudolf III of Burgundy, that he had been recognized by the suffragan bishops, and that he had carried out archiepiscopal functions. However, the appointment was challenged by Count Otto-William, and Bertald was driven from office, though he subsequently received the recognition of the pope together with the pallium and a document of investiture.

Adalbert of Hamburg acted as counsel for the alleged usurper, Archbishop Hugh. He stated that the clergy and laiety were unanimously turned against Bertald on account of simony, being convinced that he had paid King Rudolf a huge sum of money for the office. Moreover, they repudiated him on the grounds that his appointment abrogated the right of their church to free election of its bishop. Hugh, on the other hand, had been canonically elected and had exercised the

19 Steindorff, *Jahrbücher*, II, 94–5.
20 *Ibid.*, p. 97.

office of archbishop for eighteen years without the opposition of anyone. Why had Bertald not brought up the matter at a single Church council in all that time?

The case hinged upon Bertald's own defence against the charge of simony, and since he could not prove his innocence, opinion turned against him. The pope issued a document which the emperor also signed, reconfirming Hugh as archbishop of Besançon.[21] The charge of simony was obviously not to be taken lightly during the reign of Henry III and his reforming popes.

It seems incongruous that payment for office was considered a great sin by a monarch who himself named bishops and popes. Yet this power was consistent with his idea of the kind of empire over which he presided, the *societas Christiana*. 'If ever a monarch acted in consonance with the functions and principles that animated his policy, it was Henry III. As a Christian monarch in the most literal meaning of the term, Henry, by exercising his protective functions, demonstrated how a true monarchic form of government could be practised. He gave his Christian empire an episcopacy and a papacy, in short, ministers who were commensurate to their calling.'[22] To be sure, he was not the first to make such appointments. Otto I had deposed the notorious John XII and installed his own candidate, Leo VIII; and Otto III had put in his tutor Gerbert as Sylvester II. Yet the violation of what Ullmann calls 'one of the most cherished hierocratic tenets' sowed the seeds of the investiture controversy which was to erupt during the reign of Henry's son.

The future Henry IV was born at Goslar on 11 November 1050, and in 1051 his father invited Abbot Hugh of Cluny to come to Cologne at Easter to baptize him. It was the same Abbot Hugh who acted as Henry IV's sponsor at Canossa. Shortly after the baptism the emperor set out on a campaign against the Hungarians, which though ruthless was ultimately indecisive. Lotharingia was also giving trouble to the German overlord. The bishops of Utrecht, Metz, and Liége had helped the emperor in the campaign of 1048–9 against Count Dietrich of Upper Lorraine. Leo IX had aided the emperor by excommunicating Godfrey of Lorraine and Baldwin of Flanders. But perhaps the most helpful of all ecclesiastical supporters was Archbishop Adalbert of Hamburg, who negotiated a treaty with King Svein of Norway and Denmark. Svein was an ardent Christian, whose desire to see the spread of the faith matched Henry's own ideas about the *imperium Christianum*. The Scandinavian king sent his fleet to the coast of the Netherlands in aid of the emperor. The campaigns in Upper Lorraine came to an end after Henry devastated the area and when the principal antagonists, Godfrey and Baldwin, now excommunicated, fell into disarray.

[21] *Ibid.*, p. 98. [22] Ullmann, *Growth of Papal Government*, p. 252.

By 1052 the Hungarian revolt was again in the forefront. Henry made another expedition, culminating in the siege of Pressburg, about 35 miles east of Vienna. To raise the siege King Andrew of Hungary induced Pope Leo to intervene, and the pope travelled to Regensburg to carry out his function as mediator. He extracted from Andrew a promise that he would pay tribute and otherwise satisfy the German emperor, but after the siege was lifted, the Hungarian king reneged, and for this act of perfidy Pope Leo excommunicated him.

Despite this disturbing activity on the eastern front, Henry did not neglect other parts of the empire. In June of 1052 he held court at Zürich and issued a law for the Lombards (Doc. 42). With the consent of the bishops, counts, and margraves at the council, Henry decided that secret types of murder, especially poisoning, needed to be punished. The murderer who uses poison, or his accomplice, is to suffer the death penalty and to lose all his property both movable and immovable. Ten pounds (of what is not stated) is to be paid as an indemnity, half as a wergild to the relatives of the victim, and half as a fine to the royal treasury. Whoever wishes to defend himself against the charge of murder may try to do so: the freeman by duel, the unfree by ordeal. If anyone gives aid and comfort to such a criminal, he forfeits all of his property to the fisc and incurs the disfavour of the emperor. This law says nothing about murder in general, only about the particular variety that gives no warning to the victim in advance.

From this same council Henry issued a law about forbidden marriages, directed 'to everyone', though the document says the synod was composed of Italian magnates only (Doc. 43). The law states that a woman whose fiancé or husband dies cannot be subsequently wed or betrothed to any of the close relatives of the deceased. Any woman guilty of joining in such a union must sacrifice half her property, one-half to go to the royal treasury and one-half to the near legal relatives of the deceased. Any child of such a forbidden union would be liable to disinheritance of his parents' property. In this way the property of a married woman could not remain in her possession if she subsequently married a relative of her deceased husband.

Women's rights to inherit their husband's property differed widely from place to place and from century to century during the Middle Ages.[23] But at least one generalization is possible: women were by no means universally excluded from receiving a fief.[24] It was common, especially in Lotharingia, for a man and his wife to hold land jointly. When the man died, the wife often became his heir, reflecting the close

---

[23] Heinrich Mitteis, *Lehnrecht und Staatsgewalt*, Darmstadt, 1958, p. 645.
[24] Waitz, *Deutsche Verfassungsgeschichte*, VI, 88.

relationship between the marriage partners in respect to property which characterized Frankish law.[25]

Then, as now, one might marry a rich widow for her wealth, as when Robert of Flanders won the county of Holland by marrying the count's widow. But sometimes the ambitions of the new husband were foiled: when the widow of the count of Cambrai remarried, her new husband was supported by the emperor in his claim to the fief but was repudiated by the bishop, who favoured the nephew of the deceased.[26] Any widow was expected to obtain the consent of her overlord to a new marriage. Often the king himself gave the hand of a prominent girl in marriage. Henry III was apparently displeased when he learned about the wedding of Beatrice of Tuscany, for Lambert of Hersfeld reports that 'the marriage was contracted without his [Henry's] being consulted'. The monarch for his part could run the risk of criticism if he married off a noblewoman to a man of considerably lower rank, a charge levelled at Henry IV.

Feudal law in Italy under the Germans was not especially clear cut until the twelfth century, by which time the fief was simply inherited through the direct male line, whereas the property of a woman without heirs went to the Church.[27] According to Henry's law of 1052 the violator's property was to be split between the crown and the close relatives of her deceased spouse, thus enriching the family of her first marriage partner. It would seem to have been Henry's intent to nullify the political power of a rich woman by this statute, and it is possible that the edict was inspired by the case of Beatrice of Tuscany, mother of the famous Matilda. A cousin of Henry III, she was left a widow in 1052 when Duke Boniface of Tuscany was assassinated.[28] Since the properties of the Countess Beatrice were crucial to an effective Italian policy, we may wonder if the laws issued at the council of Zürich in 1052 were not directly inspired by the murder of Duke Boniface. We know that he died on 6 May, eleven days before the synod, and that his death was most likely caused by the wound of a poisoned arrow.[29] Immediately upon his death a legation including two Tuscan bishops approached the emperor asking that their spheres of influence be enlarged, presumably at the expense of the Countess Beatrice. We

[25] *Ibid.*, p. 89.   [26] *Ibid.*   [27] *Ibid.*, p. 91 and n. 2.
[28] In 1055 she married the exiled duke of Lorraine, Godfrey the Hunchback, son of Duke Godfrey the Bearded, an inveterate foe of the emperor. Upon hearing of her remarriage, Henry went to Italy and imprisoned both Beatrice and Matilda. Godfrey had already escaped out of the country; afterwards he became a staunch ally of the emperor. When he met an untimely end in February, 1076, at the hands of a murderer, Matilda, now an orphan, was left in control of Tuscany.
[29] Steindorff, *Jahrbücher*, II, 172-3.

deduce this from two documents issued at the council, one to the bishop of Volterra and one to the bishop of Arezzo, expanding their authority in secular affairs. '. . . they unambiguously reveal the intention of the emperor to reduce the official power of Boniface, especially the Tuscan imperial principality, before it definitively and formally passed to the heirs of the allod.[30]

At the same council then, Henry issued both a law against the crime of poisoning, only a matter of days after the murder of Duke Boniface (Doc. 42), and also a law forbidding the remarriage of a widow to a close relation of her husband (Doc. 43). Perhaps Henry wished to keep Beatrice from marrying a relative of Boniface and so consolidating her holdings in Tuscany, but this she did not do. Instead, she claimed the duchy of Tuscany outright as the widow of Boniface, though it is possible that she did so in the name of her minor son Frederick.[31]

Beatrice succeeded in retaining her property and passing it on to her daughter Matilda, who, at her mother's death, was the only surviving heir. Matilda bequeathed her holdings to the Church, receiving them back as a fief of the papacy for her lifetime. She too could 'spiritualize the secular' and vice versa when it was advantageous. It was at her castle of Canossa that Gregory VII took refuge in 1077, where the penitent Henry IV came to seek forgiveness. Yet later on Matilda changed sides and left her property to Henry V, not as emperor but as a blood relative.

This ultimate triumph of the grandson would no doubt have pleased Henry III, who was obviously trying at the council of Zürich in 1052 to exert control over Tuscany. By outlawing certain marriages he might prevent the continued aggrandizement of powerful families like that of the Countess Beatrice. By expanding the spheres of influence of two Tuscan bishops he was necessarily encroaching upon the authority of the secular power there. But Beatrice managed to retain control. When she did remarry, it was without imperial consent, to a man considered a public enemy in Germany – Godfrey of Lorraine – and for this *faux pas* she was imprisoned. Henry, though 'the apotheosis of medieval kingship', could be ruthless. In order to effect the kind of Christian empire he had in mind, it was necessary to create a firm power base. His drive for reform impelled him at times to put down insubordinate or inconvenient subjects.

Though Henry III was profoundly influenced by the Cluniac reformers and helped their cause throughout the empire even to the extent of appointing reform popes, he was poorly repaid for his devotion.

[30] Steindorff, *Jahrbücher*, p. 174.
[31] Frederick and a second daughter died before their mother's marriage to Godfrey of Lorraine, leaving Matilda the sole heir.

So says James Westfall Thompson. 'The Cluny reform which he so favored was at bottom insidiously destructive of secular government. The pro-Cluniac monks who surrounded Henry III were secretly hostile to the German theory of government of a strong church within a strong state and were determined to reverse the relation.'[32]

The latent conflict over spheres of influence became active when Pope Leo IX, former bishop of Toul and an appointee of the emperor, tried to expand papal influence in south Italy. Leo and Henry were both reform-minded and could theoretically have worked together to govern the Christian empire if the pope had been more like the devoted Gerbert under Otto III. But Leo was not content to follow the emperor's lead. He had ideas of his own. A sign of his independence was that he presided over the synod of Mainz together with the emperor in 1049, when the usual practice was to turn over this function to a legate.

The Normans were successfully driving out the Greeks in southern Italy, which could not fail to please the pope, for he could see the waning of Byzantine power as a prelude to the extension of the Roman Church into that area. Yet the Normans were not willing to have Pope Leo seize political power away from themselves. A struggle broke out over Benevento, which out of self-protection had sworn an oath of fealty to the pope in 1051.[33] The pope marched south in 1052 with a ragtag army that scattered and disappeared before the battle had started. Undaunted, Leo called on the emperor for reinforcements, and Henry at first seemed willing to support papal ambitions. He recognized the pope's claims to Benevento and sent an imperial army to defend it. But before the troops could act as papal allies, Henry withdrew them on the advice of the German bishops, who opposed the use of imperial forces to secure foreign goals.

Leo, thinking that his alliance with the Byzantines of south Italy was firm, went to battle with the remainder of his troops and suffered a crushing defeat at Civita in 1053. Worse still, he was taken prisoner by the Normans, became mortally ill, and died in Rome the following year, shortly after his release. The first attempt of the papacy to establish

---

[32] *Feudal Germany*, I, 101. In origin the Cluniac movement and Church reform were separate. '. . . the congregation of Cluny as such had no spiritual programme that demanded more than the keeping and improving of the monastic rule and the founding of new houses more thoroughly imbued with the spirit of St Benedict and more closely related to the mother house, nor was there a systematic encroachment of Cluniac monks into ecclesiastical or secular politics.' See Gerhart Ladner, *Theologie und Politik vor dem Investiturstreit*, p. 61. But the Cluniac movement and the drive for Church aggrandizement began to overlap late in the reign of Henry III, especially in the person of Leo IX (*ibid.*, pp. 62–3).

[33] Hampe, *Deutsche Kaisergeschichte*, p. 28.

G

hegemony over south Italy had crumbled, whereas the Norman demand before the battle to receive all conquered territory as a fief foretold the future in that area.[34]

Yet part of the blame for the breakdown in papal–imperial relations can be laid at Henry's door. His desire to reform the papacy in order to reform the Church had led to the appointment of strong administrators who were bound to question the right of the secular monarch to rule the Christian empire. 'Could the king or emperor be a monarch in a completely Christocentric world that acknowledged the primatial function of the Roman Church, the epitome of the whole Christian world ?'[35] The failure to answer this question in a satisfactory way was to characterize not only Henry III's reign but even more dramatically that of his son.

[34] Hampe, *Deutsche Kaisergeschichte.*
[35] Ullmann, *Growth of Papal Government*, pp. 252–3.

8

The Reign of Henry IV (1056-1106)

The reign of Henry III marks the highpoint of secular control of the Church. The Germanic concept of private ownership of the Church as a part of the lord's property had become ever stronger and can be seen as a major contribution to ecclesiastical law. Never seriously challenged under the Saxons or the first three Salians, it threatened to reduce the Church to a mere instrument of national policy.

With Henry IV the papacy began a vigorous campaign of self-defence and finally established its independence from the German emperor. This was at first possible because Henry was only five years old when his father died, and his mother, Agnes of Poitou, had no talent for power politics. Hers was a pious, retiring nature, and the regency period neither advanced the kingdom nor served to educate the young king for his future responsibilities. It was no wonder that lay and clerical princes alike found intrigue irresistible and plotted to usurp the role of the empress-regent. In April 1062, Archbishop Anno of Cologne enticed the young king aboard a boat on the Rhine and spirited him away to Cologne. In charge now both of the person of the king and of the regalia, Anno became official regent, and Agnes surprisingly did not protest. She retired to the religious life, seemingly relieved to bow before the audacious archbishop.

Anno had been a counsellor and confessor of Henry III, and during the five years of Agnes's regency he exercised some control over affairs of state. In a diploma to a monastery in Goslar dated 1057 both he and Agnes are listed as intercessors (Doc. 44). The monks of SS. Simon and Jude are promised several estates plus the rents therefrom just as they had received them from Henry III, whose *Lieblingsstift* it had been. This reconfirmation is made 'for the salvation of the soul of our most kind father . . .'. Anno functioned as regent from 1062 to 1064, and afterwards continued to be a powerful adviser to the king. He believed in a strong Church, and for his work on its behalf was canonized in 1183. The *Annolied*, composed in the later eleventh century in a German dialect, eulogizes the archbishop and already describes him as a saint.[1]

Another diploma dating from Henry's minority under Agnes is a patent forgery as well as an amusing bit of historical evidence (Doc. 45). Henry, king augustus of the Romans, has received the petition of Lord Ernest, margrave of Austria, asking for a charter of confirmation for the grants and privileges given to him not by Henry III, as we would expect, but 'by the ancient emperors of the pagans', Caesar and Nero! Quoted within the body of the diploma are the texts of two alleged charters from these emperors. The first one begins, 'We Emperor Julius, we Caesar and worshipper of the gods, we highest imperial Augustus on earth, we supporter of the whole earth, grant Roman grace and our peace to you, the zone of the eastern land, and to its inhabitants. . . .' This intitulation is followed by a grant to Caesar's uncle, the governor of Austria, and his successors (who would include Margrave Ernest), bestowing 'all uses of the renowned eastern land'. The people of Austria, to whom the charter is addressed, receive the right to hold feudal property in perpetuity, a statement that does not really sound very classical somehow.

The second 'ancient' charter begins: 'We Nero, friend of the gods and promoter of the faith, preceptor of Roman power, Emperor and Caesar and Augustus.' Having deliberated with the Senate, Nero has decided to exempt Austria from taxation 'because she and her inhabitants laudably shine forth before all those who are subjects of the Roman Empire'. He also guarantees her protection from invasion; anyone molesting her falls under the imperial ban and must retreat forthwith. Nero's charter was supposedly issued from the Lateran on the day of Mars, 'that great god'.

Because of this pagan reference the Christian king Henry has decided to renew the charters, 'which were written in the language of the pagans [whatever that may be!] and which we have converted and translated into the Latin tongue . . .'. To the author of the spurious diploma 'pagan' obviously meant not only non-Christian but non-Roman as well, and we may assume that his 'originals' were written in Proto-Germanic for the immediate comprehension of the primitive Austrians.

Finally, in true proprietary fashion, the forger donates the bishoprics of Austria to Margrave Ernest, who becomes their lord and advocate. All of this largesse is corroborated by a seal, which unfortunately is now so mutilated that neither picture nor writing is decipherable. The diploma is supposedly signed with the monogram of Henry IV and countersigned by Chancellor Gevehardus for Archchancellor Liutpold. This latter reference happens to be accurate. Liutpold, chapter provost

[1] Wattenbach–Holtzmann, *Deutschlands Geschichtsquellen im Mittelalter*, II, 653. It is disputed whether the dialect is Franconian or Bavarian.

at Bamberg, succeeded to the see of Mainz and the archchancellorship in 1051.[2] Contrary to custom he was not accorded the honour of crowning young Henry IV at Aachen. That office was performed by Archbishop Herman of Cologne, one of the closest advisers of Henry III and even a comrade in arms against the Hungarians.[3] Still, Liutpold was primate of Germany, and the author of the spurious diploma had him rightly listed as archchancellor in 1058.

Liutpold is also remembered for his part in the so-called 'tithe war', a feud between himself and the abbots of Hersfeld and Fulda. Part of the territory of Thuringia, though technically subject to the see of Mainz, paid a tithe to the two abbeys. Liutpold attempted to tax this formerly exempt area, claiming that Henry III stood firmly behind him. He also tried to extend the tithe to the lands of secular nobles in Thuringia, but here as with Hersfeld and Fulda, he was understandably repudiated. 'The triangular conflict dragged along for years without settlement and finally became one of the eddies in the war of investiture.'[4]

Though Austria was not created a duchy until 1156 under Henry the Lion, and though the diploma attributed to Henry IV was actually fabricated in the winter of 1358–9, it is none the less a genuine piece of evidence for medieval history. As Paul Kehr said of some spurious documents attributed to Henry III, '. . . the content of the forgeries is for the most part more interesting to peruse than the genuine documents in their honourable monotony'.[5]

Archbishop Anno remained guardian of young Henry until he attended a synod in Mantua in 1064. When Anno returned to court, he found Archbishop Adalbert of Hamburg as the new regent, a man even more powerful and ambitious than himself. Leo IX had appointed him papal vicar of the Baltic territories, with the authority to create bishoprics at will. He was so effective in ruling the northern coast that secular nobles accepted his overlordship in return for his protection. Having already made a reputation as missionary to the Slavs and Scandinavians, he did not hesitate to advance his position by taking the regency away from Anno.

Adalbert remained in charge until Henry came of age on 29 March 1065, in his fifteenth year. A diploma issued by the young king in 1063 confirms to 'our beloved and faithful Adalbert, archbishop of the holy church of Hamburg', a forest previously donated by Conrad II together with hunting rights, plus another forest that is on the king's property

---

[2] Fleckenstein, *Hofkapelle*, II, 239.
[3] *Ibid.*, pp. 243–4.
[4] Thompson, *Feudal Germany*, I, 134.
[5] 'Vier Kapitel aus der Geschichte Kaiser Heinrichs III.', appendix to Steindorff, *Jahrbücher*, II, 560.

(Doc. 46). Moreover, the members of the church family, that is the sharecroppers who belong to it, are given the right to inherit, hold, sell, or grant whatever property they have acquired, as long as they do so only among themselves, a feudal practice called *Inwärts-Eigen*. Henry also reconfirms certain privileges going back to Charles the Great, including markets, coinage, and tolls.

After Henry came of age, Adalbert continued to exercise a powerful influence over him until in 1066, at the diet of Tribur, the young king, under pressure from a faction headed by Anno, dismissed him. This marked the turning-point in Henry's career: he was now independent, and he began to exert his authority. The dismissal also marked a change in Adalbert's fortunes. His biographer Adam, a canon of the cathedral chapter in Bremen, divides his life into two distinct parts: the early years of fantastic accomplishment and power; the later years full of failure, misfortune, and even madness. Both of these phases were linked to Adalbert's character, for he had great ability flawed by personality traits such as vanity, arrogance, and boundless ambition.

'Adalbert was proud of the Greek blood he thought flowed in his veins, of his noble birth, worth, and wealth. Hence, his wanting everything bigger and better and more splendid than anything others had, his extravagant hospitality, his grandiloquence, his tireless energy, and much else. Unable to comprehend actuality, he surrounded himself with flatterers, spurned men to whom the adulation he craved was nauseating, believed in prophecies that fitted in with his desires, in fables, in dreams, in the golden age he would bring about if he could direct affairs unhindered.'[6]

Yet he also had a positive side. He favoured reform during the days when Henry III and Leo IX were actively trying to eradicate clerical abuses. After attending the synod of Mainz in 1049, which proscribed simony and clerical marriages, he attempted to enforce the newly promulgated decrees, driving the wives of priests from the town of Bremen. Adam, who knew him personally, is as charitable as a biographer can be, and yet the resulting picture is of a man with gargantuan longings for power and prestige. In his account of Adalbert's downfall and death, Adam shows us a broken man whose missions were in ruins, who had been driven from Hamburg by his political enemies in Saxony, and yet who remained loyal to the king and never gave up hope of a return to eminence (Doc. 47).

The see of Hamburg–Bremen offers a paradigm of episcopal fortunes in the eleventh century. Adalbert was appointed archbishop of Bremen

---

[6] Adam of Bremen, *History of the Archbishops of Hamburg–Bremen*, trans. Francis J. Tschan, New York, 1959, p. xxii.

by Henry III, and in this strategic position he was prepared to build an empire of his own in the north. His missionary power extended eastward into the newly conquered Slavic territory and westward to Iceland. In the early years Adalbert's enterprise in Bremen went very well. His administrative flair was put to good use in reorganizing the diocese, and his cosmopolitan personality flourished in the court which he set up. Travellers with an astonishing array of talents and professions came to Bremen from all parts of the empire and even beyond. A cathedral was begun, and the church can be said to have prospered in every way with the accession of Adalbert in 1043.

In 1030 the see of Bremen had been favoured by a sizable legacy on the part of its deceased archbishop, Unwin, and the two subsequent heads of the church had managed this inheritance carefully. Adalbert was in a good position to build on the work of his predecessors. With his noble background (he was the son of a Saxon count), his good looks, and boundless energy, he could rival any secular prince in splendour and authority. He was so successful that the Saxon duke, Bernward Billung, began to fear that Henry III might actually turn over the duchy to Adalbert. During the minority of Henry IV he acquired several pieces of property, including counties in the neighbourhood of Bremen. He also received important rights like market, mintage, and tolls, and, as we have seen (Doc. 46), the right to hunt in certain royal forests. But once the king reached his majority, Adalbert found it more difficult to extract concessions.

When the king formally dismissed the archbishop as counsellor at the diet of Tribur (13 January 1066), the dukes, says Adam, 'were filled with great joy and thought the time to take vengeance on him was also at hand, to deprive him of his bishopric altogether. . .'. Duke Bernward's son Magnus and a band of adventurers set out to capture Adalbert, but he escaped to his ancestral estate in Goslar, where he stayed in hiding six months while his enemies plundered his diocese. In order to return he was forced to pay Magnus a thousand hides of church land and to divide the see of Bremen into three parts, of which he kept only one scant share.

Having returned under such straitened circumstances, Adalbert could not aspire to his own former brilliance, though he tried. The revenues which had previously gone to feed the poor were now retained and apparently went to line the pockets of the archbishop's dishonest vicars. This was especially unfortunate, says Adam, for a famine ensued, 'and many poor people were found dead everywhere in the streets'. Gone was the archbishop's old thoroughness and conscientious attention to the pressing affairs of his church. He whiled away the hours, turning night into day, and schemed for his return to power at the royal court.

Adalbert came to grief because he aroused the envy, the suspicion, and finally even the fear of the Saxon princes. He represents the obverse of the investiture struggle: just as the king was challenged in his right to appoint bishops, so could the bishops be challenged in their claims to exert secular control. Adalbert's church owned land, acquired more, and gained commercial advantages. Adalbert himself advised the king, went on diplomatic missions, and held his own splendid court in Bremen. He styled himself 'Patriarch' and controlled as many dependants as any secular magnate. It is no wonder that the ducal family of Saxony wanted to put him down.

In fact, Henry III had appointed Adalbert for the express purpose of keeping the rebellious Saxons at bay. Adam of Bremen gives us copious details about the generous donations made by Henry to his favourite: the county of Frisia, 700 manors and other estates besides, navigation rights along the coast and on the lower Weser. 'It was evident that the machinery of the metropolitanate of Bremen and that of the fisc were to be utilized to coerce Saxony.'[7] In 1065 Bavaria was required to produce only 150 chickens; Franconia, 200; but Saxony, 1,000.[8] This is a typical example of the discrepancy in exactions of kind. The king was equally arbitrary with respect to required days of service, which put an extra burden on the Saxon peasants. By 1074 both the nobles and freemen of Saxony were literally up in arms against Henry IV, and though Henry placated them as best he could, the populace stormed his castle Harzburg, destroyed as much property as they could, and desecrated the tombs of the king's brother and son. This wanton outrage drew sympathy for Henry. He was shortly joined by the merchants of the towns along the Rhine. Some of the bishops remained loyal as did the *ministeriales*, who represented a lower type of noble of unfree origin. Some of the abbots sided with Henry too, especially those who were unenthusiastic about the vigorous Cluniac reforms being pushed by Pope Gregory VII.

At Christmas time 1073 the king visited Worms, and when the local archbishop tried to keep him out, the townspeople rebelled and turned their archbishop out instead. For this demonstration of loyalty Henry rewarded the 'Jews and other citizens of Worms' by granting them a charter of exemption from all tolls in each of seven royal villages, including Goslar, Frankfurt, and Nuremburg (Doc. 48).[9] By virtue of the

---

[7] Thompson, *Feudal Germany*, I, 187.   [8] *Ibid.*, p. 196.

[9] The words 'Jew' and 'merchant' were almost synonymous: *Mercatores id est Judaei et ceteri mercatores*, from the *Leges portoriae* (A.D. 906), cited by Karl Theodor von Inama-Sternegg, *Deutsche Wirthschaftsgeschichte bis zum Schluss der Karolingerperiode*, Leipzig, 1879, p. 447, n. 3. The other merchants at this time were for the most part Frisians, with the Lombards and Franks running a poor third.

political situation, he did not issue the diploma to the bishop, the usual practice, but to the inhabitants of the town. The striking innovations in this diploma illustrate the urban spirit of the burghers, who had everything to gain by being loyal to the central government. Protection and trading privileges throughout the empire could not be guaranteed by feuding nobles but only by a strong monarch.

Other Rhenish towns followed suit; Archbishop Anno was driven out of Cologne. But the revolt continued to smoulder in Saxony, and on 9 June 1075 the royal forces slaughtered thousands of foot soldiers in the army of the rebels. The first phase of the 'Saxon War' ended with the acceptance of the king's harsh terms by the beaten nobles: confiscation of their fiefs, six months in prison, and public humiliation. The whole conquered army trooped barefoot between the ranks of the victors in the plain of Speyer and delivered their surrender in person to the victorious king.

Broken and defeated though they were, the Saxons were not through fighting, any more than when Charles the Great had attempted to convert them. But there was a truce immediately after the battle, at least for a time. At Goslar the king announced his amnesty for one of the main leaders, Otto of Nordheim, whom he made his representative in Saxony. The former autonomy of the duchy was to be replaced by the status of a conquered land.

The highlights of Henry's career are covered in the anonymous *Vita Heinrici IV imperatoris*, which is pro-German in orientation though generally respectful of the pope (Doc. 49). At one point the author says that a certain action of the Holy See displeased many people but immediately adds the qualification, 'if one may be displeased with what the pope does . . .'. He exhorts Henry's foes in stern tones:

'What did it profit you to have accused him with fabricated crimes, when he should have scattered your accusation with easy response, as the wind scatters the dust? Nay more, what madness armed you against the king and the ruler of the world? Your conspiratorial malignity profited nothing, accomplished nothing.'

The biographer continues his sermon with dire hints and portents to those who were disloyal to the monarch.

Still another version of these events is offered by Helmold in *The Chronicle of the Slavs* (Doc. 50). Writing in the twelfth century, after the investiture contest had run its course, he gives an unflattering portrait of Henry, marred by several errors of fact. The crux of Helmold's criticism is that 'the king condemned the divine law and deprived the churches of God of all liberty of canonical election by appointing their bishops and forcibly seating the bishops whom he chose . . .'.

This practice was not the whole story, though it was certainly the major theme. In addition to Henry's duel with Gregory VII over the investiture of bishops, there was the continuing wrangle between the king and his rebellious feudal vassals, and a separate though related struggle between the king and the surly peasants of Saxony.

The investiture struggle was 'the most important turning-point in the history of medieval Germany between Charlemagne and the Reformation. It was as important for Germany as was the Norman Conquest for England, or the Crusades for all Europe.'[10] It forms a separate era from the one which we have undertaken to describe, running from 1075 to 1122 and dramatized by the self-imposed humiliation of the king at Canossa. The problem demands separate treatment and is beyond the scope of this book. Yet the issues can clearly be seen to have been present in the reigns of Henry's predecessors.

[10] Thompson, *Feudal Germany*, I, 217.

SELECTED DOCUMENTS

DIPLOMATIC KEY: PARTS OF A 'TYPICAL' DIPLOMA[1]

STRUCTURE OF DOC. 1

Present in Doc. 1

    I. Initial protocol

      1. Chrismon (C.)

      2. Invocation

      3. Intitulation

Absent in Doc. 1

      4. Address

      5. Salutation (found only in papal documents)

  II. Text

      1. Arenga or Preamble

      2. Notification

      3. Exposition

      4. Disposition

      5. Corroboration

  III. Final protocol or eschatacol

      1. Authentication, including monogram (MF. = *Monogramma firmatum*) of the king, the notary's countersign (SR.NN. = *Signum recognitionis, Notae notarii*), and the royal seal (SI. = *Sigillum impressum*.)

        Seals of the Merovingians and Caroligians were generally impressed on the document itself (*en placard*) rather than being suspended by thongs or cords, a practice which became the norm, probably under French influence, in the eleventh century. The matrix, most often of circular shape, was usually made of bronze, and this was impressed on wax. However, the seal matrices of Henry I, Otto I, and Otto II (like most of the Carolingian ones) were probably carved from gems or rock crystal.[2] The facial

---

[1] There is no such thing as a 'typical' diploma. There are royal, imperial, papal diplomas, and so-called 'private' charters, whose styles differ according to the chancery and the era whence they issued. However, some generalizations can be made about the structure of the diplomas which follow. There are three major parts in every case unless the document exists in an unofficial copy. In such cases (e.g. Doc. 37, which is preserved on a strip of parchment sewn between two folios of a codex in the library at Montecassino) the first and third parts – initial and final protocol – are often partially omitted, leaving only the content or text. See Harry Bresslau, *Handbuch der Urkundenlehre für Deutschland und Italien*, I, 3rd edn, Berlin, 1958, 47–8, 'Formeln des Protokolls und des Textes'. Bresslau distinguishes only two major parts to the diploma, counting the initial and final protocol as one. The abbreviations in the scheme above are those used in the *MGH*.

[2] Bresslau, *Handbuch der Urkundenlehre*, II, 551.

features of these seals do not reflect individual portraits but represent idealized royal types, and this continued to be the case into the eleventh century.[3]

The usual method of inserting the wax seal into the document was as follows: a cross cut was made in the lower right-hand corner of the parchment. The four corners were then folded back, resulting in a square opening, into which a lump of wax was placed. Before the wax could harden, the corners of parchment were pressed into it, and thus the resulting seal could not be removed without injuring it.[4]

2. Date
3. Apprecation

[3] *Ibid.*, p. 599.   [4] *Ibid.*, pp. 584–5.

DEFINITION OF TERMS

Chrismon: Chi rho as a monogram of Christ, but in German diplomas a C. came to be the norm from the second half of the ninth century onward.

Invocation: Pious opening naming the deity.

Intitulation: Name and title of grantor, oftentimes including his divine authorization (Devotion Formula). Also called Superscription.

Address: Person receiving the information, oftentimes 'all the faithful'.

Salutation: 'greeting' or 'your health'.

Arenga or *Preamble*: Introduction composed of general motives for issuing deed.

Notification: Also called Promulgation. The purport of the deed, introduced by *notum sit* or similar phrase.

Exposition: Specific motives for issuing the deed.

Disposition: Content of the deed and stipulations of the grantor.

Corroboration: Announcement of the means of authentication.

Authentication: The first part is the subscription, consisting of the name, signature, and description of the person signing, usually a monogram in the case of great personages. Then the notary's countersign with the words *recognovi et subscripsi*, 'I have verified and countersigned'. The word *subscripsi* was usually abbreviated to an elaborate *S*, which came to be known as the *ruche* in French, meaning 'beehive'.

Date: Day of the year reckoned since the birth of Christ; indiction, an old Roman dating system of fifteen-year intervals used for tax purposes; imperial or regnal year (or both), and place whence the document was issued.

Apprecation (from *apprecor*, 'pray'): Prayer-like words, sometimes just 'amen', as a kind of benediction.

DOCUMENTS

1. Henry I confirms to the cloister of Fulda immunity, a tithe of their own goods, and the right to elect their own abbot (Fulda, 3 April 920): DH.I.1, from *Monumenta Germaniae historica, Diplomatum regum et imperatorum Germaniae*, I, *Conradi I. Heinrici I. et Ottonis. I diplomata*, ed. Theodor Sickel, 2nd edn, Berlin, 1956, 39–40.[5]

(C.) [Invocation] In the name of the holy and indivisible Trinity. [Intitulation] Henry, by God's grace king. [Arenga] It is undisputed that with divine grace disposing, we rise above other mortals, whence it is necessary that we strive to obey in every way the will of Him whose favour we excel in. [Notification] Therefore let all of our faithful, present as well as future, know that the venerable man Haicho, abbot of the monastery named Fulda, which is situated in the district of Grapfeld, built in honour of St Boniface, martyr to Christ, there where the same glorious martyr rests bodily, he [Haicho], approaching the excellence of our Highness when we first came there on account of his request, produced for us a certain diploma of our predecessors Louis and Conrad, in which was contained how those most esteemed princes established the same aforementioned monastery under their deference and protection with the monks serving God there and with those things and men rightly belonging to it. And the aforementioned abbot asked that likewise we should take the same monastery into our protection with the monks there serving God and with the things and men legally belonging to it and that we should join our diploma to the diploma of the aforesaid kings, and since we have judged his petition to be eminently just and reasonable, we have freely accommodated and have given assent to the benefice which he asked for. [Exposition] And therefore on account of divine love and veneration towards the holy place of him [St Boniface] and the tranquility of the brothers dwelling there in the same monastery, we have decreed that this diploma be made by which [Disposition] we ordain and order in the future that no royal official or anyone from the judiciary power dare to enter into the churches, villas, dwellings, or fields – possessions which, divinely granted to us during our reign, the aforesaid monastery possesses in modern times justly and reasonably or which hereafter divine piety might wish to be augmented – for the hearing of cases at any time by judiciary rule or the

[5] Hereinafter abbreviated *MGH Diplomata*. The reference DH.I.1 means diplomas of Henry I, doc. no. 1 in the *MGH* edition. DO = diplomas of Otto; DK = diplomas of Konrad.

exacting of fines or the furnishing of lodging or victuals [for the royal household] or the raising of oath-helpers or for compelling men of that monastery, free as well as unfree living on the land [to submit to judgement], nor for demanding any revenues or illegal taxes in our time and in the future, or presume to exact what are recalled above, but the same abbot and his successors may possess [those things] of the same monastery with those subject to it under defence of our immunity, and whatever the law of the fisc has been able to exact concerning the aforesaid, we have conceded to the abovementioned monastery and monks for eternal remuneration.

We also order that concerning the villas of the church of St Boniface, which it appears in modern times to hold – also the serfs[6] and *coloni*[7] dwelling there – and which thereafter the divine piety might wish to amplify in the law of that holy place, the aforesaid abbot and his successors may have the tenth part for completing and restoring the buildings and replenishing the candle supply, and so that they may grant necessary customs of asylum to themselves and to their own faithful, to the poor, and to travellers at the time of reception, besides that which the precept and mandate of the holy rule command the monks to be prepared to offer in the care of the tenants and of the poor. And when the said abbot and his successors should go from this light by divine call, as long as those same monks can discover men among themselves who are capable of ruling that congregation according to the rule of the pious father Benedict, they may have by this our diploma the permission and license to elect abbots. [Corroboration] In order that this diploma may obtain more complete validity in the name of God, we have confirmed it below with our own hand and we have ordered it to be sealed with our ring. [Authentication] Sign of Lord Henry (MF.) most serene king. I, Simon the notary, have verified it and countersigned for Archbishop Heriger (SR.NN.) (SI.).

[Date] Given the third before the nones of April in the year of the Incarnation of the Lord 920, the seventh year of the indiction, in the first year

---

[6] The difficulty of translating the word *servus* is discussed by Edmund E. Stengel, one of the most perceptive writers on the meaning of diplomatic terms. See 'Grundherrschaft und Immunität', in *Abhandlungen und Untersuchungen zur mittelalterlichen Geschichte*, Cologne, 1960, pp. 54–7. *Servus* has two possibilities, the one meaning unfree person, the other meaning a person who serves, without reference to his condition.

[7] *Colonus* in late classical times meant serf, one attached to the soil, and this meaning was retained into the medieval period. However, in Germany the *colonus* represented more often a person whose status was somewhere between that of a serf and a freeman, and particularly someone under the protection of a church. See 'Colonus', in J. F. Niermeyer, *Mediae Latinitatis lexicon minus*, Leiden, 1960, p. 203.

of the reign of the most glorious king Henry; carried out in the monastery named Fulda;

[Apprecation] in the name of God, under favourable auspices, amen.

2. Henry I sets free the priest Baldmunt (Rohr, 11 August 926):
DH.I.10, from *MGH Diplomata*, I, 47.

In the name of the holy and indivisible Trinity. Henry, by God's
grace, king. Let all of our faithful, both present and future, know that
at the request of our faithful and beloved duke Arnulf, we, for the
magnification of our eternal reward, have freed a certain priest by the
name of Baldmunt (our serf, born of the family[8] of the monastery of
Kempten) by striking a penny out of his hand in the presence of our
faithful, according to Salic law, and we have released him entirely from
the yoke of forced servitude. And by this diploma we have corroborated
his manumission, which we desire to remain firm and unshakeable
for ever. Wherefore we order by the sceptre of our royal authority that
the said Baldmunt, reverend priest, shall acquire such rights and liberty
henceforth as other manumitted persons have had up to now who
received their freedom from the kings or emperors of the Franks. And
in order that this diploma of ours should remain firm and stable, we
have ordered it to be marked below with our ring.

I, Simon the notary, have verified it and countersigned for Archchaplain Heriger.

Given the third before the ides of August in the year of our Lord's
Incarnation 926, the fourteenth year of the indiction, in the eighth year
of glorious King Henry's reign; carried out at Rohr; under favourable
auspices, in the name of God, amen.

3. The coronation of Otto I (936): from Widukind of Corvey, *Rerum
gestarum Saxonicarum Libri tres*, ed. G. Waitz *et al.*, 5th edn., in
*Scriptores rerum Germanicarum in usum scholarum ex monumentis Ger-
maniae separatim editi*, Hanover, 1935, pp. 63-7.

After the death of Henry [936], the father of his country and greatest
and best of all kings, the Franks and Saxons chose as their prince his son
Otto, who had already been designated king by his father. They ordered

[8] The *familia* comprised the dependants who worked on cloister property,
both free and unfree. See Stengel, *Zur mittelalterlichen Geschichte*, p. 53.

H

the coronation to be held at the palace in Aachen, the place of universal election. . . .

And when they had arrived, the dukes and the great lords with a force of the chief vassals gathered in the portico of the basilica of Charlemagne. They placed the new ruler on the throne that had been constructed there, giving him their hands and offering fealty; promising their help against all his enemies, they made him king according to their custom.

While this part of the ceremony was being carried out by the dukes and other magistrates, Archbishop Hildibert of Mainz awaited the procession of the new king with all the priestly order and the commoners in the basilica. The archbishop awaited the procession of the king, holding the crozier in his right hand and wearing the alb, the pallium, and the chasuble. When the king came forward, he advanced to meet him, touching the king's right hand with his left. Then he led the king to the middle of the sanctuary and turned to the people standing about them (ambulatories had been constructed above and below in that round basilica so that all the people might have a good view).

'Lo,' Hildibert said, 'I bring before you Lord Otto elected by God, formerly designated by Henry, now made king by all the princes. If this election pleases you, signify by raising your right hand to heaven.' To this all the people raising their right hands on high loudly called down prosperity on the new ruler.

The king, dressed in a close-fitting tunic according to the Frankish custom, was escorted behind the altar, on which lay the royal insignia – sword with sword-belt, cloak with bracelets, staff with sceptre and diadem.

Archbishop Hildibert, the highest bishop at this time, was a Frank by race, a monk by profession, brought up and educated in the monastery of Fulda. Because of his superior ability he was made abbot of Fulda, after which he attained the most exalted rank, that of the archbishop of Mainz. He was a man of wonderful sanctity and superior intellect. Among other divine gifts he was said to possess the ability to prophesy.

When the question of who should crown the king arose, two bishops besides Hildibert were considered eligible: the bishop of Trier because his city was the most ancient and had been founded by St Peter, and the bishop of Cologne because the place of coronation – Aachen – was in his diocese. But both of these men who would have enjoyed the honour deferred to the pre-eminence of Archbishop Hildibert.

Going to the altar and taking from it the sword with sword-belt and turning to the king, he said: 'Accept this sword, with which you may chase out all the adversaries of Christ, barbarians, and bad Christians, by the divine authority handed down to you and by the power of all the empire of the Franks for the most lasting peace of all Christians.'

Then taking the bracelets and cloak, he clothed him saying, 'These points [of the cloak] falling to the ground will remind you with what zeal of faith you should burn and how you ought to endure in preserving peace to the end.'

Then taking the sceptre and staff, he said: 'With these symbols you may be reminded that you should reproach your subjects with paternal castigation, but first of all you should extend the hand of mercy to ministers of God, widows, and orphans. And never let the oil of compassion be absent from your head in order that you may be crowned with eternal reward in the present and in the future.'

After having been sprinkled with holy oil and crowned with a golden diadem by the bishops Hildibert and Wikfried [of Cologne] and all legal consecration having been completed, the king was led to the throne, to which he ascended by means of a spiral staircase. The throne of marvellous beauty had been constructed between two marble pillars, and from there the king could see and be seen by all.

After the divine praise was intoned and the mass was solemnly celebrated, the king descended from the throne and walked to the palace. Going up to a marble table decorated with royal utensils, he sat down with the bishops and all the people while the dukes waited on them.

Gilbert, duke of the Lotharingians, in whose district Aachen lay, made all the arrangements; Eberhard [duke of Franconia], presided over the table; Herman the Frank [duke of Swabia], supervised the cupbearers; Arnulf [duke of Bavaria], oversaw the order of knights and the choice of the camp site. Count Siegfried, highest of the Saxons next to the king and brother-in-law of the former king [Henry I], administered Saxony during this time against enemy attack, and he also took care of the young Henry [Otto's brother and duke of Bavaria, 947–55].

The king, after honouring each of the great lords according to royal munificence by an appropriate gift, dismissed the multitude with great good cheer.

4. Gero against the Slavs (939–55): from Widukind of Corvey, *Rerum gestarum Saxonicarum Libri tres*, ed. Waitz, pp. 84, 91–2, 133–5, 141–2.

[A.D. 939] The barbarians being elated by our necessity nowhere left off burning, slaughtering, and pillaging, and they considered entrapping Gero, whom the king had appointed over them.

He himself prevented the trap by a ploy [of his own] one night and killed almost thirty of the barbarian leaders while they were besotted at a great banquet and entombed in wine.

But when this did not suffice against all barbarian nations (indeed, at that time the Apodriti were making war again, and with our army destroyed, they destroyed the commander himself by the name of Haica), an army led often by the king himself destroyed them, afflicting many and bringing them almost to the last calamity.

They nevertheless preferred war to peace, disregarding all that misery for dear liberty. For this race of men is hard and patient of labour, satisfied by the lightest food, and what seems to us a grave burden the Slavs held as a certain sort of pleasure.

Several days went by, the Saxons fighting for glory and for a great and wide empire, the Slavs fighting over the issue of liberty or ultimate servitude with varying luck.

For in those days the Saxons were afflicted with many enemies, the Slavs to the east, the Franks to the south, the Lotharingians to the west, the Danes and also the Slavs to the north: on account of this the barbarians drew out the long struggle.

*   *   *   *   *

[A.D. 940] At that time a war of barbarians was raging. And when the soldiers' ranks were depleted by frequent expeditions, those who had been conscripted by Gero were incited to a seditious hatred of him, also because tributes were widely refused them. The king had been on Gero's side for the sake of the country's common good. And therefore the exacerbated troops turned their hatred against the king himself.

*   *   *   *   *

[A.D. 955] Gero indeed was an experienced warrior, but he also possessed a good head for civic affairs. He was eloquent and knowledgeable and showed his prudence more in deeds than in words. Though adept at acquisition, he also displayed largesse, and what was best, zeal in religion. Then [15 October] a guard of a swamp and the river which the swamp bordered saluted a barbarian. The Slav returned the greeting, to which the guard said: 'It would be enough for you if you wage war against one of us servants of my lord, and not against the lord my king himself. What army do you have, what arms, that you presume such things? If any virtue is in you, if any skill or boldness, give us leave to cross over to you, or we will give you an opportunity of coming here, and the force of battle may appear on level ground.'

The Slav gnashing his teeth in the barbarian custom and spewing forth many shouts mocked Gero and the emperor and the whole army, knowing they were sorely aggravated and troubled.

Gero was provoked at this, for he had a fiery temperament, and said, 'Tomorrow will tell whether you and your people are strong in men or not. For tomorrow you will see us attacking you without doubt.'

Gero, though formerly rendered famous by many outstanding deeds, was at this time said everywhere to be great and celebrated because he had gloriously conquered the Slavs who are called Uchri. Gero returned to camp and reported what he had heard.

[16 Oct.] The emperor, getting up at night, gave the order to provoke a battle with arrows and other machines, as if he intended to cross the river and the swamp by force.

The Slavs, however, were thinking of nothing else than yesterday's threat and were likewise planning for battle, defending the route with all their men. But Gero leaving the camp with his friends the Ruanii to a distance of one mile without being discovered by the enemy quickly constructed three bridges, and a messenger dispatched to the emperor brought back the whole army. At this sight the barbarians themselves tried to stand in the way of the legions. The infantry of the barbarians, since they ran a rather long way and went to battle, were weak from fatigue and quickly yielded to the soldiers; without delay they were cut down when they sought the refuge of flight.

Stoinef viewed the outcome of the affair with horsemen from a prominent hill. Seeing his allies turn to flight, he himself fled, and when discovered in a wood with two retainers by a soldier named Hosed, Stoinef, who was fatigued by battle and bare of arms, was decapitated. One of the retainers was captured alive and presented to the emperor by the same soldier together with the head and the spoils of the chieftain. From this episode Hosed became distinguished and famous. The wages of so famous a deed [was] an imperial donation of twenty hides of land including the revenues therefrom. On that day the camp of the enemy was invaded, and many men were killed or captured, with slaughter lasting far into the night.

[17 Oct.] At the next light the head of the feudal vassal was placed in the field, and around it seven hundred decapitated captives; their chief adviser with eyes torn out was deprived of his tongue and left for useless in the midst of the cadavers.

5. Otto gives Margrave Gero the village bounds of Trebnitz in the region of Zeitz (Allstedt, 4 May 945): DO.I.65, from *MGH Diplomata*, I, 146.

In the name of the holy and indivisible Trinity. Otto, by God's grace king. May all of our faithful, future as well as present, know that we, inclining to the petition of our dear and faithful Margrave Gero and of our brother Bruno, have given to him as his own a certain property of ours beyond the river Saale situated among the pagans in the county of Thietmar in the region called Zitice [Zeitz] in the language of the Slavs, namely, the whole march of the village named Tribunice [Trebnitz] with all of its accessories and adjacencies justly and legally pertaining thereto – freeholds, dependants, buildings, lands cultivated and uncultivated, fields, meadows, pastures, woods and watercourses, mills, fish ponds, passes and impasses, duties and incomes, land claimed and to be claimed, movables and immovables.

Therefore we have also ordered that this present diploma be written up, by means of which we wish and firmly order that, with respect to all those things conceded to him in perpetuity by our gift, our dear Margrave Gero hold unrestricted power of having, donating, selling, exchanging or whatever he pleases henceforth and hereafter.

And in order that this donation of our largesse may remain firm and stable through the course of future time, we have corroborated it below with our own hand and have ordered it to be marked with our ring.

Sign of Lord Otto, most invincible king.

I, Chancellor Bruno, have verified it for Archchaplain Frederick.

Given the fourth before the nones of May in the year of the Incarnation of our Lord 945, the third year of the indiction, our most serene king Otto reigning for the ninth year; carried out at Allstedt; in the Lord under favourable auspices, amen.

6. The achievements of Otto (*Gesta Ottonis*): from Hroswitha of Gandersheim, *Hrosvithae Liber tertius*, trans. Sister Mary Bernardine Bergman, Ph.D. dissertation, St Louis University, 1942, pp. 39–85.

To Gerberga, renowned abbess, esteemed no less for her integrity than for her illustrious descent from a royal race, I, Hroswitha of Gandersheim, the lowest of the lowly of those serving under the sway of her ladyship, wish to offer all that a servant owes to her mistress.

O my mistress, thou who enlightenest by the radiant diversity of thy spiritual wisdom, may it not irk thy kindliness to examine carefully what thou knowest has been written at thy bidding!

Thou hast indeed imposed upon me the difficult task of narrating in verse the achievements of an august emperor, which thou art well aware was impossible to gather abundantly from hearsay. Thou canst surmise what great difficulties my ignorance put in my way while engaged in this work. There were things of which I could find no written record, nor could I elicit information from anyone sufficiently reliable. I was like a stranger wandering without a guide through the depth of an unknown forest where every path was covered over and mantled with heavy snow. In vain he tries to follow the directions of those who are showing the way only by a nod. Now he wanders through pathless ways, now by chance he comes upon the trail of the right path, until at length, when he has traversed half of the thick-treed domain, he attains the peace of long sought rest. There staying his step, he dares not proceed farther, until either he is led on by someone overtaking him or follows the foot-steps of one who has preceded him. In like manner, I, bidden to under-take a complete chronicle of illustrious achievements, have gone on my way stumbling and hesitating, so great was the difficulty of finding a path in the forest of these royal deeds.

And so, wearied by my endeavour, I have lapsed into a silence as I pause in a convenient resting-place. Without guidance I propose to go no farther. If, however, I be encouraged by the eloquent treatises of the learned (either already written or in the near future to be written) I might perhaps discover the means of veiling to some degree my homely simplicity.

Now, however, in proportion as I am unsupported by any authority, I am defenceless at every point. I fear, too, that I shall be accused of temerity and that I shall encounter the reproaches of many, because I have dared to disgrace by my uncultured style matters that should be set forth with the festal eloquence of choice expression. Yet, if a person of good judgement, who knows how to appraise things fairly, examines my work, he will pardon me the more readily because of the weakness of my sex and the inferiority of my knowledge especially since I undertook this little work not of my own presumption, but at thy bidding.

Why, then, should I fear the criticism of others, since if I have erred somewhat, I become responsible only to your judgement? Or why can I not escape reproofs for those works about which I was anxious to be silent? If, because of its crudeness, I should wish the work to be shown to none, should I not deserve the blame of all? To your decision, how-ever, and that of your most intimate friend, Archbishop William, to whom you have bidden me present this testimony of my simplicity, I submit the work to be appraised for its worth and its imperfections.

Otto, mighty sovereign of the empire of the Caesars, who, renowned because thou wieldest a sceptre of imperial majesty by the indulgent kindliness of the Eternal King, surpassest in integrity all foregoing emperors, many nations dwelling far and wide reverence thee; the Roman Empire, too, bestows upon thee manifold honours! Do not reject the small offering of this poem, but may this proffered tribute of praises which the least of the flock of Gandersheim accords thee be pleasing. The kind solicitude of thy forebears has assembled it, and the constant desire of rendering service owes it to thee. Many, perchance, have written and many hereafter will produce masterful memorials of thy achievements. But none of these has provided a model for me, nor have monographs hitherto written taught me what I should set down. But devotedness of heart alone is the reason for this undertaking, and this urged me to dare the formidable task. Yet I am fearful that by verse I may be heedlessly tracing spurious deeds of thine and not disclosing authentic ones. But no baneful presumption of mind has urged me in this matter, nor have I voluntarily played falsely by a disdain of the truth as a whole. But, that the account, as I have written it, is true, those who furnished the material for me themselves declared. Let not, therefore, the benignity of august majesty despise that which a lowly suppliant, devoted of heart, has achieved. And although hereafter many books may be written praising thee duly, and may be esteemed fittingly acceptable to thee, yet let this little book which has clearly been written from no earlier copy be not the last in order of regard. And although thou holdest the honour of Caesar's emperorship, disdain not to be called by the name of king, until, the fame of a royal life having been written, the imperial splendour of the second realm may be declared in an orderly fashion and in becoming language.

[Dedication to Otto II]

Otto, resplendent ornament of the Roman Empire, bright scion of the august and revered Otto, for whom the mighty King throned on high and his eternal Son destined an empire strong in the zenith of its power: spurn not the poor composition of a poor nun! Thou, thyself, if thou deign to remember, hast lately ordered it to be presented to thy keen gaze; and when thou perceivest that it is marred with many blemishes, be then the more inclined to favour a speedy pardon, the more I am but obeying thy behest in presenting it to thee. If I were not urged by the dread command, under no circumstance should I have such self-assurance as to presume to offer to thy scrutiny this little book with its obvious lack of polish.

Thou, who by the decree of God art associated with thy father in his court and art ready to obey his paternal admonitions, holdest harmoniously a like distinction of imperial rule, bearing the kingly sceptre in thy youthful hands. But since I know that thou art loftily considered like to Solomon, son of the celebrated King David, who, in his father's presence and at his revered command, received the paternal kingdom amid desired peace, I hope that in accord with his example thou will be content. Though Solomon, as king, resided in a proud citadel, wisely establishing the decrees of sacred laws and penetrating with profound mind into the secrets of nature, yet occasionally he was disposed to relax his mind with trivial investigations. But he did not loathe duly to settle, with the determination of a just and speedy decision, the quarrel of the two women, ordering the child to be restored to its true mother.

Therefore, as a suppliant indeed, I request that thou, our Solomon, though the administration of a harassing empire occupy thee, deign to read now, for amusement, the recent account by thine own poor nun: that thus all crudeness of utterance, in this treatise on thy imperial name, may presently disappear from the badly arranged words, and that enhanced by thy revered title, they may be guarded from the breath of well-merited contempt.

After the King of kings, who alone rules forever, by His own power changing the fortunes of all kings, decreed that the distinguished realm of the Franks be transferred to the famous race of the Saxons, a race which because of its steadfast rigour of spirit fittingly derived its name from rock,[9] the stone of the great and revered Duke Otto, namely Henry [the Fowler], was the first to receive the kingly authority to be administered with moderation in behalf of a righteous nation.

Just as he was pre-eminent for distinguished excellence, just as he ruled his subject nations with great kindliness, and just as he excelled all the rulers of his time through his extraordinary achievements, so does he in like degree exceed the power of expression of this homely little poem with its many defects. For he was inexorable to the wicked and gentle to the just, guarding legal rights with the utmost zeal and measuring out to all deserving followers just compensation. To him as long as he lived, Christ, the peace-loving King, granted from on high civil peace; and he very happily retained the supreme power of the domain, if I mistake not, for a decade and twice six years of blessed memory; with him ruled his illustrious wife, Matilda, who now in the realm none will be found to surpass in exalted holiness.

Their union the triune God blessed with three sons, thereby bestowing even then a grace upon the kindly race, so that after the death of the revered King Henry no wicked men might evilly seize the control of the kingdom, but that these sons, descended from royal lineage, might rule their paternal realm in harmonious peace. Yet unlike distinctions were reserved for these princes, so that one was to rule and two be subject to him.

Otto, the first born among them, shone as the morning star, beaming with a radiance of goodness famed far and wide. Him the eternal King

---

[9] Hroswitha derives her etymology from Latin *saxum*, 'rock'. Widukind and others take it from Germanic *sahs*, 'knife' or 'dagger', the weapon they used.

with his wonted kindness destined as the ruler of a duly faithful people. He, as superior in age and likewise greater in achievements, was suited to wielding the sceptre when his father died. There is no need to express in words the full tale of his integrity, or the praiseworthy virtue of so distinguished a youth, for whom even now Christ is so increasing his renown that he with weighty right is taking possession of haughty Rome – Rome which has ever been the great capital of the established world. And with Christ favouring him he is subduing the barbarian races who heretofore often disrupted Holy Church.

Henry [father of Abbess Gerberga], born after him, was illustrious because he had received the name of his father, the king. In an equal degree the provident wisdom of Christ, the Lord, deigned to preserve him as a brave leader for his people, so that as a courageous fighter, well skilled in the arts of war, he might bravely protect Holy Church, stoutly warding off the weapons of the foe like a strong rampart.

After him was born Bruno, a priest of Mother Church. Him the sublime grace of the eternal High-priest deemed worthy to exercise care over a Catholic people. Thus at the bidding of God, the kingly solicitude of his father has dedicated him to the service of Christ, so that, withdrawn from the cherished bosom of his dear mother and withdrawn from the splendours of the realm, he might be able to stand as a soldier in the star-swept court of the ever-reigning Lord. But Christ, the true wisdom of the eternal Father, cherishing indulgently this His recruit, bestowed upon him such remarkable gifts of wisdom that there is none more utterly wise than he among the mortal sages of this perishable world.

When, therefore, the princes had been reared according to royal custom, Henry, their illustrious father and king, decided in mind and carried out in deed that, while he was himself still breathing the warm breath of life, he would at once betroth to Otto, his first born son and the future king, a suitable maiden, that she could worthily be joined in wedlock to his own son. He desired to seek her not in his own dominion, but he sent duly experienced representatives to the charming land of the nation of the Angles, instructing them forthwith to go, with accompanying gifts, in quest of Edith, daughter of King Edward. Since her father was dead, she, even at this time, resided in court while the administration of the paternal domain was managed by her brother, whom an ignoble consort had born to the king. The mother of this excellent maiden was most illustrious, but the other woman was of greatly inferior descent.

For this daughter of a king about whom I compose verses was, I say, by reputation well known to all. Influential because of her nobility and equally so because of her esteemed excellences, she was a descendant of an eminent family of great monarchs. Her calm countenance was one of remarkable sincerity, and she was resplendent with a wondrous charm of queenly bearing. Adorned with a radiance of such exceeding goodness, she merited such a meed of praise in her native land that public opinion by a unanimous decision rated her the best of all women who existed at that time. Little wonder that she was conspicuous for eminent virtues, since she was descended from a family of sainted ancestors. For they say, furthermore, that she was descended from the blessed stock of King Oswald, with whose praise the universe resounds because he submitted himself to death for the name of Christ.

But the representatives of our king, who had been commissioned with the embassy, came to the brother of the princess, who then was residing in the castle, and disclosed to him whatever official messages they bore. What he learned officially pleased him exceedingly, and presently in a kind voice he related it to his sister, urging her to obey the exemplary king who wished her to be allied to his own son. And when by friendly admonition he had poured into her heart a sweet love for Otto, the royal prince, then the brother with exceeding diligence, gathered countless treasures. But when he deemed that enough had been amassed, he dispatched the princess carefully with suitable attendants across the sea, heaping high honours upon her and bestowing upon her riches exceedingly precious. With her he sent her sister, Adiva, who was younger in years and likewise inferior in merit. Thus he bestowed greater honour upon Otto, the loving son of the illustrious king, by sending two girls of eminent birth, that he might lawfully espouse whichever one of them he wished. But at first sight the revered Edith, truly pleasing at once to all because of the endowments of her great goodness, was deemed duly worthy to be the consort of a royal prince. And this illustrious lady bore him a dear son, Liudulf by name, a son worthy of such parents. The people, praying that life for him be duly prolonged, rightly cherished him with a tender love.

Thus these matters occurred, and finally the end approached for King Henry. At his death, the whole nation subject to his rule mourned. And after his demise Otto, the venerable first born son of the king, fell heir to the kingdom. And with the responsive prayer of a unanimous people, he, with the approval of Christ, was anointed into the mighty kingship.[10] Upon him the King of Heaven bestowed gifts of such sweet

[10] The ceremony of anointment was not to be taken lightly. When Louis the German invaded the territory of Charles the Bald, Hincmar of Reims reminded those assembled at the synod of Quiercy in 858 that Charles was the anointed king, like David and Saul (note Hroswitha's comparison of Otto I to David). '. . . the bishops . . . declared their adherence to Charles, not because he was elected by the people, not so much because he was the king by the grace of God, but because he was in receipt of the sacrament of unction which had been administered by them and which had changed his being and status.' Unction

grace that he, worthily distinguished in all respects, eclipsed by the renown of his achievements all the kings whom the ocean with its reciprocal waves enfolds. Moreover, the holy hand of God protects him from great and mighty snares devised by secret treachery, and so often honours him with splendid triumphs that one may believe that even now it is the faithful King David, duly resplendent with ancient triumphs, who is seated on the throne. Not only did he maintain his power by the bonds of kindliness over the tribes who had previously surrendered to the sway of his father, but on his own part he reduced many more to his authority, subduing the pagan nations into the service of Christ, so that a firm peace might be established for Holy Church. As often as he set out for war, there was not a people, though haughty because of its strength, that could harm or conquer him, supported as he was by the consolation of the heavenly King. Nor did his army give way to any assault unless, perchance, in scorning his kingly commands it fought where the king had forbidden it to fight.

But Duke Henry, the esteemed brother of the king, respected by the people because of his goodness, was then second to the king in the peaceful realm. He in lawful wedlock duly allied himself to Judith, the noble daughter of the distinguished Duke Arnulf. Her countenance, resplendent in beauty, was the more charming by reason of the lustre of every virtue.

After these events, while the clangour of war remained stilled, there was peace far and wide for our people, which was not in perfect harmony with the warlike tendencies of the other tribes.

O what a serene age the pleasant and truly fortunate nation of our people would have enjoyed, ruled as it was by the sway of a truly wise king, had not the wicked cunning of the ancient foe disturbed our placid existence by his secret wiles!

In fine, when we had happily escaped the blows of the barbarians, a powerful dissension suddenly arose among our people, and civil war harassed the faithful folk more than the oft repeated preparations of diverse wars without. The cause of this doleful evil was no trifling one, and the struggle of certain individuals was not kept within bounds. Now of these, some who were kindly disposed towards Henry promised to the brother of the king feudal loyalty, while others promised like zeal to Eberhard. But when each sought the solace of his own master, then the strife on the part of the leaders themselves became the more serious. At last with the conflict actually progressing, the aforesaid Eberhard presently sent without warning, under cover of dark night, soldiers

alone transmitted divine grace, and Louis the German had not been anointed. See Walter Ullmann, *The Carolingian Renaissance and the Idea of Kingship*, London, 1969, p. 85.

levied with evil intent, to seize the fortress of Beleke, and he led Henry, the noble brother of the king, captive, binding with cruel chains his white hands better suited for adornment. And plundering his boundless wealth, he brought with him to his own lands the noble offspring of his feudal lord, so that he was using the son of his own superior as a hostage.

When the king learned this, he grieved in his inmost soul and wept with deep sadness over the heinous deed. Moreover, he brooked not the painful loss of his dear brother but presently followed in his own action the well-known deed of Abraham, which that patriarch in compassion performed in ransoming Lot from the enemy. With the greatest pains he chose his soldiers and a huge crowd from the whole people, and then proceeded in solemn procession to bring consolation to his princely brother in the great weariness of his grieving heart. Without delay he ransomed the brother whom he came to comfort, and he condemned the instigators of the dastardly crime, hanging some of the criminals on a scaffold, and commanding others to depart from their dear native land.

When by the order of the wise king these matters had been properly taken care of, a wicked plot of the ancient enemy again proferred a device of crime worse by far than the first one and truly for all ages a thing to be shuddered at in dread. In fine, the aforesaid leader, Eberhard, returned from exile to his cherished fatherland, the kindly favour of the king making his return possible. To Gilbert, his companion, to whom he was joined by firm ties, he had given advice (which to thee, O Christ, was displeasing), urging him to seize the Christian king, the blessed of the Lord. And he said that by making injustice prevail over justice they would soon deprive him of his own kingdom. Further, they urged this plan, product of a depraved heart, upon Henry, brother of the faithful king, wickedly coaxing him with flattering speeches not to be minded to repay the wrong he had previously suffered, but rather, by obeying their infamous desires, to depose his brother and receive the kingdom to rule.

Conquered at last by viciously delusive persuasions, Henry, alas, promised that he would be ready for their demands and this he confirmed by strong oaths; but I hope that he did not feel thus in his heart, but that he had been constrained by force to agree with them. For they, captivated with the wicked solace of an idle hope, expected to subdue to their frail sway the king ruling our various peoples. But the King of Heaven, the most just judge of the world, who alone knows the thoughts of all and is able to destroy the delusions of the human heart, brought to nought the fabrication of his heinous crime by the strength of His mighty hand which created the whole universe. He duly turned the intrigues prepared against the anointed of the Lord

against the promoters of this heinousness, and they who wove malign
snares for their lord were themselves the first to be entrapped by their
own devices.

I do not boast that I am of such great wisdom – more than is seemly –
as to hope to be able to express fully in words with what great strength
of heavenly grace Christ, again and again, arranged it that this very
king deservedly blessed passed unharmed through manifold snares and
plots prepared by a hostile faction. But I do not think it fitting for a frail
woman abiding in the enclosure of a peaceful monastery to speak of
war, with which she ought not even to be acquainted. These matters
should be reserved for the toil of qualified men, to whom wisdom of
mind has granted the ability to express all things wisely in eloquent
terms. I relate this only which I can rightly recount: He, who is of all
things the beginning and likewise the end, who alone has ever performed
wondrous deeds powerfully, and who many times snatched faithful
King David from the intrigues of Saul and gave the power of the throne
to David: He in an equal degree, amid a thousand perils, over and over
again protected Otto, the imitator of David in goodness.

And finally, when alone and supported by very few soldiers, Otto had
been surrounded on all sides by hostile forces, and in addition was
enduring with a sorrowing heart and excessive grief a wicked desertion
on the part of his own adherents and dared not entrust himself even to
his own few supporters who did not desert him, though the others had
fled, he thought many a time that he was soon grievously to die. Then
quickly supported by the strength of aid from on high, he had to marvel
that he was now overcoming the treachery of the bloodthirsty mob without hazard to his own life. If haply, with the fight progressing un-
favourably, he heard that his companions were suffering from mortal
wounds, he wept and presently made use of the words of David, words
which that ancient king had spoken when he saw with sadness of heart
that the people were to perish from the blows of an angel's sword:
'Lo,' he said, 'it is I who have sinned and I have committed the crime;
I therefore am worthy of such vengeance! What have these done, who
have suffered so great a loss ? Even now commiserate them, O Christ,
sparing those whom Thou has redeemed, lest a hostile force overwhelm
the innocent too much!' Having compassion, then, by reason of these
prayers, the Divine Power with its wonted benignity spared the servants
of the king, and in its mercy granted the wished-for triumph from the
enemy, destroying by a just test the aforesaid companions. For on that
very day on which, deceived by a vain trust, they hoped that the king,
who rightly held the royal power, would be enfettered with their chains,
Duke Udo, unexpectedly bringing with him a large force, hastened
forward and with vigourous effort entered into the mighty war. Speedily

then was Eberhard smitten by swords and destroyed, and Gilbert, flee-
ing, drowned in a raging stream. But the king, meanwhile, tarrying on
the opposite bank of the Rhine, did not know of so fierce a struggle, nor
did he then know that the solace of such powerful assistance had already,
through the mercy of God, been suddenly sent to him. Finally, when he
realized the intensity of the fight, he rejoiced not at the death of his
enemies, but rather mourned at the slaughter of so many men, lamenting
unrestrainedly in the manner of David, who had grieved piously because
of the slaying of King Saul.

But when the victors came joyfully and saw his countenance moist-
ened with flowing tears, they declared that grief was unsuited for so
signal a triumph, but that thanks ought rather to be given to the eternal
King, who by His constant kindliness had then brought about the
fulfilment of what is clearly written in the Book of King Solomon, who
says that the just shall be freed from distress and the unjust soon be
given over to justice. Soothing the mind of the king with these persuas-
ive words, they urged him to lay aside his deep sadness and to rejoice
duly with his victorious troops and to display a happy countenance
before his subjects after the wars. The king, then, exhibiting a moderate
joy of face but secretly nursing a sad grief in his soul, returned thanks to
Christ from his inmost heart because He had not given him over as
booty to his enemies, but had, by His divine power, duly protected him;
and the distinguished title of the victory he had won he attributed, not
to himself, but to the benignity of Christ.

After these events, the nation rested for a brief period, exhausted by
the struggle of civil war. But even then the guile of the ancient foe, which
always seeks to pervert feeble hearts, did not cease, but after the deed of
ill urged the addition of a worse crime. The enemy is said to have entered the breasts of certain men with such frenzy of destructive poison
that they desired to inflict death upon the faithful king and to appoint his
brother as ruler over the nation; nor did they fear to desecrate the holy
day of Easter with the shedding of the blood of the just king, if only they
could. But the Paschal Lamb, who gave Himself in death as a chosen
holocaust to His Father for our redemption, permitted not the com-
mission of that hideous crime. But presently he exposed their plan to
all men, and thus happily the blood of the innocent king was saved, and
those who were found guilty of the accursed crime were condemned to
bitter punishment in proportion to the measure of their guilt. Some
were sentenced to execution, and others were exiled far from their dear
native land.

After these events, Henry, the noble brother of the king, touched in
his inmost heart with the grace of Christ, pondered within himself and
reflected with great sorrow upon what wrong he had ever committed in

the face of justice. And he wept frequently with excessive tears over this fact also, that he had wickedly yielded to the alluring persuasions of those who by their hypocritical speeches had seduced him. But, although he bore this deep grief in his heart, nevertheless for a long period of time he dared not approach the royal presence; but keeping aloof, in the burning zeal of his sorrowing heart he longed for the granting of the sweet gift of pardon. At last, conquered by strong love, he forthwith thrust from his bosom fear of punishment; and, arriving very stealthily under cover of nocturnal darkness, he entered the royal city, in which the holy ruler, solemnly and with fitting ceremonies, had begun to celebrate the birthday of the eternal King. There, laying aside his costly jewels, he donned a garment of simple and thin texture, and amid the venerable hymns of the holy night he entered the sacred threshold of the church with bare feet, shuddering not at the bitter cold of the raging winter, but with downcast countenance prostrating himself at the sacred altar and throwing his princely form upon the icy earth. Thus, thus with the whole strength of his grieving heart he longed to have the sweet gift of a full pardon vouchsafed to him. When the king became aware of his desire, he was overcome by a benign kindliness; and mindful of the approach of the feast of universal veneration on which the heavenly hosts sang peace to the world in their joy at the birth of their King, from a tender virgin, that He might generously save the world which deserved to perish, Otto, in deference to the greatness of that peace-bringing day, pitied his repentant brother and sympathized with him in his admission of his offences. And in his kindliness he granted him the enjoyment of his favour along with the loving gift of a full pardon. And after some small interval of time he subordinated all the chiefs of the renowned tribe of the Bavarians to Henry's jurisdiction and duly appointed him their mighty leader. And now that their hearts were united in brotherly concord, there was thereafter no further disharmony between them. The fierce Avars, frequently conquered by Henry, subsequently no longer harassed the extensive realm of King Otto in their usual manner with bloody arms, nor did the neighbouring tribes, in their dread of the doughty Duke, dare molest the kingdom. Because he acted with the vigour of an understanding mind, preventing these continuous destructive wars of men, he had barred all the avenues of approach to us. Besides and foremost, safe with the strength of Christ, he courageously sought out with a troop of conquered people the native land of this same wicked race, fighting against the nation that was rebellious against all other men. For, taking possession of the various spoils which the common enemy had gathered as it laid waste very many sections of the world, he carried off also the wives and dear children of the leaders; and when he had thus vanquished his foes, he returned in joy.

When these affairs had thus occurred, the mournful day for intensify-
ing our deep sorrow speedily came for us, the day on which Queen
Edith, resplendent with eminent virtues, left the confines of this present
life, causing by her death sadness and excessive grief of heart to the
nation serving under her jurisdiction. With intense grief – and fittingly
so – the whole race mourned her, a race which she had cherished with
a love of motherly kindness rather than had dominated with the severe
ordinances of a tyrannical queen.

No one who knew the pre-eminent merit of her chaste life and the
kindly disposition which she perseveringly manifested will doubt that
rest eternal without end will be vouchsafed her by Christ and that the
joy prepared for the just will speedily be granted her. But, nevertheless,
in accordance with the way of the human heart, there can be little wonder that the nation spent itself in bitter bewailing, when such a solace
had suddenly been withdrawn from them and the queenly countenance
of their dearly beloved mistress, the resplendent glory of a conquered
kingdom, was entrusted to the earth to be preserved in earth's spacious
bosom until she could rise again and reinhabit the body, rendered
incorruptible, which the tomb now imprisons.

She, therefore, left her son Liudulf, mentioned a few lines above,
bitterly bereft, as well as her sweet and only daugther, Liutgard by
name, resplendent with the utmost excellence and like to her revered
mother in appearance and character.

Towards these children of lovable lineage the entire people was
presently drawn with great affection of heart because of the pre-
eminent merits of both parents. But more so, and even justly so, the
nation cherished the princely boy, Prince Liudulf, with a sweet love.
And he, charming as he was, gentle, indulgent, humble, and exceedingly
faithful, practising well all the traits natural to himself, predominated
over all hearts by his affability. Hence, too, with the beneficent Christ
bestowing His grace, he worthily merited and received such favour, that
whosoever, among all the tribes subjected under the sway of his father,
received, with ear ever ready, even the slightest report of his fame, was
wholly engulfed with a sweet love for his absent lord, cherishing him
with a zealous heart. Him did his renowned father, king and esteemed
sire, grieving intensely over the death of his beloved mother, exalt with
paternal affection and benign kindliness and with worthy distinction
making him rightful master of a subject race. With equal favour he
cherished, protected, and loved Liutgard, likewise respected for her
noble lineage, who was his only daughter. Her he allied in marriage to
Duke Conrad, illustrious, active, and exceedingly brave, who was clearly
worthy of the tribute of this distinction.

And in order to cause the friendly rulers of the noble race of Franks

I

and all the chieftains of the Suevi to be subjected to his son Liudulf
in the perfect love of devoted hearts, he ordered Ida, the lovely daughter
of Herman, a kindly disposed ruler and a renowned chief in those
regions, to be united to his son in lawful wedlock. This princess was
worthy to be allied to the son of a king because of her own excellence,
and she was revered with queenly honour, in accord with the accustomed
piety of the king's command. This king, duly affectionate toward his
son, did not wish her to dwell in places far removed, but wished her to
cross the extensive realm as a queen, that thus his beloved son, sharing
along with his father and his spouse the privileges of the royal court,
might always realize the kindly gifts of his father's favour.

Meanwhile, the Italian king Lothar, stricken with a fatal illness,
departed from this world, rightly leaving the kingdom of Italy to be
ruled by the will of the eminent queen whom he had made his wife.
She was the daughter of the mighty Rudolph and had descended from a
long line of renowned monarchs. The distinctive nobility of her parents
required an illustrious name for her, and she was appropriately called
Adelaide.

She was a woman illustrious in the comeliness of her queenly beauty
and solicitous in affairs worthy of her character, and by her actions she
corresponded to her regal lineage. She possessed such pre-eminent
natural abilities that she could have ruled worthily the state bequeathed
to her, if the nation itself had not presently given evidence of vile
treachery. Now when Lothar, whom I mentioned before, died, a certain
faction of the populace with perverted and hostile spirit offered resistance to their own sovereigns and restored the kingdom to the sway of
Berengar, on the ground that at the death of his father it had once been
snatched from him by violence through the instrumentality of King
Hugh. Now Berengar, exalted by the attainment of this long desired
distinction disclosed all the hatred he had nursed in his baleful breast,
deploring the while the loss of his father's kingdom. And enraged with
an inordinately bitter animosity of heart, he extended his pent-up fury
against the innocent, perpetrating unjust violence against Queen
Adelaide, who as queen had done him no harm. Not only did he seize
the throne of the illustrious court, but at the same time he unbarred the
doors of the treasury and carried off with grasping hand everything he
found; gold, jewels of various kinds, treasures, and the lordly crown to
grace a king's brow; no single detail of adornment did he pass by. He
feared not to deprive her of her own attendants and those suited for
waiting upon royal personages, and – dreadful to mention! – her queenly sovereignty. Lastly, too, he maliciously denied her all freedom of
going or likewise of abiding where she wished, commanding her to go
forth with but one lady-in-waiting and to be guarded by a minion,

subject to himself. This man, prisoner of a king whose injunctions were far from just, dreaded not to guard his own mistress, guileless though she was, and to keep her enclosed by the barriers of a prison-like cell with guards spread about the place in a manner customary for patrolling criminals. But He who freed Peter from the chains of Herod released her, when He willed, with tender kindliness.

While she was undoubtedly distressed in soul by diverse apprehensions and had no hope of certain consolation, Bishop Adelhard [of Reggio], deploring the obnoxious deed and not brooking the painful loss of his dear queen, presently sent a secret message and urged her with zealous exhortations to attempt flight and to direct her course to the city well built with strong ramparts which he had established at his episcopal see. He directed that quarters offering the safest possible protection be provided for her and that a worthy servant be given her. When these admonitions came to her royal knowledge, the illustrious queen, now the more joyful by reason of these kindly provisional bequests, longed to be liberated from the chains that bound her fast. Yet she knew not what to do, since no door stood open to allow her to escape during the nightly hours while the sentries were overwhelmed with deep sleep.

In this prison dungeon she had no one subject to her as a servant, to be solicitous in discharging her demands, except only the maid mentioned above and one priest of exemplary life. Now when, with constant weeping, she had told them with bitterness of soul all that she meditated in her grief-stricken heart, it seemed to them, under the guidance of common prayer, that their fortunes would be changed for the better, if with stealthy zeal they dug and so made a secret tunnel under the earth through which they might be able to escape from the heavy chains of bondage. Thus it is evident that these happenings were accomplished the more speedily by the present support of the benevolent Christ. For when a tunnel had been made ready according to agreement, there came a night during which while sleep stole over the limbs of mankind, the virtuous queen fled with only two companions and eluded all the snares of the guards. And under cover of night she traversed as much ground as she could upon her tender feet.

But presently, as soon as dusky night scattering its shadows had withdrawn, and the heavens began to redden with the rays of the sun, she concealed herself in secluded caverns. And now she would wander in the wilderness and now lurk in furrows amid the ripened ears of growing grain, until night returning enrobed in its wonted darkness enshrouded the earth again with its sable cloud. Then a second time she took pains diligently to pursue the path begun.

At last the guards, not finding her, apprehensively related the fact to a count upon whom the duty of safeguarding her majesty had been imposed, and he, grievously frightened in heart, proceeded with many comrades to seek her out. And when he grew weary and was as yet unable to learn whither the distinguished queen had directed her course, he with great fear of heart reported the matter to King Berengar. The king, too, immediately flew into a passion of anger and began instantly sending his subordinates in every direction, instructing them not to pass a single spot, but to examine minutely every hiding place on the chance that the queen might lie concealed in some such ambuscade. And he himself followed with the full force of a brave legion, as if he were a man out to conquer a fierce foeman. In his speedy course he passed through the very grainfield in whose winding furrows the lady whom he was tracking down was hidden under the protecting curtain of blades of growing grain. But although he ran hither and thither through the very section in which she, a victim of numbing fear, was screened from sight, and though with all his strength he tried to part the surrounding stalks with his extended spear, yet he found not her whom the grace of Christ had shielded. But when he had retraced his steps in bafflement and weariness, the holy Bishop Adelhard presently arrived and with joy in his heart conducted his queen within the goodly strong walls of the city we have already described. Here with all respect he duly attended her, until from the compassionate Christ she received the recompense of a kingdom greater than the one she had previously relinquished in distress.

Finally, some of our countrymen, perceiving then that the queen had been bereaved of her dear lord, and remembering that they had been the recipients of her beneficent kindness when they had begun their advance through Italy towards Rome, frequently repeated to Otto, then a great king, but now also augustus of the Roman Empire, her manifold benevolences. They declared that none other was so worthy as she to be conducted to his royal marriage couch, after the demise of the queenly Edith, who was mourned by all.

The monarch was overjoyed with the suavity of so wondrous a repu⁻tation, and he pondered for a long time in his inmost heart as to how he might unite this queen unto himself in marriage, surrounded as she was by the craft of a wicked king. At length the aforesaid monarch remembered that at one time when he had been expelled from his own native lands he quickly had been restored by the sympathizing support of this same queen, he would now be acting ungratefully in return for her beneficences.

Therefore he presently saw a fitting means of joining the Italian kingdom to his own. Now when Liudulf, the true love of his father and the hope of his race, had learned of this plan from conversation with his father, he proceeded to action, not under the impulse of his own ambition, but with a view to benefits towards his sire. Taking with him in secret a very few companions, he made for Italy and entered it with a small band, urging the inhabitants to submit to the sway of his father. Presently he returned, bringing with him a famous triumph without bloodshed.

King Otto became aware of this achievement from popular rumour, and with a gladsome heart he commended his loving son, who for his sake had undertaken so Herculean a task in assailing a savage nation. And in order that such a labour of love might not be in vain, he himself moved hastily to that same nation with a goodly retinue of his own folk escorting him. Adorned with all the stateliness of royal splendour, he entered the regions girded by the lofty Alps.

Berengar was astounded upon hearing of these events; he neither set in motion the machinery of war nor went to meet the king, but straight-way he betook himself for safety to an appropriate citadel situated in a secure and strongly fortified place. But our renowned king, disdainful in his valour, very courageously crossed the unfamiliar regions and seized Pavia, the capital city of the Italian kingdom. When this town had been definitely occupied, all the chieftains, as if in military formation, trooped in, seeking the new king and vying with one another to submit to his great power. For he received them in his accustomed way with a kindly disposition, promising them the remuneration of his benevolence, if thereafter they would serve him with loyal hearts.

Such was the turn of events; and with frequent ponderings of heart Otto remembered the distinguished Queen Adelaide, and longed to behold the queenly countenance of her whose excellence of character he already knew.

Therefore he dispatched somewhat confidentially messages which included both tidings of peace and words of fond love, and under the pledge of assured protection urged her (making use at the same time of friendly persuasions) to set out speedily for Pavia, a populous city, which she had forsaken previously in bitter dejection. This he did so that, under the benign kindliness of the eternal King, she might ex-perience the most distinguished honour in the very city in which she had once endured the deepest sorrow.

The queen yielded to these kindly injunctions and proceeded whither she was bidden with a very great multitude of her subjects likewise accompanying her. When the king, by whose order she was coming, realized this, he instructed his loving brother, Henry, to cross the banks of the Po to meet her, in order that a due attendance from a great leader might pay homage to her who was to be exalted to the splendour of alliance with Otto. And Henry, obeying zealously the injunctions of his elder brother, set out with a king's guard and joyfully directed his course to seek the encampment of the revered queen in which she with many companions abode. Until he could convey her to the king's presence, he duly attended her with the utmost deference. Thereafter she immediately – and rightly so – found favour with Otto and was chosen to be the worthy help-mate of his empire.

Then the king, perceiving that he would be detained by reason of the strange complexity of affairs and for a time could not return to his native land, decided to send his dear son Liudulf in advance so that the brave race of Saxons might rally to his side, and that under so stalwart a protector the kingdom might stand firm. And Liudulf, who obeyed the orders of his sire, returned to his fatherland and assumed the administration of government. He fulfilled prudently and very sagaciously all the duties of office which at that time had to be accomplished in his native land.

Meanwhile, in Italy, Duke Henry, the esteemed brother of the king, with the utmost endeavour of his heart performed the tasks required of his obedience to the king, of fulfilling in his kindly zeal not only his office as a well loved brother, but rather the duty of a vassal to his lord. Hence, he greatly pleased Otto himself and was bound in bonds of brotherly love to the queen also and duly cherished by her.

Then the king traversed the whole of the Italian kingdom subjecting the chiefs of the realm to his own sway. When he had completed these deeds and subdued the lands according to his own desire, in order that Berengar might not again seize the kingdom for himself, he bade the wise Duke Conrad to dwell in Pavia with a number of picked troops from his army and he bade his distinguished daughter to be united in marriage with Conrad. He himself, with his illustrious wife, forthwith returned home, moving with haste to the heart of his native land. With deep joy did the populace welcome his arrival, extending its ardent gratitude to God enthroned on high, who with His wonted beneficence had been compassionate to His people and had brought back in peace the king whom in His goodness He had chosen for them.

Now after these events had been joyfully celebrated, Duke Conrad arrived bringing terms of peace and conveying with him Berengar mentioned above, who had been so captivated by the depth of his profound wisdom that he had come voluntarily to submit himself to King Otto. Otto, then, who always acted wisely, received this monarch with due respect, restoring to him the dominion of the realm of which he had been bereft – but only on this very exacting condition, that in future he would on no grounds offer resistance to Otto's authority which was feared far and wide by many, but would as a vassal king be zealous to execute his commands. This, too, he prescribed most impressively, that thereafter Berengar should rule more mercifully his own subjects, over whom he had previously tyrannized with harsh despotism. Berengar, feigning that he would be quick to comply with these terms, speedily departed and directed his course in joy to his native land. But when, corrupted by the adverse persuasions of certain of his retainers, he had regained possession of the lofty citadel of his own domain, he presently imposed a heavier yoke on his unfortunate nation, in return for the treatment that had been meted out to himself. He maintained that he had bought the hegemony at a great price, and that he should not be blamed if he had infringed upon the law of his ancestors, but rather that the merit of the blame should redound to Otto himself, who had corrupted with bribes all the chieftains of the people. As soon as these matters came to the ears of the king, he was aroused to a righteous anger against Berengar, and in his grief of heart over the affliction of his distressed subjects, he yearned to ameliorate the state of the kingdom. And supported as he was by the strength of Christ, he could have done so quickly had not an event of adverse circumstances hindered him. For in the universal splendour of his realm, while he was rejoicing at being blessed with widespread favourable fortune, the recurrent plague of the ancient foe reappeared, fabricating a crafty plan to be regretted throughout the ages and striving even at that time to disrupt the peaceful domain. In order that he might achieve his end the sooner, the envious enemy first made restless all the rulers of the realm, hoping that presently the destruction of the populace would follow.

In fine, as Liudulf, the son of the renowned king, perceived through signs significant of friendship only the intense love amid perfect faithfulness which the loyal queen entertained for Henry, brother of the king, and the fact that she governed herself by all the laws that faithfulness would expect of her, he was pierced secretly by the shafts of inward grief, neither raging with anger, nor languishing in the bitterness of hatred, but heaving sighs from the depth of his sorrow-laden heart over the loss of his dear mother's love. Deluded by the wicked persuasions of many, as might be expected from his frail nature, he was afraid that thereafter he would not be destined to enjoy the return of the honours due him but would perhaps have to submit to second place. (But Christ in his justice would never have allowed this to happen, if the kingdom had remained tranquil under a just peace.)

But when he had repeatedly displayed to his father his sadness through a mournful countenance with nothing of its wonted serenity, there were some who were beguiled by the machinations of the wily serpent and who . . .

[Verses 752–1141 have been lost.]

. . . but in order that he might increase the royal prestige of his father.

When the king became aware of this state of affairs, he rejoiced because of the good fortune of his devoted son, and with all the fond affection of his heart he forthwith dispatched tidings to him, with the following message: 'May praise endure for ever and ever to the Almighty, who hath granted thee to rejoice amid great blessings; and let thanks be tendered thee, most beloved son, who, indeed, I learn hast remined absolutely loyal, since thou hast given clear indications of thy loyalty, when by thine own efforts to extend our sovereignty, thou hast confirmed for us the whole glory of thine own exertions. Therefore, accepting gratefully what thou hast done wisely, I in turn requite thee with a worthy interchange, and to thee I entrust the rule of this very dominion, which thou hast established to be brought under our sway. And I admonish thee, beloved one, with fatherly counsels, to cause without delay the nation which thou hast conquered by thy victorious hand to strike with thee a treaty sanctioned by dreadful oath.' The esteemed Duke Liudulf upon reading this message was quite happy because of such kind injunctions and in accordance with the command given him, he bound to himself with a strong oath the nation that was to be duly governed in obedience to his father.

When these matters had been well disposed of and an excellent treaty arranged, he yearned to gain sight of his absent sire; and overcome by tender love for his dear spouse and the two children left far behind, he decided to turn back to the borders of the neglected fatherland he had left, in order that there, after the excessively heavy burden of a cruel exile, he might enjoy at last the tranquility of his native land. And that he might accomplish this end speedily without any delays, he suffered no baggage to retard his intended journey; his treasures he ordered to be gathered and sent in advance of him, and the entire force which he had brought thither with him for the sake of war, to precede him, promising that he himself, if he but lived, would in a brief space of time be at the bounds of his homeland. This, too, he indicated with honied utterance; namely, the castles and abodes in which he wished preparations worthy of his entertainment to be made ready. Our countrymen, roused by this welcome report, rejoiced with deep affection of heart. Dispelling from their souls the whole weight of sorrow and of grief which heretofore they had endured because of the absence of their honoured prince, they all unanimously agreed that the occasion was one for heartiest rejoicing, if after the course of a few days they were according to the message of gladsome promise to gain . . .

[Verses 1189–1479 have been lost.]

. . . in like manner bearing the sceptre and wearing the beautiful diadem upon her head and clad in all the magnificence of her royal apparel. But she who, together with the sovereign king, was soon blessed, received distinction of even greater honour.

Although but a poor Muse, I have up to now chanted in verse the achievements of the far-famed Otto. Now there remain to be recorded further deeds of this same monarch, who retains his throne in the zenith of his power – this I fear to treat because I am withheld by my womanly nature, nor ought these matters be rehearsed in homely discourse: how, namely, in the cruel struggle of an unremitting war he gained the fortress built at the seashore which Berengar and his wife had possessed, and how, under the compulsion of oath, he sent him with his wretched spouse, Willa, into exile; how, prompted by the sense of righteous zeal, he caused the supreme pontiff, who was perpetrating certain irregular acts and disdaining to heed his frequent admonitions, to be deprived of the dignity of the chair of the apostle, adjudging another worthy of the name of ruler; and how, passing in undisturbed peace with his kingship undisturbed, to our country and returning again to Italy, and retaining the glory of both kingdoms, he raised his son, who came after him, namely Otto, a king from infancy, to the highest offices of hallowed nobility, and by his own example caused him to be duly blessed. These matters, then, cannot be recounted in our verses, since they require for themselves a far more eloquent account. Hence I, hindered by the weightiness of these great themes, proceed no further, but prudently make an end, lest hereafter I be shamefully overcome and fail in my attempt.

Now that my recital has been completed and its story cursorily recounted, I must invoke the great goodness of the eternal King that He in His kingliness may grant our sovereigns to prolong happily the whole span of life still remaining, and that He may protect the custodians of Holy Church for many years, supported always in all matters favourable to their prayers, thereby granting unto us a more merciful consolation. *Amen.*

7. Liudprand of Cremona, A chronicle of Otto's reign (*Liber de rebus gestis Ottonis*): from *The Works of Liudprand of Cremona*, trans. F. A. Wright, London, 1930, pp. 215–32.

Berengar and Adalbert were reigning, or rather raging, in Italy, where, to speak the truth, they exercised the worst of tyrannies, when John [XII], the supreme pontiff and universal pope, whose church had suffered from the savage cruelty of the aforesaid Berengar and Adalbert, sent envoys from the holy church of Rome, in the persons of the cardinal deacon John and the secretary Azo, to Otto, at that time the most serene and pious king and now our august emperor, humbly begging him, both by letters and a recital of facts, for the love of God and the holy apostles Peter and Paul, who he hoped would remit his sins, to rescue him and the holy Roman Church entrusted to him from their jaws, and restore it to its former prosperity and freedom. While the Roman envoys were laying these complaints, Waldpert, the venerable archbishop of the holy church of Milan, having escaped half-dead from the mad rage of the aforesaid Berengar and Adalbert, sought the powerful protection of the above-mentioned Otto, at that time king and now our august emperor, declaring that he could no longer bear or submit to the cruelty of Berengar and Adalbert and Willa, who contrary to all human and divine law had appointed Manasses bishop of Arles to the see of Milan. He said that it was a calamity for his church thus to intercept a right that belonged to him and to his people. After Waldpert came Waldo bishop of Como, crying out that he also had suffered a like insult at the hands of Berengar, Adalbert, and Willa. With the apostolic envoys there also arrived some members of the laity, among them the illustrious Marquess Otbert, asking help and advice from his most sacred majesty Otto, then king now emperor.

The most pious king was moved by their tearful complaints, and considered not himself but the cause of Jesus Christ. Therefore, although it was contrary to custom, he appointed his young son Otto as king, and leaving him in Saxony collected his forces and marched in haste to Italy. There he drove Berengar and Adalbert from the realm at once, the more quickly inasmuch as it is certain that the holy apostles Peter and Paul were fighting under his flag. The good king brought together what had been scattered and mended what had been broken, restoring to each man his due possessions. Then he advanced on Rome to do the same again.

There he was welcomed with marvellous ceremony and unexampled pomp, and was anointed as emperor by John, the supreme bishop and universal pope. To the church he not only gave back her possessions but bestowed lavish gifts of jewels, gold, and silver. Furthermore Pope John and all the princes of the city swore solemnly on the most precious body of Saint Peter that they would never give help to Berengar and Adalbert. Thereupon Otto returned to Pavia with all speed.

Meanwhile Pope John, forgetful of his oath and the promise he had made to the sacred emperor, sent to Adalbert asking him to return and swearing that he would assist him against the power of the most sacred emperor. For the sacred emperor had so terrified this Adalbert, persecutor of God's churches and of Pope John, that he had left Italy altogether and had gone to Fraxinetum [on the southern coast of France] and put himself under the protection of the Saracens. The righteous emperor for his part could not understand at all why Pope John was now showing such affection to the very man whom previously he had attacked in bitter hated. Accordingly he called together some of his intimates and sent off to Rome to inquire if this report was true. On his messengers' arrival they got this answer, not from a few chance informants, but from all the citizen of Rome:

'Pope John hates the most sacred emperor, who freed him from Adalbert's clutches, for exactly the same reason that the devil hates his creator. The emperor, as we have learned by experience, knows, works, and loves the things of God: he guards the affairs of church and state with his sword, adorns them by his virtues, and purifies them by his laws. Pope John is the enemy of all these things. What we say is a tale well known to all. As witness to its truth take the widow of Rainer his own vassal, a woman with whom John has been so blindly in love that he has made her governor of many cities and given to her the golden crosses and cups that are the sacred possessions of St Peter himself. Witness also the case of Stephana, his father's mistress, who recently conceived a child by him and died of an effusion of blood. If all else were silent, the palace of the Lateran, that once sheltered saints and is now a harlot's brothel, will never forget his union with his father's wench, the sister of the other concubine Stephania. Witness again the absence of all women here save Romans: they fear to come and pray at the thresholds of the holy apostles, for they have heard how John a little time ago took women pilgrims by force to his bed, wives, widows and virgins alike. Witness the churches of the holy apostles, whose roof lets the rain in upon the sacrosanct altar, and that not in drops but in sheets. The woodwork fills us with alarm, when we go there to ask God's help. Death reigns within the building, and though we have much to pray for, we are prevented from going there and soon shall be forced to abandon God's house altogether. Witness the women he keeps, some of them fine ladies who, as the poet says, are as thin as reeds by dieting, others everyday buxom wenches. It is all the same to him whether they walk the pavement or ride in a carriage and pair. That is the reason why there is the same disagreement between wolves and lambs. That he may go his way unchecked, he is trying to get Adalbert, as patron, guardian, and protector.'

When the envoys on their return gave this report to the emperor, he said: 'He is only a boy, and will soon alter if good men set him an example. I hope that honourable reproof and generous persuasion will quickly cure him of these vices; and then we shall say with the prophet, "This is a change which the hand of the Highest has brought." ' He added, 'The first thing required by circumstances is that we dislodge Berengar from his position on Montefeltro. Then let us address some words of fatherly admonition to the lord pope. His sense of shame, if not his own wishes, will soon effect a change in him for the better. Perchance if he is forced into good ways, he will be ashamed to get out of them again.'

This done, the emperor went on board ship and sailed down the Po to Ravenna. Thence he advanced to Montefeltro, sometimes called St Leo's Mountain, and beseiged the fort in which Berengar and Willa had taken refuge. Thereupon the aforesaid Pope John sent Leo, then the venerable chief notary of the holy Roman Church and now in that same see successor to St Peter, chief of the apostles, together with Demetrius, one of the most illustrious of the Roman princes, as envoy to the holy emperor. By their mouths he declared that it was not surprising if in the heat of youth he had hitherto indulged in childish follies; but now the time had come when he would fain live in a different fashion. He also cunningly alleged that the holy emperor had sheltered two of his disloyal subordinates, Bishop Leo and the cardinal deacon John, and that he was now breaking his sworn promise by letting them take an oath of allegiance not to the pope but to the emperor. To the envoys the emperor gave this answer:

'I thank the pope for the change and improvement in his ways that he promises. As for the violation of pledges that he charged me with, judge yourselves if the accusation be true. We promised to restore all the territory of Saint Peter that might fall into our hands: and for that reason we are now striving to drive Berengar with all his household from yonder fort. How can we restore this territory to the pope, if we do not first wrest it from the hands of violent men and bring it under our control ? As for Bishop Leo and the cardinal deacon John, his disloyal subordinates, whom he accuses us of having welcomed, we have neither seen them in these days nor welcomed them. The lord pope sent them to Constantinople to do us damage, and on their way, we are told, they were taken prisoners at Capua. We are also informed that with them was arrested a certain Saleccus, a Bulgarian by birth and an Hungarian by training, who is an intimate friend of the lord pope, and also a reprobate named Zacheus, a man quite ignorant of all literature sacred or profane. whom the lord pope has recently consecrated as bishop, with the intention that he should preach to the Hungarians a campaign against us. We would not have believed that the lord pope would have acted thus, whoever told us; but his letter, sealed with leaden seals and bearing his signature, compels us to think that it is true.'

This done, the emperor sent Landohard, the Saxon bishop of Minden, and Liudprand, the Italian bishop of Cremona, to Rome in company with the pope's envoys, to satisfy the lord pope that no blame attached to him. Furthermore the righteous emperor bade the soldiers of their guard to prove the truth of his words in single combat if the pope refused to believe him. The aforesaid bishops Landohard and Liudprand came before the lord pope at Rome, and although they were received with all due honour they saw clearly with what scorn and indifference he was prepared to treat the holy emperor. They explained everything in order, as they had been told to do, but the pope refused to be satisfied either with an oath or with a single combat and persisted in being obdurate. Still, a week later he craftily sent John, bishop of Narni, and Benedict, cardinal deacon, back to the lord emperor with his envoys, thinking that by their tricks he could delude a man whom it is exceptionally difficult to deceive. Before they got back, however, Adalbert at the pope's invitation had left Fraxinetum and reached Civita Vecchia; whence he set out for Rome and there, so far from being repudiated by the pope, as he should have been, received from him an honourable welcome.

While these things were going on, the fierce heat of the dog days kept the emperor away from the hills of Rome. But when the sun had entered the sign of the Virgin and brought a temperature change, he collected his forces, and at the secret invitation of the Romans drew near to the city. Yet why do I say 'secret', when the greater part of the Roman princes forced their way into the castle of St Paul and giving hostages invited the holy emperor to enter. Why make a long tale? When the emperor pitched his camp in the vicinity, the pope and Adalbert made their escape together from Rome. The citizens welcomed the holy emperor and all his men into their town, promising again to be loyal and adding under a strong oath that they would never elect or ordain a pope except with the consent and approval of the august Caesar Otto, the lord emperor, and his son King Otto.

Three days later at the request of the bishops and people of Rome a synod was held in the church of St Peter, attended by the emperor and the Italian archbishops. The deacon Rodalf acted in place of Ingelfred, patriarch of Aquileia, who had been seized by a sudden sickness in that city; Waldpert came from Milan, Peter from Ravenna; Archbishop Adeltac and Landohard, bishop of Minden, represented Saxony; Otker, bishop of Speyer, France. The Italian bishops were Hubert of Parma, Liudprand of Cremona, Hermenard of Reggio; the Tuscans, Conrad of Lucca, Everard of Arezzo, the bishops of Pisa, Siena, Florence, Pistoia, Peter of Camerino, the bishop of Spoleto; the Romans, Gregory of Albano, Sico of Ostia, Benedict of Porto, Lucidus of Gavio, Theophylact of Palestrina, Wido of Selva Candida, Leo of Velletri, Sico of

Bieda, Stephen of Cervetri, John of Nepi, John of Tivoli, John of San
Liberato, Romanus of Ferentino, John of Norma, John of Veroli,
Marinus of Sutri, John of Narni, John of Sabina, John of Gallese, the
bishops of Civita, Castellana, Alatri, Orte, John of Anagni, the bishop of
Trevi, Sabbatinus of Terracina. There were also present: Stephen,
cardinal archpriest of the parish Balbina, Dominic of the parish Anas-
tasia, Peter of the parish Damasus, Theophylact of the parish Chryso-
gonus, John of the parish Equitius, Peter of the parish Pamachius,
Adrian of the parish Calixtus, John of the parish Caecilia, Adrian of the
parish Lucina, Benedict of the parish Sixtus, Theophylact of the parish
Four Crowned Saints, Stephen of the parish Sabina, Benedict cardinal
archdeacon, John deacon, Bonofilius chief cardinal deacon, George
second cardinal deacon, Stephen assistant, Andrew treasurer, Sergius
chief warden, John sacristan, Stephen, Theophylact, Adrian, Stephen,
Benedict, Azo, Adrian, Romanus, Leo, Benedict, Leo, Leo, Leo
notaries, Leo chief of the school of singers, Benedict subdeacon in charge
of the offertories, Azo, Benedict, Demetrius, John, Amicus, Sergius,
Benedict, Urgo, John, Benedict subdeacon and steward, Stephen arch-
acolyte with all the acolytes and district deacons. Representing the
princes of Rome were Stephen son of John, Demetrius Meliosi, Cres-
centi de Caballo Marmoreo, John Mizina, Stephen de Imiza, Theodore
de Rufina, John de Primicerio, Leo de Cazunuli, Rikhard, Pietro de
Canapanaria, and Benedict with his son Bulgamin. The commoner Peter,
also called Imperiola, together with the whole body of Roman soldiery
was in attendance.

When all had taken their seats and complete silence was established,
the holy emperor began thus: 'How fitting it would have been for
the lord Pope John to be present at this glorious holy synod. I ask you,
holy fathers, to give your opinion why he has refused to attend this
great gathering, for you live as he does and share in all his interests.'

Thereupon the Roman bishops and the cardinal priests and deacons
together with the whole populace said: 'We are surprised that your
most holy wisdom deigns to ask us this question: even the inhabitants
of Iberia and Babylonia and India know the answer to it. John is not
now even one of those who come in sheep's clothing and within are
ravening wolves: his savegeness is manifest, he is openly engaged in the
devil's business, and he makes no attempt at disguise.'

The emperor replied: 'It seems to us right that the charges against the
pope should be brought forward seriatim, and that the whole synod
should then consider what course we should adopt.'

Thereupon the cardinal priest Peter got up and testified that he had
seen the pope celebrate mass without himself communicating. John,
bishop of Narni, and John, cardinal deacon, then declared that they had

seen the pope ordain a deacon in a stable and at an improper season. Benedict, cardinal deacon, with his fellow deacons and priests said that they knew the pope had been paid for ordaining bishops and that in the city of Todi he had appointed a bishop for ten years. On the question of his sacrilege, they said, no inquiries were necessary; knowledge of it was a matter of eyesight not of hearsay. As regards his adultery, though they had no visual information, they knew for certain that he had carnal acquaintance with Rainer's widow, Stephana his father's concubine, the widow Anna, and his own niece, and that he had turned the holy palace into a brothel and resort for harlots. He had gone hunting publicly; he had blinded his spiritual father Benedict who died of his injuries; he had caused the death of cardinal subdeacon John by castrating him; he had set houses on fire and appeared in public equipped with sword, helmet, and cuirass. To all this they testified, while everyone, clergy and laity alike, loudly accused him of drinking wine for love of the devil. At dice, they said, he asked the aid of Jupiter, Venus, and the other demons; he did not celebrate matins nor observe the canonical hours nor fortify himself with the sign of the cross.

When he had heard this, as the Romans could not understand his native Saxon tongue, the emperor bade Liudprand, bishop of Cremona, to deliver the following speech in the Latin language to all the Romans. Accordingly he got up and began thus:

'It often happens, and we know it by experience that men set in high positions are besmirched by the foul tongue of envy: the good displease the bad, even as the bad displease the good. For this reason we still regard as doubtful the charge against the pope which the cardinal deacon Benedict read out and communicated to you, and we are uncertain whether it originated from zeal for righteousness or from impious envy. Therefore, unworthy as I am, by the authority of the position that has been granted me I call upon you all by the Lord God, whom no one, even if he wishes, can deceive, and by His holy mother the pure virgin Mary, and by the most precious body of the chief of the apostles, in whose church this is now being read, cast no foul words against the lord pope nor accuse him of anything that he has not really done and that has not been witnessed by men on whom we can rely.'

Thereupon the bishops, the priests, the deacons, the rest of the clergy, and the whole Roman people cried out as one man,

'If Pope John has not committed all the shameful crimes that the deacon Benedict read out to us and done things even worse and more disgusting than those, may the most blessed Peter, whose verdict closes the gates of heaven against the unworthy and opens them for the righteous, never free us from the chains of our sins; may we be held fast in the bonds of anathema and at the last day be set on the left hand with those who said to the Lord God, "Depart from us, we would have no knowledge of thy ways." If you do not give us credence, at least you ought to believe the army of our lord the emperor, against whom the pope advanced five days ago, equipped with sword, shield, helmet, and cuirass. It was only the intervening waters of the Tiber that saved him from being taken prisoner in that garb.'

Then the holy emperor said, 'There are as many witnesses to that as there are fighting men in our army.'

So the holy synod pronounced: 'If it please the holy emperor, let a letter be sent to the lord pope, that he come here and purge himself from all these charges.'

Thereupon a letter was sent to him as follows:

'To the supreme pontiff and universal pope lord John, Otto, august emperor by the grace of God, together with the archbishops and bishops of Liguria, Tuscany, Saxony, and France, sends greeting in the name of the Lord. When we came to Rome in God's service and inquired of your sons, the Roman bishops, cardinal priests and deacons, and the whole body of the people besides, concerning your absence, and asked them what was the reason that you were unwilling to see us, the defenders of your church and your person, they brought out such foul and filthy tales about you that we should be ashamed of them, even if they were told about actors. That your highness may not remain in complete ignorance we set down some of the them briefly here; for though we would fain give them all seriatim, one day is not enough. Know then that you are charged, not by a few men but by all the clergy and laity alike, of homicide, perjury, sacrilege and of the sin of unchastity with your own kinswoman and with two sisters. They tell me too something that makes me shudder, that you have drunk wine for love of the devil, and that in dice you have asked the help of Jupiter, Venus, and the other demons. Therefore we earnestly beg your paternal highness not to refuse under any pretence to come to Rome and clear yourself of all these charges. If perchance you fear the violence of a rash multitude, we declare under oath that no action is contemplated contrary to the sanction of the holy canons.'

After reading this letter, the pope sent the following reply:

'Bishop John, servant of God's servants, to all the bishops. We hear say that you wish to make another pope. if you do, I excommunicate you by Almighty God, and you have no power, to ordain no one or celebrate mass.'

When this answer was read in the holy synod, the following clergy, who had been absent at the previous meeting, were present: from Lorraine, Henry archbishop of Trier; from Aemilia and Liguria, Wido of Modena, Gezo of Tortona, Sigulf of Piacenza. The synod returned the following reply to the lord pope:

'To the supreme pontiff and universal pope lord John, Otto, august emperor by the grace of God, and the holy synod assembled at Rome in God's service, send greeting in the Lord's name. At our last meeting of the sixth of November we sent you a letter containing the charges made against you by your accusers and their reasons for bringing them. In the same letter we asked your highness to come to Rome, as is only just, and to clear yourself from these allegations. We have now received your answer, which is not at all of a kind suited to the character of this occasion but is more in accordance with the folly of rank indifference. There could be no reasonable excuse for not coming to the synod. But messengers from your highness ought certainly to have put in an appearance here, and assured us that you could not attend the holy synod owing to illness or some such insuperable difficulty. There is furthermore a sentence in your letter more fitting for a stupid boy than a bishop. You excommunicated us all if we appointed another bishop to the see of Rome, and yet gave us power to celebrate the mass and ordain clerical functionaries. You said, "You have no power to ordain no one." We always thought, or rather believed, that two negatives make an affirmative, if your authority did not weaken the verdict of the authors of old. However, let us reply, not to your words, but to your meaning. If you do not refuse to come to the synod and clear yourself of these charges, we certainly are prepared to bow to your authority. But if – which Heaven forbid! – under any pretence you refrain from coming and defending yourself against a capital charge, especially when there is nothing to stop you, neither a sea voyage, nor bodily sickness, nor a long journey, then we shall disregard your excommunication, and rather turn it upon yourself, as we have justly the power to do. Judas, who betrayed, or rather who sold, Our Lord Jesus Christ, with the other disciples received the power of binding and loosing from their Master in these words: "Verily I say unto you, whatsoever ye shall bind on earth shall be bound in heaven: and whatsoever ye shall loose on earth shall be loosed in heaven." As long as Judas was a good man with his fellow disciples, he had the power to bind and loose. But when he became a murderer for greed and wished to destroy all men's lives, whom then could he loose that was bound or bind that was loosed save himself, whom he hanged in the accursed noose?'

This letter was written on the twenty-second day of November and sent

K

by the hand of the cardinal priest Adrian and the cardinal deacon Benedict.

When these latter arrived at Tivoli, they could not find the pope: he had gone off into the country with bows and arrows, and no one could tell them where he was. Not being able to find him they returned with the letter to Rome and the holy synod met for the third time. On this occasion the emperor said:

'We have waited for the pope's appearance, that we might complain of his conduct towards us in his presence; but since we are now assured that he will not attend, we beg you earnestly to listen to an account of his treacherous behaviour. We hereby inform you, archbishops, bishops, priests, deacons, clerics, counts, judges, and people, that Pope John being hard pressed by Berengar and Adalbert, our revolted subjects, sent messengers to us in Saxony, asking us for the love of God to come to Italy and free him and the church of St Peter from their jaws. We need not tell you how much we did for him with God's assistance: you see it today for yourselves. But when by my help he was rescued from their hands and restored to his proper place, forgetful of the oath of loyalty which he swore to me on the body of St Peter, he got Adalbert to come to Rome, defended him against me, stirred up tumults, and before my soldiers' eyes appeared as leader in the campaign equipped with helmet and cuirass. Let the holy synod now declare its decision'.

Thereupon the Roman pontiffs and the other clergy and all the people replied:

'A mischief for which there is no precedent must be cauterized by methods equally novel. If the pope's moral corruption only hurt himself and not others, we should have to bear with him as best we could. But how many chaste youths by his example have become unchaste? How many worthy men by association with him have become reprobates? We therefore ask your imperial majesty that this monster, whom no virtue redeems from vice, shall be driven from the Holy Church, and another be appointed in his place, who by the example of his goodly conversation may prove himself both ruler and benefactor, living rightly himself and setting us an example of like conduct.'

Then the emperor said, 'I agree with what you say; nothing will please me more than for you to find such a man and to give him control of this holy universal see.'

At that all cried with one voice: 'We elect as our shepherd Leo, the venerable chief notary of the holy Roman Church, a man of proved worth deserving of the highest sacerdotal rank. He shall be the supreme and universal pope of the holy Roman Church, and we hereby reprobate the apostate John because of his vicious life.' The whole assembly repeated these words three times, and then with the emperor's consent escorted the aforesaid Leo to the Lateran Palace amid acclamations, and later at the due season in the church of St Peter elevated him to the supreme priesthood by holy consecration and took the oath of loyalty towards him.

When this had been arranged the most holy emperor, hoping that he could stay at Rome with a few men and not wishing the Roman people to be burdened with a great army, gave many of his soldiers leave to return home. John, the so-called pope, hearing of this and knowing how easily the Romans could be bribed, sent messengers to the city, promising the people all the wealth of St Peter and the churches, if they would fall upon the pious emperor and the lord pope Leo and impiously murder them. Why make a long tale? The Romans encouraged, or rather ensnared by the fewness of the emperor's troops and animated by the promised reward, at once sounded their trumpets and rushed in hot haste upon the emperor to kill him. He met them on the bridge over the Tiber, which the Romans had barricaded with wagons. His gallant warriors, well trained in battle with fearless hearts and fearless swords, leaped forward among the foe, like hawks falling on a flock of birds, and drove them off in panic without resistance. No hiding place, neither basket nor hollow tree trunk nor filthy sewer, could protect them in their flight. Down they fell, and as usually happens with such gallant heroes, most of their wounds were in the back. Who of the Romans then would have escaped from the massacre, had not the holy emperor yielded to the pity which they did not deserve, and called off his men still thirsting for the enemies' blood.

After they were all vanquished and the survivors had given hostages, the venerable pope Leo fell at the emperor's feet and begged him to give the hostages back and rely on the people's loyalty. At the request of the venerable Pope Leo the holy emperor gave back the hostages, although he knew that the Romans would soon start the trouble I am about to relate. He also commended the pope to the Romans' loyalty, a lamb entrusted to wolves; and leaving Rome hastened towards Camerino and Spoleto where he had heard that Adalbert was to be found.

Meanwhile the women, with whom the so-called Pope John was accustomed to carry on his voluptuous sports, being many in numbers and noble in rank, stirred up the Romans to overthrow Leo, whom God and they themselves had chosen as supreme and universal pope, and bring John back again into Rome. This they did; but by the mercy of God the venerable Pope Leo escaped from their clutches and with a few attendants made his way to the protection of the most pious emperor Otto.

The holy emperor was bitterly grieved at this insult, and to avenge the expulsion of the lord Pope Leo and the foul injuries done by the deposed John to the cardinal deacon John and the notary Azo, one of whom had his right hand cut off, and the other his tongue, two fingers and his nose, he got his army together again and prepared to return to Rome. But before the holy emperor's forces were all assembled, the Lord decreed that every age should know how justly Pope John had been repudiated by his bishops and all the people, and how unjustly afterwards he had been welcomed back. One night when John was disporting himself with some man's wife outside Rome, the devil dealt him such a violent blow on the temples that he died of the injury within a week. Moreover at the prompting of the devil, who had struck the blow, he refused the last sacraments, as I have frequently heard testified by his friends and kinsmen who were at his death bed.

At his death the Romans, forgetful of the oath they had taken to the holy emperor, elected Benedict cardinal deacon as pope, swearing moreover that they would never abandon him but would defend him against the emperor's might. Thereupon the emperor invested the city closely and allowed no one to get out with a whole skin. Siege engines and famine completed the work, and finally in spite of the Romans he got possession of the city again, restored the venerable Leo to his proper place, and bade Benedict the usurper to appear before him.

Accordingly the supreme and universal pope, the lord Leo, took his seat in the Church of the Lateran and with him the most holy emperor Otto, together with the Roman and Italian bishops, the archbishops of Lorraine and Saxony, the bishops, priests, deacons, and the whole Roman people whose names will be given later. Before them appeared Benedict, the usurper of the apostolic chair, brought in by the men who had elected him and still wearing the pontifical vestments. To him the cardinal archdeacon Benedict addressed the following charge:

'By what authority or by what law, O usurper, are you now wearing this pontifical raiment, seeing that our lord the venerable Pope Leo is alive and here present, whom you and we elected to the supreme apostolic office when John had been accused and disowned? Can you deny that you swore to our lord the emperor here present that you and the other Romans would never elect nor ordain a pope without the consent of the emperor and his son King Otto?'

Benedict replied, 'Have mercy upon my sin.'

Then the emperor, revealing by his tears how inclined he was to mercy, asked the synod not to pass hasty judgement upon Benedict. If he wished and could, let him answer the questions and defend his case:

if he had neither the wish nor the power but confessed his guilt, then let him for the fear of God have some mercy shown to him.

Thereupon Benedict flung himself in haste at the feet of the lord pope Leo and the emperor, and cried out, 'I have sinned in usurping the holy Roman see.' He then handed over the papal cloak and gave the papal staff which he was holding to pope Leo, who broke it in pieces and showed it to the people. Next the pope bade Benedict to sit down on the ground and took from him his chasuble and stole. Finally he said to all the bishops:

'We hereby deprive Benedict, usurper of the holy Roman apostolic chair, of all pontifical and priestly office: but by reason of the clemency of the lord emperor Otto, by whose help we have been restored to our proper place, we allow him to keep the rank of deacon, not at Rome but in exile, which we now adjudge against him.'

8. The *Ottonianum*; after the imperial coronation Otto I confirms territories to Pope John XII (Rome, 3 February 962): DO.I.235, from *MGH Diplomata*, I, 322–7.

In the name of the Almighty Lord God, Father and Son and Holy Spirit. I Otto, by God's grace emperor augustus, together with our son Otto, by divine providence king, [1] we vow and promise by this pact of our confirmation to you, blessed Peter, prince of apostles and key-bearer of the kingdom of Heaven, and through you to your vicar Lord John, highest bishop and universal twelfth pope [of that name], just as you have held them from your predecessors and have administered them up to the present in your power and jurisdiction: the city of Rome with its duchy and all its suburbs, villages, and territories, mountains and shores, coasts and ports, [2] and all cities, castles, towns, and villages which belong to Tuscany, that is, Porto, Civita Vecchia, Ceri, Bieda, Monteranno, Sutri, Nepi, castle Gallese, Orte, Bomarzo, Ameria, Todi, Perugia, with its three islands, that is the greater and the lesser, [and] Pulvensis, Narni, and Otricoli with all territories belonging to the aforesaid communities. [3] Likewise the Exarchate of Ravenna in its entirety including the cities, towns, citadels, and castles which Lord Pippin of pious memory and Lord Charles, most excellent of emperors, our predecessors, granted to the blessed apostle Peter and to your predecessors at one time by a deed of donation, the city of Ravenna and [in] Emelia: Bobbio, Cesena, Forumpopuli, Forli, Faenza, Imola, Bologna, Ferrara, Comacchio, and Adria and Gavello with all marches, territories, and islands, on land and on sea, belonging to the above-mentioned towns. [4] And likewise the Pentapolis, to wit Rimini, Pesaro, Fano, Sinigaglia, Ancona, Orsino, Umana, Jesi, Fossombrone, Monte-feltre, Urbino and the territory of Balba, Cagli, Lucioli, and Gubbio with all the marches and territories belonging to these towns. [5] In the same way, the Sabine territory just as it was conceded in its entirety by the emperor our predecessor Lord Charles to the blessed apostle Peter by a document of donation. [6] Also in the region of Lombard Tuscany, Città di Castello, Orvieto, Bagnorea, Ferentum, Viterbo, Orchia, Marta, Toscanella, Sovana, Populonia, Rosello with all their suburbs and villages and maritime territories, the citadels and their villages and all marches. [7] And likewise from Luna [Spezia] with the island of Corsica, then to Sarzana, then over the pass of La Cisa, then to Berceto, then to Parma, then to Reggio, then to Mantua and Mon-selice, and the provinces of Venetia and Istria and also the entire duchies of Spoleto and Benevento together with the church of St Christina situated on the Po about four miles from Pavia. [8] Likewise in the territory of Campagna – Sora, Arces, Aquino, Arpenio, Teano, and Capua. [9] And also the patrimonies under your power and authority, the Beneventan patrimony, and the Neapolitan patrimony – from the town of Naples with the castles, territories, marches, and islands per-taining to it just as they appear to belong – and the patrimony of upper and lower Calabria; also the patrimony of Sicily, if God should give it over to our hands. [10] In the same way the cities Gaeta and Fondi with all that belongs to them. [11] Moreover, we offer to you, Blessed Apostle Peter, and your vicar Lord Pope John and his successors, for the salvation of our soul and that of our son and of our forebears, from the kingdom belonging to us towns and citadels with their fishing rights: that is, Rieti, Amiterno, Aquila [Furcone], Norcia [Nursia], Valva, and Marsica, and elsewhere the community of Teramo with whatever belongs to it. [12] We confirm now to the end of time all these above-mentioned provinces, cities and towns, citadels and castles, villages and territories and at the same time the patrimonies, for the salvation of our soul and that of our son and our forebears and our successors, and on behalf of all the people of the Franks, who have been preserved and will be preserved by God, for the said church of yours, Blessed Apostle Peter, and through you to your vicar, our spiritual father, Lord John, highest pontiff and universal pope, and to his successors, that they may possess them lawfully in their dominion and authority. [13] In the same way we confirm through this pact of our bestowal the donations which Lord King Pippin of pious memory and afterwards Lord Charles, most excellent emperor, conferred on the blessed apostle Peter of his own free will, likewise the revenues or taxes or other tributes which have

customarily been brought into the palace of the king of the Lombards
every year from Tuscany and the duchy of Spoleto, just as it is contained
in the above-mentioned donations and as it was decided between Pope
Hadrian of holy memory and Lord Charles, emperor, when that pope
confirmed for him a diploma of his own authority concerning the above-
mentioned duchies, that is, Tuscany and Spoleto, in such a way that the
above-mentioned revenue be paid every year to the church of the blessed
apostle Peter, our domination in all things over those same duchies
remaining secure as well as their subjection to us and our son. [14]
Besides just as we have said, we validate for you through this diploma
of our confirmation all those things named above, so that they may remain
rightfully under your authority and dominion and so that your power
may not be diminished in any way by our successors through any
argument or machination whatever, or anything then be taken away
from you of the above-mentioned provinces, cities, towns, citadels,
fortresses, villages, islands, territories, and patrimonies, and likewise the
taxes and revenues, with the result that we will not make them over or
consent them to be made over to anyone who may want them.[11] But
rather we testify that we will be defenders as far as we are able of all
those things named above, that is, provinces, towns, cities, citadels,
castles, territories, patrimonies, and islands, and the revenues and taxes,
for the church of the blessed apostle Peter and of the popes residing
in the most Holy See in order that they may keep them in their control
to use, to enjoy, and to administer. [15] In all things our power and that
of our son and our descendants is to be secure according to what is
contained in the deed and constitution and sworn promise of Pope
Eugene and his successors, that is, that all the clergy and nobles of the
Roman people take an oath that the future election of the popes be
carried out canonically and legally as far as it can be determined in each
case, on account of various constraints and the unreasonable harshness
of the popes *vis-à-vis* the people subject to them. And whoever is
elected to this holy and apostolic office, let no one consent to his being
consecrated pope until he makes a promise in the presence of our legates
or our son or the whole populace for the satisfaction of all, now and in
the future, such as our venerated spiritual father Leo is known to have
done voluntarily. [16] Moreover, we have seen to it that other minor
items be inserted in this work, to wit that in the election of the popes
neither free nor unfree man should presume to come to the election to

---

[11] . . . *ita ut neque nos ea facturi simus neque quibuslibet ea facere volentibus
consenciamus.* Cf. Thatcher and McNeal, *Source Book,* pp. 117–18: 'We will
never do so, nor allow others to do so. . . .' Their translation overlooks the object
ea and requires that one supply the idea of diminishing the territories named
above. I have taken an alternate meaning of *facere,* 'to bequeath'. See Niermeyer,
Lexicon minus, p. 402.

impede the Romans, whom antique custom admits through the authorization of the holy fathers. And if anyone should presume to go against
our orders, let him be banished. In addition, we prohibit any of our
legates from daring to cause any impediment to the above-mentioned
election. [17] We have determined to implement this fully so that those
who have at one time under special protection of the Apostolic See or
of us might legally use the protection thus acquired. And if anyone
should presume to violate anyone of those who earned it, let him
know that he will run the risk of his life. [18] We also confirm this
so that they may render just obedience in all things to the apostolic
lord or to his dukes or judges in order for justice to be carried out. [19]
We have ascertained that this should be added to this serviceable charter;
legates of the apostolic lord or of us always be appointed so that they
may be able to report to us or our son every year how individual dukes
and judges carry out justice toward the people and how they observe
this imperial decree. As soon as these legates ascertain all the complaints
which may have arisen through the negligence of the dukes or judges, let
them bring them to the notice of the apostolic lord, and he himself will
select one of two possibilities: either the difficulties may be immediately
corrected by those same legates or, after our legate has reported to us,
they may be corrected by our legates as directed by us. [20] In order
that this be believed to be firm by all our faithful of the holy church of
God, we have confirmed this pact of confirmation with a seal of our own
hand and by the signature of our highest nobles, and we have ordered
it to be sealed with the impression of our bull.

Sign of the most serene emperor Lord Otto and of his bishops,
abbots, and counts.

Sign of Adaldag, archbishop of the church of Hamburg. Sign of
Hartbert, bishop of the church of Chur. Sign of Druogo, bishop of the
church of Osnabrück. Sign of Voto, bishop of the church of Strasbourg.
Sign of Otwin, bishop of the church of Hildesheim. Sign of Landwart,
bishop of the church of Minden. Sign of Otger, bishop of the church of
Speyer. Sign of Gezo, bishop of the church of Tortona. Sign of Huc-
bert, bishop of the church of Parma. Sign of Wido, bishop of the church
of Modena. Sign of Hatto, abbot of the monastery of Fulda. Sign of
Gunther, abbot of the monastery of Hersfeld. Sign of Count Eberhard.
Sign of Count Gunther. Sign of Count Burghard. Sign of Count Uto.
Sign of Count Conrad. Sign of Ernest. Sign of Dieter, Ricdag, Liupen,
Hartwig, Arnolues, Ingilthies, Burchart, Retinges.

In the year of the Incarnation of our Lord 962, the fifth year of the
indiction, month of February, the thirteenth day of the same month, in
the twenty-seventh year of Lord Otto, most invincible emperor of the
empire, this document was made under favourable auspices.

9. With Pope John XIII and Otto I presiding in the royal court, Archbishop Peter of Ravenna charges Rainerius with invading Ravenna and violating his person and property (Ravenna, 17 April 967): DO.I.340, from *MGH Diplomata*, I, 464–6.

In the name of the Father and of the Son and of the Holy Spirit. In the second year in which it pleased God for Lord John to reign as highest pontiff and universal pope in the most sacred apostolic see of St Peter[12] and in the reign of the very pious and ever august Lord Otto, the great and pacific emperor crowned by God, in the sixth year of his reign of piety in Italy, on the seventeenth day of the month of April, in the tenth year of the indiction, in the city formerly called Classis, within the residence where the Lord Emperor Otto was staying near St Severus.[13]

Since everything that has taken place over a long period of time cannot be retained by memory, it is prudent to pin it down in written form. When Lord John, most sacred and coangelic universal pope, along with Lord Otto, his spiritual son, the great emperor crowned by God, sat in judgement at an imperial *placitum*[14] held in the residence attached to the cathedral, which is located behind the sanctuary of the monastery of St Severus, the rights of each man were stated and deliberated in accordance with long-standing custom. Sitting with them were Romans, Franks, Lombards, Saxons, and Alemanni, and first of all, namely, Lord Peter, the most holy and coangelic archbishop of the holy church of Ravenna; Gualpert, archbishop of Milan; Rodoald, patriarch of Aquileia; Bishop Landward, Bishop Otherius, Bishop Guido of Modena, Bishop Hubert of Parma, Bishop Liudprand of Cremona, Bishop Ermenald of Reggio. Also Odbert, glorious margrave and count palatine; Conrad, son of King Conrad; Bucco, duke and imperial vassal; Margrave Adelramus, Count Amizo, Count Eriprand, Count Atto of Modena, Bernard and Ugo and Guido, the sons of the late Count Mainfred of Parma, count Gandulf of Verona, Dato of Milan; John, judge[15] of the city of Rome; Stefan, papal almoner; Paul, judge

[12] John XIII, former bishop of Narni, followed Leo VIII in 965, but the Romans drove him into exile. Otto restored him in 966 and punished the rebels. At Christmas of 967, Pope John crowned Otto II king in Rome, confirming him as his father's successor.

[13] '. . . hubi domnus Otone imperatore residebant . . . .' This is a sample of the perplexing Latin of the document, whose editor says, 'It is difficult to draw a line between scribal errors and surprising speech forms. . . .' (Sickel, *MGH Diplomata*, I, 464). Many characters have been omitted, which in some cases seem to represent elision in pronunciation.

[14] *Placitum*, a word of many meanings, but most commonly a general assembly or the session of a law court.

[15] *Judex*, in classical Latin simply a judge, but in medieval parlance a *judex* could be any public official. Dukes and counts, the magnates of the realm, could

of the city of Ravenna; Ursus, judge of the city of Ferrara; Peter,
dativus;[16] John, *dativus* of the city of Ferrara; Leo, *dativus* of the city of
Faenza, Peter *dativus* of the city of Ferrara, Stefan, *dativus*; Gualpert,
judge of the lord kings; Gaulterius, Astulfus, and Acius; Griffo, judge
of the lord emperor; Counts Peter and Severus, called Sigizo, who are
brothers; Count Lambert, their son and nephew; Counts Gerard and
Erard, brothers; Count Guarinus of Ferrara; Aginoni, Paul, and Peter,
duke of Traversaria; Duke John; John, notary and archivist; Sergius,
notary; and Lord John, consul[17] and father of the city,[18] and also Leo
the chancellor, who is named *de Cisterna*, and . . . . . and others.

Coming into the presence of all of us listed above, the said Lord
Ursus, well-known judge of the city of Ferrara and advocate of Lord
Peter, most holy and coangelic archbishop of the church of Ravenna,
lodged a complaint and brought a charge on behalf of the person of the
aforesaid archbishop Peter against Rainerius, a deacon and son of the
late Count Tendegrimo and his wife Countess Ingelrada, to the effect
that, 'Rainerius the deacon came with his troops and entered by force
into my diocese of the holy church of Ravenna, violated my see, arrested
my person, and put me in chains in prison. He took the treasure from
my churches and my residence, which cannot be reckoned. Therefore
he was charged by you many times on my behalf: the first time in the
city of Rome in your presence, most holy Lord John, and also before the
clergy of Rome; the second time in the 'new' basilica of Sant' Apollinare,
a bishop and martyr for Christ, where they sat in judgement at a general
placitum.[19] And he was charged by you at a third *placitum* for the same
crime.'

The aforesaid Lord John, coangelic and most holy pope, with Otto
the great emperor, his spiritual son, addressed the members of the court:
'We have sent a letter and a legate to them so as to get them to come to

also be referred to as *judices*. However, in our document the *judices* are clearly
functioning as judges.
    [16] *Dativus*, literally 'appointed', the title of a functionary in the Byzantine
provinces of Italy.
    [17] *Consul*, outside of Rome, designated an office whose duties are not clear.
In some Italian cities the consul was a magistrate elected for a year. Eduard
Brinckmeier suggests *Bürgermeister*. See *Glossarium diplomaticum*, I, Aalen, 1967,
540.
    [18] *Pater civitatis* is equivalent to *curator civitatis* according to Niermeyer
(*Lexicon minus*, p. 772), who cites our diploma as evidence. The curator was a
municipal officer of the late Roman Empire.
    [19] Sant' Apollinare Nuovo was built by Theodoric the Great in the early sixth
century. First used as a cathedral for Arians, it was converted in 560 into
a Roman Catholic church. The label 'new' was applied in the eighth or ninth
century, distinguishing it from Sant' Apollinare in Classe Fuori, the largest
basilica still extant in Ravenna.

our synod and *placitum* and to make amends to you, Archbishop Peter, the plaintiff, but he absolutely refused to come.' Then they inquired of the aforementioned officials and *dativi*, both Roman and Lombard, what the law was on this point, and these officials and *dativi* replied, 'Since Rainerius the deacon refused to come to your synod and *placitum* concerning the crime which you have charged him with so many times, the law demands that you invest Lord Peter's advocate with all his property and possessions, that is, with whatever the deacon Rainerius has held up to the present time, including both the rights of property and rentals, within the whole kingdom of Italy and wherever else you are able to find anything that is his.'

Then Lord Otto, the great emperor, by means of the gilded staff which he and the archbishop held in their hands, in accordance with the above, invested in perpetuity the said lord Archbishop Peter, as well as his advocate, and also the bishops who would succeed him; and furthermore the emperor by handshake gave certain property to Archbishop Peter, to wit, in the same symbolic form in which John, the consul and father of the city, had invested him [the archbishop], with all these very same things and properties. And when this was done, the same lord emperor ordered the said Otbert, marquis and count palatine, to place the ban in turn on all that property.[20] So the said Lord Otbert, well-known marquis and count palatine, said in a loud voice to all, 'By order of my lord the emperor I place his ban on all the property and possessions with which Archbishop Peter's advocate was invested, so that no one may dare to divest him of it for any reason or on any pretext. Whoever presumes to divest him is to be fined two thousand gold *mancusi*, one-half to the treasury of the lord emperor and one-half to you, the said Lord Archbishop Peter, and your successors.'

And this was done on the day and in the month and in the tenth year of the indiction as written above at Ravenna.

I Otbert, count palatine, have signed. I Count Adelbert, was present. Sign of the hand of the count of Milan, who was present. Sergius, by God's grace duke, was there and signed concerning everything stated above. Paul, son of the late Duke Peter, was present and signed for all those named above. Stephan, judge, was present and signed concerning everything stated above. Peter, consul, was present and signed.

---

[20] *Bandum mitere* (=*bannum mittere*): '*judicial warranty* of the possession of an estate and generally of possessory rights deriving from a judgment'. See Niermeyer, *Lexicon minus*, p. 83, item 10 under *bannus*, where DO.I.340 is cited as evidence.

10. Otto I confirms donations to Bishop Rather of Verona and puts him under his protection (Balsemado [later Monzambano], 5 November 967): DO.I.348, from *MGH Diplomata*, I, 474–5.

In the name of the holy and indivisible Trinity. Otto, by God's grace emperor augustus. Let all of our faithful, future as well as present, know that, by the intervention of our most beloved son of the same name for the love of God, of His holy mother, and of S. Zeno, we have granted to the church of Verona, over which Bishop Rather is known to preside by our imperial clemency and the authority of God, whatever remains from that which our predecessors conferred upon his predecessors pertaining to the two gates of the same city, one, to wit, which is called S. Zeno, the other which is called by the name of S. Fermo, with customs house for wagons and all revenues owed to us from the same.

We also concede, or rather we return to it [the church of Verona], the market on S. Zeno's day and on Palm Sunday just as our predecessors are said to have granted to the same church; we also grant it two portions of the river toll[21] and the same river toll completely from the castle which is called Portus;[22] and whatever our precedessors conferred upon the church up to our time and confirmed through diplomas, we concede entirely and confirm by this diploma.

We also rescind and remove all exactions of labour service from the castles which now belong in perpetuity to the same church, so that neither count nor viscount nor *sculdahis*[23] may have any power of staying in them or distraining anyone, but all those living in them may thus remain under the power of whoever has been in charge of the said church through the succession of time, so that no power subject to our rule may ever have permission to exercise judicial authority. But if anything should be done against the law either by manse-dwellers or castle-dwellers or homesteaders, or *incensiti*[24] or *commendati*[25] or clerics or serfs of him [Rather], it may be corrected justly and legally either by himself or by a *ministerialis*[26] of his. Furthermore, no one may presume

[21] *Ripaticum*, a tribute collected on river banks, either a coast and dike tax, or a tax on goods displayed and sold on shore. See Brinckmeier, *Glossarium diplomaticum*, II, 481. Verona is located on the banks of the river Adige.

[22] Portus is now part of the town of Legnago, south-east of Verona.

[23] *Sculdahis*, with many variant spellings, was a village mayor or a local judge – akin to modern German *Schultheiss*.

[24] *Incensitus*, one who owes a tribute in incense (*incensum*). See Niermeyer, *Lexicon minus*, p. 519, who cites this document as evidence. However, Brinckmeier defines *incensitus* as one who has to pay taxes (*census*); see *Glossarium diplomaticum*, I, 1034.

[25] *Commendatus*, one of a class of dependants created by acts of recommendation to a patron.

[26] *Ministerialis*, an administrative official peculiar to feudal Germany. Origin-

to fish in his waters, unless he has a license from ancient times

And because he is a man of modest means and an alien lacking everything except the help of God and of us, and because he has had to
endure many hardships, we wish to relieve him in this way so that our
bishop is protected beyond what others have in the realm by our
guardianship [*mundiburdis*[27]] as by a special prerogative. If anyone should
presume to harass him further or to be rebellious to him or prevent his
ministry from rendering service to God, let him be compelled, if a
cleric, to give all that he has collected from the church to him as legitimate and worthy compensation; if a serf, he must submit to whatever
the lot of serfs is and remain in his power as is proper; and let the faithful friends have license to do what they can to help without fear of any
fine; if a count, a viscount, a *sculdahis* or any other secular power should
do this and infringes his property against his [Rather's] wishes, that is,
he holds land without its being given or he receives a cleric or serf in
commendation without his [Rather's] permission or he undertakes anything similar to this, he should pay a hundred pounds of gold to us.
Furthermore, he should make good to him as a penalty whatever he
owes him by law; nor may he ever remove an occupant of a castle from
the castle of that one [Rather] to his own [castle], because this is most
unjust; let him pay for the violation of the immunity [*fractura*] if he
has done this; and let him be compelled to pay the regal fine to us; he
will be legally liable who refuses to do what is proper to him [Rather]
and pleasing to God, concerning the property of the church and who
presumes to be protector, defender, and patron of anyone else of those
who commit so great a crime.

If any *libellaria, commutationes,* or *precariae*[28] are contracted fraudulently in the bishop's diocese, we order and command that they be
entirely rescinded and that they be emended according to the will of

---

ally of unfree origin, they functioned as administrators of both secular and
ecclesiastical estates or as armed retainers of bishops and abbots. The land which
they held from their lords was still the property of the lord, but their servile
position changed in the course of time so that the *ministeriales* were ultimately
absorbed into the lesser nobility. Moreover, they came to be employed by the
monarch and held increasingly important administrative posts under the
Salians. '. . . when the chroniclers of the period complain that Henry [IV] is
surrounded by *vilissimi* and *infimi homines,* that he listens only to low-born
counsellors and spurns the advice of highborn princes, they are voicing the
complaints of the aristocracy against Henry IV's consistent and exclusive use of
ministeriales.' See Geoffrey Barraclough, *Origins of Modern Germany,* p. 82. See
also Stengel, 'Über den Ursprung der Ministerialität', *Zur mittelalterlichen
Geschichte,* pp. 69–86.

[27] *Mundiburdis,* royal protection given to various ecclesiastics and others. The
word has at least a dozen alternate spellings.

[28] Three types of precarial contracts and of charters.

God, inasmuch as we are able to free him [Rather] from any injuries, Christ being favourable, so that he may be able to perform the divine service for God in the interest of our well-being and that of our most dear wife and all legitimate progeny so that we obtain [divine] mercy.

Sign of Lord Otto, most serene emperor.

I Ambrose, chancellor, for Hubert, bishop and archchancellor, have verified it and countersigned. Given on the nones of November in the year of our Lord's Incarnation 967, the sixth of the empire of our most pious Lord Otto, the eleventh year of the indiction; carried out at Balsemado; under favourable auspices, amen.[29]

11. Otto I renews the treaty with the Venetians (Rome, 2 December 967): DO.I.350, from *MGH Diplomata*, I, 478–83.

In the name of the holy and indivisible Trinity. In the 967th year from the Incarnation of our Lord Jesus Christ, the _____[30] of the empire of Lord Otto, most pious Caesar, eleventh year of the indiction, the fourth day before the nones of December, in the city of Rome. At the instigation and request of Peter, doge of Venice, he [Otto] determined and ordered this treaty to be drawn up between the Venetians and their neighbours so that oaths might be given by both parties concerning those regulations to be observed and so that afterwards by the observation of these regulations a firm peace might last among them.

The neighbours of the Venetians to whom the business of this treaty pertains are: the inhabitants of Istria, Forumiulii [Cividale], Cenetum, Treviso, Vicenza, Monselice, Gauelenses, Commachio, Ravenna, Cesena, Rimini, Pesaro, Fano, Sinigaglia, Ancona, Numana, Fermo, and Picenum, those who are settled in these places at the present time or will have settled in the future, both upper-class and lower-class.

The most pious emperor determined that they, with Peter [Candiano IV], doge of the Venetians and with the people of Venice (that is, the inhabitants of the Rialto, Oliboli, Murano, Metamauco, Albiola, Torcello, Amianas, Burano, Ciuitas noua, Equilo, Caprulas, Bibiones, Grado,

[29] 'This well-meaning document [DO.I.348] hardly achieved its aim since the deep division between the bishop and the Veronese, which was supposed to be healed by this means, still existed. The attempt to better the paltry condition of the lesser clergy at the expense of the higher, which Rather undertook right away by means of a manifesto signed by the patriarchs and other Lombard bishops present in Verona, raised a general storm of protest against him and soon undermined . . . his position completely.' See Köpke–Dümmler, *Kaiser Otto der Grosse*, p. 427.

[30] The imperial year is not written in the copies.

Caput Argeles [Caorle], Laureto, and with bishops and priests as well as magnates and the rest of the people belonging to the duchy of Venice) ought to observe this treaty through the course of all the years so that no crime or violation should take place among the parties and if anything wrong is committed between the parties (God forbid), they promise to make good according to the terms of this treaty and to keep justice.

And if any Venetian carries out a raid into your territory of Venice, the person who was in charge of perpetrating the crime is to be turned over to you within sixty days and everything that has been stolen is to be restored twofold; and if we have not paid the double to you or turned over the same person into your hands, let him pay 500 gold *solidi* for each person who has perpetrated that injury.

And we add that we promise to return to you all your men who took refuge with us after the previous treaty was executed at Ravenna, if we can find them.

If captives are found in your duchy, those malefactors who transported those captives are to be handed over with all their goods and families; and if this is not done, then the justice of that place may offer an oath where those dependants are claimed with twelve free men [as oath-helpers] that the dependants were not taken in nor transported thence to foreign parts.

If your men take refuge in our duchies, we promise to return them to you by all means with all their goods, whether serf or freeman.

If any enemies or robbers or the like should attempt to come through our territory against you to your detriment or to your territories and he comes to our notice, we will report it to you right away without delay.

And if any robbery has taken place between the parties, it is to be restored fourfold.

If male or female serfs during this period should flee between the parties, they are to be returned with all the goods which they have taken with them, and the justice who returns these fugitives is to receive a gold *solidus* for each one, and if more is required, satisfaction may be given to their lord by a suitable oath. If the justice takes in those fugitives and neglects to return them and they then take refuge in another territory, he is to pay seventy-two gold *solidi* for each fugitive.

Moreover, no one at all is permitted to accept a pledge in other territories except where fugitives or a lawsuit is demanded; from there a pledge may be accepted; and if a pledging takes place, one party may not presume to distrain another party for security, but he is to wait until the cases have been heard, so that within the space of six months when the cases are at an end, he returns first what was condemned by judgement, and he receives his own pledge back.

If anyone should presume to carry away a pledge concerning another place or should bear it away without legal proceedings or if anyone should presume to seize something as a pledge, he is to restore twofold what he has taken.

If horses or mares or cattle or other quadrupeds are stolen, they are to be restored twofold.

Lawsuits: the parties are permitted to give what has been agreed on between them without either party doing a violence.

Concerning the river toll: according to antique custom the fortieth part is to be retained, and your men may have the license to move about the land wherever they might wish to do business or whatever their work might be, and similarly our men should have freedom of movement for business purposes.

But this is arranged so that if any damage eventuate between the parties, envoys should not be detained, but should return safe to their own territory; and likewise if couriers are detained, they should be released and 300 *solidi* should be paid to them; and if (God forbid) they are put to death, 1,000 *solidi* are to be paid to their relatives for them, and that person [the murderer] should be handed over to them.

If anyone among the parties has a claim, he is to go right away once or twice with a letter to his justice, and if satisfaction has not been done within fourteen days and if the man himself whence satisfaction is required is within the same place or has returned from another place, he may have license within seven days to distrain the justice who was appointed in the same time during his case however much is owed.

We add, if anyone has committed murder and the treaty is in force, all the accomplices everywhere who were involved in the murder are to be handed over, and if they postpone handing them over, let him pay 300 gold *solidi* for each person; and if he should wish to make any pledge in woodland, let it be done without murder, and if (God forbid) the homicide was done to a free man, let him pay 300 *solidi* for him and fifty *solidi* for each serf; and if a wound has been inflicted on a free man, let him pay similarly fifty *solidi* and for a serf thirty *solidi*.

We are willing that an oath by one man be accepted instead of six *mancusi*,[31] and an oath by two men would do in place of twelve *mancusi*, and thus up to twelve Venetian pounds through twelve chosen oath-helpers – up to as many oath-helpers as there are pounds; and if a claim exceeds twelve pounds, the oath-helpers should not exceed twelve.

We have determined concerning pledges which are made between the parties that if any dispute has arisen concerning them, the one who has retained the pledge should take the oath on behalf of himself alone.

---

[31] The Arabic gold denar was called *mancus* in Christian Europe, and was the equivalent of thirty silver denars. It appears first in Italy in the year 778, and is mentioned in Venetian documents until the end of the eleventh century.

Likewise, it has been agreed that in matters affecting the saints and churches of God there ought to be no booty or pledging, except in the case of priests of those same churches; and a demand may be made once and then again; afterwards a pledge ought to be made; and if anyone should presume to do otherwise, he is to pay twofold, and if he has ignorantly pledged, let him offer an oath and be absolved so that he restores the same pledge in full.

And this has been agreed concerning the right to cut wood, which the inhabitants of Rialto, Oliboli, Murano, Metamauco, Albiola, Torcello, and Amianas have done for thirty years: where they have cut wood, they have the right of cutting, just as has been their custom for the aforesaid number of years, whether along a river or by the sea; and the rivers which have been opened in the area of Treviso today after thirty years, let them be rediscovered according to custom in the future.

The inhabitants of Equilo have the right to cut every tree from the shore of S. Zeno all the way to the embankments of Metamaurum and Gentio, where they have had the task of cutting wood and allowing to grow what might better be left standing, and you may pasture and graze your cattle in those areas with security.

Concerning the borders of Ciuitas Noua we have determined that the limits which were made at the time of King Liudprand[32] between Duke Palutio and Marcellus, *magister militum*, ought to remain hereafter, that is from the greater river Piave all the way to the dry Piave; and also to pasture their herds of cattle with security.

The Caprisani may cut wood in the Foroiulian forest where they have always cut wood.

Similarly the inhabitants of Grado may cut wood in the Foroiulian forest according to antique custom.

And the whole duchy of the Venetians promised us and our successors for the conclusion of this treaty that it would pay annually every month of March fifty pounds of their *denarii* and one *pallium*.[33]

We confirm that one party should do justice to another party in every way concerning claims of the churches or monasteries of God.

We are willing that for one pound of *denarii* an oath be taken by one man, and thus twelve elected oath-helpers be added, up to twelve pounds of Venetian *denarii*; and if a claim is made beyond twelve pounds, oath-helpers beyond twelve should not be added.

We have also determined concerning pledges that are set between the parties that if there is any dispute concerning them, control of swearing

---

[32] King of the Lombards, died 744.
[33] A *pallium* could be a liturgical garment, an altar cloth or any decorative material, especially of Byzantine silk or brocade.

L

is awarded to the one who has the pledge, alone without oath-helpers. Bonds are to be handled in the same way.

If anyone therefore should become a violator of this our diploma, which we can scarcely believe, or he does not wish to observe it, let him know that he is to pay 1,000 pounds of the best gold, half to our treasury and half to the above-mentioned Venetians. In order that this more readily be believed and more diligently be observed by all, we order this charter to be marked with the impression of our sign manual, confirming the same with our own hand below.

12. Otto I announces his intention of making Magdeburg an arch-bishopric (968): DO.I.366, from *MGH Diplomata*, I, 502–3.

In the name of the holy and indivisible Trinity. Otto, by God's grace emperor augustus. To all our faithful, namely bishops and counts and our other co-provincials, eternal salvation and everything good in the Lord.

Since we believe that the augmentation of the divine religion affects the safety and welfare of our kingdom and empire, we intend and desire to amplify it in all possible ways. Therefore desiring that an archiepis-copal see be created in the city of Magdeburg, as you all knew, and find-ing the time now opportune for carrying this out, with the counsel of the venerable Archbishop Hatto, Bishop Hildeward, and other of our faithful, we have decreed and chosen the venerable Bishop Adalbert, once destined and sent as missionary to the Russians, as archbishop and metropolitan of all the people of the Slavs beyond the Elbe and Saale, lately converted and to be converted to God, and we have directed him to Rome to receive the *pallium* from the lord pope.

And in order that our election should be made more firm and depen-dable, we direct him to your charity and we desire by all means that he be installed as head of the see by all of you, after having been elected by the acclamation of voices and the elevation of hands.

Lest his election and his installation in the future be impugned by the envy of others (God forbid), we want him to ordain three bishops – one in Merseburg, the second in Zeitz, the third in Meissen – in the presence of the papal legates and of you so that your presence may be a future witness before God and the saints of this our intention.

And because the venerable man Boso toiled so greatly to convert the Slavic people to God, he may have the choice that he wishes between the church of Merseburg and Zeitz; the other one may go to the disposi-tion of our archbishop according to our convenience.

Moreover, we call to witness and admonish you our margraves

namely Wigbert, Witger, and Gunther, since fealty is owed to us, not to let anything obstruct this ordination of our archbishop, but let it be done according to our direction and his, as he tells you, and you may be sure that we agree with whatever you may hear from him.

Lest indeed those same bishops who are to be ordained should be esteemed paupers and peasants, we wish you would be on your guard and take counsel from the archbishop and the bishops and counts with him at Christmas to find out how they should be supported.

For whatever is distributed to them is offered to God for our salvation and yours, and the reward will not be lessened with God.

Over and above these things we wish that the lord bishops Dudo [of Havelburg] and Dodelin [of Brandenburg] should sign in the election of our archbishop and that they should promise him fealty and deference.

And in order that this our election and yours should remain firm and stable in the sight of God we have ordered that this diploma be perpetually retained in the church of Magdeburg and that a future witness be written of those whom we have mentioned above, which we have strengthened below with our own hand, and we have ordered it to be marked by the impression of our ring.

Sign of Lord Otto, great and invincible emperor augustus.

13. Otto II gives his wife Theophano great properties on both sides of the Alps (Rome, 14 April 972): DO.II.21, from *MGH Diplomata*, II, Pt. 1, *Ottonis II. diplomata*, ed. Theodor Sickel, 2nd edn, Berlin, 1956, 28–30.

In the name of the holy and indivisible Trinity. Otto, by God's grace emperor augustus. God, the creator and founder from eternity of all things that are, the most greatly good maker who brought forth primordial natural things in perfect elegance from the beginning of the nascent world, wished man, who was to surpass and dominate all things created by Himself, to attain His own image and likeness.[34]

Since He did not wish him to remain alone and in order that lasting posterity might be sufficient in multiple progeny forever in restoring the angelic order, which had been diminished on account of pride, he fabricated a conjugal helpmate for the same man from a rib taken from his body and by a wonderful providence ordered thereafter two to be

---

[34] Thus the opening of an arenga or preamble, a more elaborate literary digression than is found in the other charters in this collection. In its train of thought and biblical allusions it is wholly in keeping with other so-called *libelli doti* (Sickel, *MGH Diplomata*, II, Pt 1, 29). See Heinrich Fichtenau, *Arenga: Spätantike und Mittelalter im Spiegel von Urkundenformeln*, Graz, 1957.

in one flesh, decreeing that by most sacred law the father and mother
were to be abandoned and that one must cling to one's wife.

To this He Himself, the author of both testaments, mediator of God
and men, Lord Jesus Christ coming in human flesh, emerging from the
immaculate uterus of the virgin, the bridegroom as it were from the
bedchamber, in order that the church as a bride be joined with Himself,
and so that He might show that marriage celebrated in a legitimate
manner was good and holy and that he was the author of it, He wished
to come to it and to gladden it by the first miracle of His majesty, when
He turned water into wine, and He also wished to sanctify it. Finally
showing that the wedding was done by God with His own edict, He
says in the Gospel: What God has joined, let no man put asunder.
Likewise, the apostolic sentence: honourable marriage and immaculate
wedlock. Also by the testimony of many holy books it is affirmed that
the connection of the nuptial bond ought to be carried out by God the
author and should persist in mutual and indissoluble love for the pro-
creation of the race.

Wherefore I too, Otto, emperor augustus by the supernal will, the
Lord favouring me with His most gracious clemency, with the consul-
tation of our great and most holy and most serene parent Otto, most
pious emperor augustus, and the faithful of the holy Church of God
and of our empire, have decided to take as my wife Theophano, most
renowned niece of John, emperor of Constantinople, in the great city of
Romulus, since blessed Peter the apostle, holy and highest prince of
the churches, is favourable to our vows, and the benediction of Lord
John XIII, most holy and universal pope, will follow, Christ being
propitious to the fortunate and the auspices being favourable, and [I
have decided] to take her in the bond of legitimate matrimony and as
empress-consort.

Therefore let all of the faithful of the holy Church of God and of us,
both present and future, know how we have granted to the same most
beloved bride of ours by legal endowment in the custom of our ancestors
certain properties within the Italian borders and in the Transalpine part
of our realm to have and lawfully to possess in perpetuity: Istria, a
province of Italy with the county of Pescara, beyond the Alps the provinces of Walcheren, Wicheren [near Ghent] with the abbey of Nyvel,
with 14,000 manses[35] belonging to it and the worthy imperial manors,
ours by prosper sovereignty, Boppard [on the Rhine], Tiel on the Waal,
Herford, Tilleda, and Nordhausen, which is known to have belonged to

[35] *Mansus*, originally 'dwelling, homestead', but then extended to signify
the square measure of property that a manse and its arable land would comprise.
Somewhat analogous to the English word 'hide' and likewise without any precise
definition.

our grandmother, the forever august Lady Matilda until it was admitted that divinity lived in her.[36]

Therefore by this document of our deed we concede to the same most holy and beloved Theophano our wife, we donate and entirely grant, and from our right and dominion we transfer and delegate to her dominion and right, together with castles, houses, serfs, male and female, lands, fields, vineyards, meadows, woods, mountains and plains, waters and watercourses, mills, fisheries, and all things belonging to those estates *in toto* whether provinces or abbeys, as far as she may have all those things by the right of property and may firmly hold and possess and have the power of donating, selling, commuting, or whatever she might finally decide to do legally, the contradiction of all men being removed.

If anyone is tempted to infringe the diploma of our endowment, let him know that he is obnoxious to our majesty, and let him pay 1,000 pounds of the best gold to our most beloved bride Theophano and to our heirs.

In order that this might be believed more truly and be more diligently observed in the future, we have ordered it to be confirmed by our own hand and to be signed below with the impression of our ring.

Sign of the most invincible lord, great and pacific, likewise the sign of the lord perennially august.[37]

I Chancellor Willigis have verified it for Archchaplain Ruotbert.

Given the eighteenth day before the kalends of May in the year of the Lord's Incarnation 972, the fifteenth year of the indiction, the twelfth of the holy empire of our most holy parent Otto, the fifth of ours; carried out in Rome at the church of the Twelve Apostles; under favourable auspices.

[36] 'One of the many foundations of Queen Matilda was the nunnery in Nordhausen on the southern edge of the Harz, in Thuringian Helmegau. Here the memory of the founder was particularly cherished, and her life was twice written up there. The older Vita, composed possibly by a nun around 975 at the instigation of Otto II, grandchild of the queen, is like so many medieval Vitae more of a work of edification than a worthy biography of the historical figure of its heroine; moreover, it is badly distorted by the plagiarizing of older authors, from whom not only the style but also the content was lifted and transferred in most improbable fashion to Queen Matilda. The later Vita originated at the behest of Henry II (before 1012), probably composed by an active member of the cloister with the help of the older version but with striking alterations, which have to do with Matilda's second son Henry. Henry, the grandfather of the ruling king, was to be especially celebrated and praised, and the revisions or additions that follow this aim are for the most part unreliable. [Compare Hroswitha's treatment of the same character.] On the whole neither life is pleasing as literature. Each attempted to praise and eulogize the queen and fell wide of the mark in providing a true understanding of the significance of this high-spirited Saxon lady.' See Holtzmann, *Geschichte der sächsischen Kaiserzeit*, p. 500.

[37] That is, monograms of both Otto I and Otto II.

14. Otto II gives to the monks of St Emmeram's in Regensburg an estate which they had bought from the Jew Samuel (Rome, 2 April 981): DO.II.247, from *MGH Diplomata*, II, Pt I, 278–9.

In the name of the holy and indivisible Trinity. Otto, by God's grace emperor augustus.

If we confer any benefice on those serving the Lord in places devoted to the divine religion for the love of God, we do not doubt that the prize of eternal reward with God will be repaid to us. Therefore let all of the faithful of the holy Church of God and of us, both present and future, learn that, through the intercession of our dear nephew Duke Otto and the venerated Wolfgang, bishop [of Regensburg], and the amiable Ramwold, abbot [of St Emmeram's], we have granted as a property a certain estate named Scierstat in the district of Nordgau in the outskirts of Regensburg in the county of Henry to St Emmeram, holy martyr of God, and to the monks serving God therein, which [property] they previously had purchased for a price from a certain Jew named Samuel, by our permission with the courtyards, lands, meadows, pasturage, duties and incomes, passes and impasses, woods, lands cultivated and uncultivated, claimed and unclaimed, and all things duly belonging thereto, with the proviso that those same brothers may hold or commute it just like other property of the Church, and no one shall contradict or disturb them. And in order that this diploma of our authority be held more firmly and be more truly believed in posterity, we have ordered it to be written, and we have confirmed it, signed by the impression of our ring, with our own hand.

Sign of Lord Otto, great and invincible emperor augustus, I Hildibold, bishop and chancellor, have verified it for Willigis, archchaplain.

Given the fourth day before the nones of April in the year of our Lord's Incarnation 981, the ninth year of the indiction, in the twenty-first year of the reign of Otto II, fourteenth of the empire; carried out at Rome.

15. With Otto II presiding in royal court the dispute between Abbot John of the cloister of S. Vincenzo at Volturno and Count Landulf about property is decided in favour of the monastery (Salerno, 5 December 981): DO.II.266, from *MGH diplomata*, II, Pt I, 308–10.[38]

I John, by God's grace humble abbot of the monastery of St Vincent,

[38] This document records a *placitum* rather than a deed. Note that it is the plaintiff who speaks, in the first person. The Latin almost defies translation in places as when in the opening lines the adjective 'situated' (*situs*) agrees with 'abbot' (*abbas*) instead of the word it is intended to modify, 'monastery' (*monasterio*).

located on the bank of the river Volturno bordering the city of Benevento, came to trial against Landulf, son of the deceased Count Landulf, before Lord Otto, emperor augustus. Sitting in judgement with
him were Lord Ceso, by God's grace bishop of the city of Pavia, Lord
Giselbert, by God's grace bishop of the city of Bergamo, Margraves
Gunzolino and Azzolino, counts of Teatino, and other magnates of his
standing before him.

I the aforesaid abbot John, with Audoald, advocate of our monastery,
showed him in the presence of the court sealed diplomas of Duke Gisulf
and Prince Arechis, diplomas of Prince Gremoald and of Prince
Sicardus, a diploma of Emperor Louis, a diploma of Princes Pandulf
and Landulf, and a diploma of Emperor Otto, and charters of donation
to our monastery as well as other diplomas and documents.

When the aforesaid diplomas, documents, and deeds were read
containing the obligatory penalty of a thousand gold pieces to be paid
by the same Landulf if in the future he should cause any damage at all
to that church, the aforesaid abbot John with Audoald, the advocate of
his monastery, brought charges against Count Landulf in the presence
of Lord Otto, emperor augustus, in order to get control of the lands
which the monastery was supposed to possess for thirty years, namely,
the lands, cultivated and uncultivated, mountains and woods, in the
region of Samnie where the old monastery building stands.

Whereupon the above Landulf said to the abbot that he should get
from that monastery the lands and mountains and woods because he
said they were royal[39] and belonged to his county of Isernia, whose
boundaries were listed in the aforesaid diplomas, grants, and confirmations – the aforesaid diploma of Emperor Louis, the aforesaid
diploma of Princes Pandulf and Landulf, and the diploma of Lord Otto,
emperor augustus – those limits beginning first from the river which is
called Sangro, then through the royal mountains to the mountain called
Acze, and around the same mountain to the river called Melfa, and
following the river until it joins a stream called Mellarino; from here
to the top of the mountain called Balvola and along another peak of the
same mountain to Mount Archanus, Mount Marthe, and Mount Casale.
Those mountains surround a place with a brook called Ravennola, and
from the source of that same brook along the royal mountains up to the
mountain which rises above the city of Benafranum, around that mountain to the ridge of the mountain above the territory called Arcora,
which belongs by hereditary right to the holy church of the Mother of
God called Oliveto, which belongs to the above-mentioned monastery,
and also the church of St Cristina with all of its territories and the rest

[39] . . . *eo quod dicebat puplice esset.* . . . For examples of the word *publicus*
meaning 'royal', see Niermeyer, *Lexicon minus*, p. 869.

of the lands that form part of its inheritance up to the river Volturno; and beginning in another direction now from the Sangro and leaving it as it runs down from the hill Paru to the river town of Forli, and from there to the river Vandra, and as it runs into another river which is called Volturno, which flows by the land of that same monastery to the aforesaid territories and lands of the church of St Mary just as is stated in those deeds.

And since this was demonstrated by the said diplomas, documents, and deeds, we have stated our case against that same Landulf saying that those diplomas, documents, and deeds had been presented on behalf of that monastery, and that same Landulf and his son and all of his party appropriated lands and mountains and woods from our monastery, and they said that those same diplomas, documents, and deeds were in error; therefore we asked him to answer in court so that the case might be settled.

When the aforesaid Landulf heard us argue our case against him in this matter, he now stated in front of the aforesaid court that the said diplomas, documents, and deeds which we showed him were accurate in every respect; that none of the lands, mountains, and woods in the aforesaid territories belonged to him; that none of the property in these parts was royal; and that it belonged entirely to the said monastery. From now on neither he nor his heir nor any other man may allege a legal claim on his behalf at the expense of the same monastery, either by producing documents or by taking possession or by representing the monarch or for any other reason, under penalty of having to pay 100 gold pounds to our heirs and successors and to the aforesaid monastery. Through this settlement decreed by the said pious emperor augustus the same Count Landulf voluntarily gave me, Abbot John, a pledge handing over half of it so that he or his heir would always fulfil all of the aforesaid to us and our successors. Through this guarantee which was divided between us we Abbot John made Landulf know that he should give us charters of confirmation, drawn up and legally validated, and if he has not sent them to us within three days, he must undergo the established punishment written above, and he must see that the fine is paid to us as has been agreed between us.

This was done by a *placitum* on Monday, the fifth day of December, the tenth year of the indiction, near the city of Salerno where the aforesaid emperor resided with his court, in the year of our Lord 981, in the eighteenth of the reign of Lord Otto II. By command of the aforesaid Lord emperor, I John, chancellor, have written it.

16. Thietmar of Merseburg, Otto II's fight for southern Italy (981–3): from *Thietmari Chronicon*, ed. Johannes M. Lappenberg, in *MGH, Scriptores*, III, Stuttgart, 1963, 765–7.

Meanwhile the Caesar ruled the Roman Empire so that he maintained all the former property of his father, bravely resisting the Saracens' attack and forcing them far back from his territory. When he heard that Calabria suffered greatly from frequent Greek invasions and Saracen plunder, he called out the Bavarians and the battle-hardened Alemanni [Swabians].

He and Duke Otto, the son of his brother Liudulf, hurried to the city of Tarento, which the Greeks had secured by an occupation force, and he was shortly able to subdue them in a courageous raid. In order to put down the Saracens, who had covered the territory with numerous troops, he sent out trained spies to collect information about the enemy.

First he bottled them up in a town and forced them to flee, totally beaten, and afterwards meeting them in an open field, he killed countless of them in a brave attack and now hoped to destroy them. But unexpectedly they collected themselves once more, proceeded in closed ranks against our troops, and on 13 July defeated them since our side put up very little resistance – what a disaster! Among the slain was Richer, the lance-bearer, and Duke Udo, my mother's uncle; Count Thietmar, Bezelin, Gebhard, Gunther, Ezelin and his brother Bezelin, with Burkhard, Dedi, Conrad, and many others, whose names God only knows.

The emperor, however, fled with the aforesaid [Duke] Otto and others by way of the sea, and seeing in the distance a ship of the 'Salandria' type, he tried to reach it on the horse of the Jew Calonimus.[40] But it refused to take him aboard and passed by. Upon his return to dry land he saw the Jew, who was apprehensive and wanted to await the fate of his beloved lord. And when the emperor saw that the enemy was approaching, he was upset and asked him what would become of him now; but then he saw a second Salandria and recognized a friend among the crew on whose help he could count, so he plunged once more into

---

[40] This man became a rabbi in Mainz. Some of his descendants turn up as prominent citizens of Speyer in the reign of Henry IV. Having emigrated from Mainz, they took part in negotiating privileges for the Jewish community in Speyer. 'Some, or all of these leaders, apparently belonged to the Kalonymide family originally transplanted from Lucca to Mayence because one of its members had saved Otto II's life during the battle against the Saracens at Cotrone, Calabria (982). Although found only in Thietmar's *Chronicle* . . . we have no reason to doubt the authenticity of Otto's escape with the aid of Kalonymos, since the Merseburg divine certainly did not invent that story for the benefit of Jews.' See Baron, *History of the Jews*, p. 273.

the sea on horseback, reached the ship, and was taken on board. Only his knight Henry (with the Slavic named Zolunta) knew who he was; they laid him on the bed of the ship's commander, who finally recognized him and asked if he was the emperor. After a lengthy disclaimer he finally had to admit it. 'It's me,' said he; 'my sins have rightly brought me to this misfortune. But listen to what we should do now together. Miserable me, I have just lost the best men of my empire, and driven by this grief, I cannot and will not ever set foot on these lands again nor see their friends again. Let's go to Rossano where my wife awaits my return. We will pick her up and all the money, a vast sum, and look up your emperor, my brother.[41] Surely he will be a good friend in need to me, or so I hope.' The commander of the ship agreed, delighted over such pleasant conversation, and hurried day and night to reach that place.

When they were near, the knight with the double name was sent ahead by the emperor to get the empress, together with Bishop Dietrich, who was with her, and the many pack animals laden with much gold. When the Greeks saw the empress leave the town with the aforesaid gifts, they anchored and let Bishop Dietrich on board with a few attendants. On the advice of the bishop the emperor took off his poor clothes and put on better ones. Standing on the prow of the ship, he suddenly trusted to his strength and agility and jumped into the sea. One of the Greeks standing around wanted to grab him by his garment and hold him fast; but transfixed by the sword of the good knight Liuppo, he fell down backwards.

Then they fled to the other side of the ship, but our forces went into the boats with which they had come, following undisturbed behind the Caesar, who was waiting on the dry land and was ready to fulfil the promised reward to the Greeks by means of rich presents. But since they were greatly frightened and full of mistrust, they went home, contrary to their promises. . . . With what joy the emperor was greeted by those present and the ones coming later, I need not describe.

In order to inform you precisely about everything, dear reader, I will now give a brief report on what a Salandria is and why it came to the coast. As I have already said, it is a ship of astounding length and speed, and on each side it has two rows of oars and 150 sailors. Both the boats which were sent to Calabria by Basileus [II] Nicephorus [976–

[41] Presumably brother-in-law is meant, i.e. the brother of Theophano. But this reference to her family connections is apparently erroneous. The reigning emperors in Byzantium in 982 were Basil II and Constantine VIII, sons of Romanus II. For a long while it was thought that Theophano was the daughter of Romanus, the *porphyrogenita* Liudprand had requested in his embassy to Constantinople in 968. Now she is thought to have been the niece of John Tzimisces, who ruled till 976, immediately before the accession of Basil and Constantine.

1025] to collect tribute were of this type. Although this land is service-able to the Roman Empire, it voluntarily pays a certain sum of gold every year to Constantinople in order not to incur the risk of any annoyance by the Greeks. The emperor had taken these ships, which carried fire on board that can only be extinguished by vinegar, into his service when they arrived and sent them to sea in order to set fire to the Saracen fleet.[42] One of them, as reported, refused to take the conquered emperor; perhaps they did not recognize him, or perhaps they were afraid of enemy pursuers. The other, however, which had accepted him on the order of Henry, only later gave him up unwillingly, as I explained.

After this short digression I will now take my subject to the end. After receiving the unfortunate news, all our princes came sorrowfully together and sent a note via a messenger unanimously demanding to see him again. After hearing their news the Caesar consented to their demand. In the city of Verona a meeting was convoked to which all princes were invited to discuss many pressing problems. Only Duke Bernhard turned back on the way, for one of his fortresses, which the emperor had secured against the Danes with a wall and occupation force, had been newly taken by them treacherously and burned down after the murder of the defenders.

In the year 983 of the Incarnation of the Lord, the emperor held a meeting in Verona, and Henry the Younger, free of banishment, was made duke of Bavaria. In this same year too the Slavs carried out unbroken opposition to the Caesar and Count Dietrich. Moreover, the emperor's son was elected as lord by all.

A few days later they said their last farewells and went home, for hardly did the emperor reach Rome, after taking leave of his esteemed mother in the city of Pavia, when he fell seriously ill. When he felt that the end was near, he divided his money into four parts: he donated one part to the churches, a second to the poor, a third to his beloved sister Matilda, who lived at the abbey of Quedlinburg as devoted servant of Christ, and a fourth part to his sorrowing attendants and soldiers. Then he confessed in Latin to the pope, his fellow bishops, and priests, obtained the desired absolution from them and departed this life on 7 December. He was commended to the earth, where the eastern portal of paradise of the house of St Peter is open to all believers and an excellent statue of the Lord blesses everyone who enters.

For my own part, I am mindful of human destiny and the great need of mercy; I pray the Lord God on earth and in heaven that whatever sins he committed against my church [Merseburg] be mercifully for-

---

[42] Greek fire was 'the chief weapon in the Byzantine armoury, whose compo-sition was a closely guarded secret. . .'. See *Cambridge Medieval History*, IV, Pt 1, 98. It was used to advantage against the Arabs.

given,[43] for he gave a hundred times over in benefices, and since power has been granted to my unworthy self, I ask you the successor with all my strength that you always grant favour from the heart to everyone.

His famous progeny [Otto III], born in the forest that is called Kessel [near Cleves], was consecrated king at Aachen by Archbishop John of Ravenna and Willigis of Mainz at Christmas, and after the ceremony a legate brought the sad news, greatly disturbing the joy of the occasion. An unspeakable sadness moved every heart, and tested courage was sought by fragile uncertain man, who always hopes to find it unharmed. Twice five solar years had he ruled after the death of his father, as protector of the kingdom and the empire, a terror to all enemies and an unshakeable bulwark for the flocks entrusted to him. Probably the opinion of the people wavered frightfully in such important times, but the compassion of the divine majesty bolstered it rapidly.

17. Gerbert of Aurillac, Letter to Archbishop Willigis of Mainz asking him to support Theophano and to use his influence to have Gerbert recalled to the German court (Reims, 26 June 984): from *The Letters of Gerbert*, trans. Harriet Pratt Lattin, New York, 1961, pp. 83–4.[44]

To Willigis, Archbishop of Mainz

Many things we do not trust to letters but do entrust to messengers, just as [now] my father Adalbero, archbishop of Reims, faithful to you in all respects, has entrusted to his intimate friend, this Abbot Ayrard, much information about the condition and peace of the kingdoms that you should keep to yourself. Furthermore, as to those matters that he made known to you by letter, he invokes God as a witness that [these] things are so. Place faith in this messenger as in himself, therefore, and make such answer as seems good to you; if it is not suitable for the written word, then by the spoken word.

[43] The bishopric of Merseburg was founded by Otto I in 968 when he established the archdiocese of Magdeburg (Doc. 12). When Bishop Gisiler of Merseburg wanted to accept the archbishopric of Magdeburg – a transfer that was looked upon as invalid – he induced Otto II to dissolve the see of Merseburg. The pope obliged at a Lateran synod in 981, arguing speciously that the bishop of Halberstadt had never given his written consent to the creation of Merseburg in the first place. Henry II resurrected the defunct see in 1004 upon the death of Archbishop Gisiler. See Johnson, *Secular Activities of the German Episcopate*, pp. 44–5 and 255.

[44] This [letter] . . . was written a few days before the news reached Reims that Henry had surrendered Otto III to Empress Theophano at Rohr on 29 June [Lattin's note].

But, O my father, with what words shall I address a grieving person when I grieve for the same reason? Deprived of Caesar, we are the prey of the enemy. We thought that Caesar had survived in the son. O, who has abandoned us, who has taken this other light from us? It was proper that the lamb [Otto III] be entrusted to his mother [Theophano], not to the wolf [Duke Henry of Bavaria]. My boundless grief does not allow me even to look after my own affairs. Now my mind is carried quickly to my Italian enemies who completely plundered my possessions [at the abbey of Bobbio]. Now, in thought my mind turns to distant places of the earth as if they were better. But, as long as Otto [II] comes back to my mind, and as long as his features remain imprinted in my heart, and as long as his Socratic disputations[45] recur frequently to my mind, the violent impulse is destroyed and the weariness of my journeying among the Gauls is somewhat alleviated.

Advise me, father, for even if I possess no merits in the sight of your majesty, my affection has not been absent, nor will I fail in achievement if fortune should smile as formerly. When you will have found an opportune moment either with the empresses or with those persons to whom you may remember to propose it, pray recall me from exile who have been a faithful servant of Caesar and who have committed no crime unless it be that I have been faithful to Caesar. Thus you alone will bear my burden because I have not cared to communicate with my friends the princes until I should try what could be done through him [Willigis] whom I judge most influential.

18. Otto III writes his grandmother, Empress Adelaide, about his elevation to imperial office (Pavia?, 996): DO.III.196, from *MGH Diplomata*, II, Pt II, *Ottonis III. diplomata*, ed. Theodor Sickel, 2nd unaltered edn, Berlin, 1957, 604–5.

To Lady A., the always august empress, O., by God's grace emperor augustus. Because following your prayers and desires the Divinity has conferred the rights of empire upon me by fortunate succession, we adore the Divinity, indeed, and we render thanks to you. For we recognize and understand your maternal affection and zealous piety, for which we cannot fail to be in your debt. Therefore since we have been promoted and your honour has been raised, we pray and desire greatly

[45] Richer [of Reims] states that Otto II 'in arguing could propound questions skilfully and arrive at credible conclusions' and that Otto II 'had heard him [Gerbert] dispute not infrequently' [Lattin's note].

that the state will be advanced by you,[46] and having been advanced, will be fortunately ruled in its [new] status.

Farewell.

19. Otto III confirms immunity to the cloister of Hornbach and gives them indemnity and compensation for slain churchmen (993): DO.III.124, from *MGH Diplomata*, II, Pt II, 536.

In the name of the holy and indivisible Trinity. Otto, by God's grace king. If we grant adequate benefices to places devoted to the divine religion for the use of the servants of God living there, we trust that such donations will help us in the acquisition of the rewards of eternal blessedness.

Therefore let all our faithful both present and future know that the venerable Adalbert, abbot of the monastery of Gamundias which is called by another name, Hornbach, built in honour of the holy Mother of God and of St Peter, prince of the apostles, came to us and presented diplomas of King Lothar and King Charles, our predecessors, and of our grandfather Otto of blessed memory and of our father of the same name, both emperors augusti, in which we found written down how they had often visited that place on account of divine love, and they warmly regarded the congregation living there under regular habit with profound love of heart, and how for the salvation of the free men living on the lands of that monastery who were obliged to pay into the royal treasury either fines, tributes, taxes, or *heribannus*[47] or any other exactions or dues, they agreed to restore the candle supply of the above-mentioned monastery; for the said abbot recommended that we again renew [the deed] by this diploma of our authority for the increase of our reward.

And we, kindly accepting his petition, have ordered this present diploma to be drawn up by which we wish and strongly order that no royal official exercise any power of constraint or of exacting taxes, fines, tributes or *heribannus* or any other exactions or dues whatsoever from those free men who hold and possess the land of the said monastery, but for our salvation just as the kings who preceded us long ago confirmed them for the said monastery, and henceforth for all time by a donation

---

[46] Lattin says that *vos* is confused with *nos* in the manuscripts and therefore translates 'that the commonwealth is being enlarged through us', which she thinks makes better sense. See *Letters of Gerbert*, p. 271, n. 2. The letter was apparently written for the emperor by Gerbert.

[47] A tax in lieu of labour service.

of our largesse let them firmly persist and endure there without the obstacle of any contradiction.

On account of the love and intercession of our beloved nephew of the same name, Duke Otto, we have granted to the said abbot Adalbert and his church and his successors peace-money and fine-money which is to be paid from the royal treasury for men of the church who have been slain so that he and his successors according to church law may receive fine-money and peace-money as a wergild according to royal law concerning the slain, just as it had been granted to the same church earlier by our predecessors.

And in order that this deed of ours should remain more firm and stable and be truly credited by our faithful and those of God, we have confirmed it below with our own hand and have ordered that it be sealed with our ring.

Sign of Lord Otto, most glorious king.

I Hildibald, bishop and chancellor, have verified it for Archbishop Willigis.

20. Otto III grants his *ministerialis* Sigibert the locality of Emmikenrot in the Mark of Pöhlde including serfs (Gandersheim, 9 July 977): DO.III.248, from *MGH Diplomata*, II, Pt II, 664–5.

In the name of the holy and indivisible Trinity. Otto, by God's grace emperor augustus of the Romans. May all of our faithful both present and future know how, on account of the intercession and petition of our faithful chaplain and chancellor Heribert, we have given to a certain *ministerialis*[48] of ours, Sigibert, bringing to mind the service which he constantly rendered us, a certain property of ours located between the rivers Bretenbech and Crummumbech in the mark of Pöhlde adjoining the county of Count Henry—a certain place called Emmikenrot with all appurtenances, that is, with serfs of both sexes named below – Reginhard, Waldric, Alfwart, with their wives, sons, and daughters, with lots, buildings, lands broken up and to be broken up, fields, meadows, pastures, woods, ponds and streams, claimed and unclaimed, and all other appurtenances which up to now have been stated, discovered, or named, we have handed over to him as a possession with proviso and condition that the said Sigibert may have free power henceforth of doing what he wants with the same property, whether he should wish to donate, trade, sell, give to his wife, or keep it rather for himself.

And in order that this deed of our mandate should now and in the

[48] See note 26 above.

future remain in effect we have ordered that this diploma be sealed, corroborating below with our own hand.

Sign of Lord Otto, most invincible emperor augustus.

I Hildibald, bishop and chancellor, have verified it for Archbishop Willigis.

Given the seventh day before the ides of July in the year of our Lord's Incarnation 997, the tenth year of the indiction, in the fourteenth year of Otto III's reign, second of the empire; carried out at Gandersheim.

21. Otto III informs Gerbert about the journey of his opponent Arnulf to the pope (997): DO.III.260, from *MGH Diplomata*, II, 677–8.

Otto, most faithful of pupils, offers constancy and steadfastness to Gerbert, teacher beloved beyond all others, and most benevolent archbishop. If events should follow your prayers, no mortal would be happier than we; if, though we hope not, they should accord ill with your just deserts, we would be similarly affected by sorrow for you. We also know that the industry of your cautious providence has been greatly concerned in the condition of our affairs. Therefore we wish to reach you, however you may be, and we will tell you truly, though admittedly under compulsion, that your adversary Arnulf, son of deception, journeyed to see the pope, a fact which we found out from Abbot Leo.

On account of this, it was our decision that an envoy be sent to the pope together with the same Leo so that he may act as a faithful intercessor on your behalf.

May you live, fare well, and remain eternally fortunate.

22. Otto III, through the pen of Gerbert, announces to Pope Gregory V his departure from Italy and his arrangements for the eight counties under dispute (Pavia, 5 August 996): from Lattin, *Letters of Gerbert*, pp. 271–2.[49]

From august Emperor Otto by the grace of God to the very reverend Pope Gregory.

I am overcome by vehement grief because the unseasonable weather has prevented me from satisfying your desires. For I am urged on by

[49] This letter has been placed out of chronological order so that it may immediately precede the diploma concerned with the same topic.

an affectionate piety towards you, but the necessity of nature, which restricts everything by its own laws, puts into opposition the quality of the Italian climate and the frailty of my body. Changed only bodily are we on this account; mentally we remain with you, and we are leaving the foremost men of Italy as aid and comfort to you – Hugh of Tuscany, faithful to us in everything, and Cono, count of Spoleto and prefect of Camerino,[50] to whom, because of our love for you, we have entrusted the eight counties which are under dispute.[51] For the present, furthermore, we have placed our representative[52] in charge of them in order that the people may have a ruler and render to you the works and services due.

23. Otto III grants eight counties to the Church of St Peter (Rome, January 1001): DO.III.389, from *MGH Diplomata*, II, Pt II, 818–20.

In the name of the holy and indivisible Trinity. Otto, servant of the apostles, and by the will of God the Saviour, emperor augustus of the Romans. We acknowledge Rome as head of the world; we testify that the Roman Church is the mother of all churches, but the negligence and stupidity of the popes have for a long time obscured the titles of her fame. For not only do they [the popes] sell those things which seem to be outside the city, but they have also sold things to certain dregs of society and traded by sale from the treasury of St Peter, though we do not say this without pain: whatever they had in this royal city they scattered with greater license and gave up both St Peter and St Paul to the common use, money being the decisive factor in every case; they also despoiled the altars and always introduced disorder for their own

[50] Hugh, margrave of Tuscany from 970 to 1001, was a major support of Ottonian power in Italy. Cono (a nickname for Conrad) was a faithful and powerful vassal in north Italy before he became lord of Spoleto and Camerino.

[51] Pesaro, Fano, Sinigaglia, Ancona, Fossombrone, Cagli, Jesi, and Osimo, which Otto III later bestowed upon Sylvester II (DO.III.389), over which, as here, he was to exercise only a partial control. They were counties whose possession in friendly hands was very important to Otto III to assure him safe access from Ravenna down the Adriatic coast on the way to Rome. In 962 Otto I had bestowed these counties upon the papacy (DO.I.235), and Gregory V wished to make good these claims. Otto III claimed the counties as imperial property and entrusted their military defence to Margraves Hugh and Cono and their financial and judicial administration to a legate or *missus* [Lattin's note].

[52] *Legatus*, the emperor's representative in judicial and financial administration, who was to hold court and collect the public imposts, especially those for provisioning the ruler's soldiers and animals (*fodrum*). However, he must permit Pope Gregory V to enjoy the usufruct of these counties [Lattin's note].

M

renewal. Indeed, since the papal laws were confused and the Roman Church was now cast down, certain of the popes went on the attack in such a way that they joined the greater part of our empire to their Apostolic See, not asking what and how much they lost by their faults, not caring how much they squandered through willful vanity, but since they were giving away what had been despoiled by themselves, as if casting back their guilt into our empire, they transferred their property mostly to others, that is, into our hands and those of our empire.

They fabricated stories, one of which was written down with gold letters in a charter by John the Deacon, nicknamed 'the one with the mutilated fingers',[53] which contrived the circumstances of the long-standing lie under the title of Constantine the Great. They also lied when they said a certain Charles gave our royal property to St Peter. To this we answer that that same Charles could not rightfully give away anything since he was put to flight by a better Charles, deprived of the empire, hence was destitute and nullified;[54] therefore he gave away what he himself did not possess. He gave as he doubtless was able to give – as one who had acquired badly and did not hope to possess it for long.

Therefore having disdained these forged deeds and false writings, we give to St Peter out of our largesse what is ours, not what is his, just as if we are conferring our own property. And for the love of St Peter we have elected Lord Sylvester our teacher as our pope, and God willing we have ordained and created him most serene. Thus for the love of that same Lord Pope Sylvester we confer on St Peter gifts from our property, so that the teacher may offer on the part of his pupil something to our prince Peter.

Therefore we Otto confer and donate certain counties to St Peter for the love of our teacher Lord Pope Sylvester so that he may hold them, for he holds his salvation and ours, and may administer them for the augmentation of his apostolate and our empire. We concede for his administration: Pesaro, Fano, Sinigaglia, Ancona, Fossombrone, Cagli, Iesi, and Osimo, so that no one may ever dare to make any trouble for him and St Peter or disturb him in any way.

Whoever presumes to take them away is to lose all he has and St Peter will receive what is his. So that this may be preserved in eternity by all, we confirm this deed with our victorious hand, so help us God,

[53] The career of Johannes digitorum mutilus is intriguingly explored by Horst Fuhrmann in 'Konstantinische Schenkung und abendländisches Kaisertum', *Deutsches Archiv*, XXII (1966), 128–54.

[54] Charles the Bald made two trips to Rome, one in 875–6 and another in 877, the year of his death. It was during the latter that his cousin Carloman (the 'better Charles' of the diploma) drove him to flight. Schramm conjectures that the donation was made after Charles had returned to France in 877. See *Kaiser, Rom und Renovatio*, p. 165 and esp. n. 4.

and we order it to be marked with our seal, so that it may be valid for him [the pope] and his successors.

Sign of Lord Otto, most invincible emperor augustus of the Romans.

24. Pope Sylvester II to Erkambald, abbot of Fulda, confirming him as abbot and exempting the monastery from all control except that of the Holy See (Rome, 31 December 999): from Lattin, *Letters of Gerbert*, pp. 324–6.

Sylvester, bishop, servant of the servants of God, to his very beloved son Erkambald,[55] venerable abbot of the sacred monastery of our Saviour, Jesus Christ, and to all of your abbot successors of this same monastery in perpetuity.

Pontifical duty compels us to favour the utility of all the holy churches of God and to render suitable decisions to them according to which each may remain in its proper condition.

Wherefore, dearly beloved son, we confirm to you and to your successors in perpetuity everything which your predecessors legally and reasonably requested from our predecessors. Therefore, through the authority of our privilege we grant and confirm to you the monastery of Fulda,[56] that Boniface, most holy martyr of Christ, first constructed and [then] enriched magnificently by the votive offerings of kings and princes and by his own means, with all cells, churches, manors, and all their appurtenances, so that henceforth no future abbot shall presume ever to receive consecration except from this Apostolic See. Of all the monasteries of Germany we assign to you and to your successors the first rank of sitting and of judging and of holding a council. No bishops, archbishops, nor, by chance, patriarchs, may celebrate the solemnities of the Mass on an altar under your protection. Let the person of no prince presume to subject to any mortal either a whole or a part of the possessions of the monastery, nor to give such under the name of a benefice, but let the church of Fulda, always free and secure, zealously serve the Roman see alone. If, though God forbid, any abbot of your monastery shall become notorious through any crime, we decree and command that he not incur the judgement of an accusation until he shall be heard and examined by our Apostolic See.

It is granted to you, dearest son, and to your successor abbots to call

[55] 997–1011. Erkambald later became archbishop of Mainz, 1 April 1011–15 September 1020 [Lattin's note].

[56] Fulda was the first German monastery exempted from the jurisdiction of the bishop, through the privilege granted in 751 by Pope Zachary [Lattin's note].

upon the Apostolic See to defend you and your church, according to the custom of bishops, and to defend yourself by the shield of the Roman majesty against all your rivals. As we weigh this matter, we direct that at convenient times you may satisfy our solicitude as to whether the monastic life is being carried on in regular fashion and whether harmony among the brothers is being maintained with ecclesiastical zeal, lest perchance, under the pretext of this privilege, though God forbid, both your disposition to uprightness and its direction may be twisted from the norm of justice. In accordance with the decree of Zachary, our predecessor [4 November 751], we forbid any woman to enter this same monastery.

But above all we direct and warn that no one shall carry off or give to anyone any of the revenues and incomes or tithes and other donations offered to God by St Boniface Martyr and many other princes, except the legitimate benefices of the *ministeriales*,[57] but that just as your sainted patron established, all revenues shall be apportioned and regulated, as much those apparently belonging to the dwelling for the poor and the gate for guests as those [belonging] to the brothers' necessities.

Over all of these items we decree through the document of this privilege, which we confirm by the authority of the prince of the apostles, that if anyone shall dare violate this charter of our privilege, let him be accursed and, incurring the wrath of omnipotent God, be excommunicated from the company of the saints, and let the dignity of the said monastery as indited by us remain in every case forever inviolate.

Written by the hand of Anthony, notary and secretary of the holy Roman Church.

Farewell.

Given on the 31st of December through the hand of John, bishop of the holy church of Albano and librarian of the holy Apostolic See, in the first year, with God's favour, of the pontificate of Lord Sylvester the Younger, pope, with the pacific Otto III ruling, in the third [fourth] year of his reign, the thirteenth year of the indiction.

25. In the presence of Otto III the law of the emperor and the empire is recognized with respect to the cloister of the Holy Saviour and of St Felix of Pavia against Countess Rotlind and her son (Pavia, 14 October 1001): DO.III.411, from *MGH Diplomata*, II, Pt II, 844–6.

In the name of God in the city of Pavia in the portico of the palace of the

57 See note 26 above.

lord emperor, which is in front of the chapel of St Maurice where the Lord Emperor Otto III was present, Otto, *protospatharius*[58] and count palatine and count of this county, chaired a session of court in order to make and deliberate justice for certain individuals, and with him presided Duke Otto, Peter of Como, Wido of Pavia, Adalbert of Brixen, Warmund of Ivrea, Rainfred of Bergamo, Otbert of Verona, John of Genoa, Constantine of Albi, Gerolimus of Vicenza, bishops of the holy churches of God; Adalbert and Mainfred, margraves; Count Wibert, the son of the Count Dadonus of good memory; Alberic, judge and *missus* of the emperor; Walpert, Raidulfus, Gerolimus, Ebbo, Andreas, Arman, Atto, Walfred, Sigefred, Waltari, Adalbert, Almo, Olphari, and Volman, judges of the sacred palace; Otbert, son of the late Aponus, Adam of Corpello, Odelo of Corneliano, Walderic of Bagnolo, and Umfred, vassals of Countess Ferlende, and many more.

And coming into their presence Lanfranc, judge of the sacred palace, son of Walpert of good memory who was also judge advocate of the same lord emperor and the same realm, declared:

'I have and hold from the same lord emperor and his realm a monastery called Regine with the area around it, located within the city of Pavia and dedicated to the Lord Saviour and St Felix, with all the cottages, ramparts, chapels, mills, fisheries, and all property within and without the city of Pavia together with all serfs and bondmaids, and freedmen both male and female, pertaining and belonging to the same monastery, completely and fully.

'And if anyone wishes to bring a charge concerning this property against me or to challenge that it belongs to the emperor and his realm, I am prepared to present my evidence in court and let the case be settled as the law provides.

'And furthermore I demand that Countess Rotlind, daughter of Lord King Hugh of good memory, and Hubert, deacon of the holy church of Pavia, son of Count Bernard of good memory – mother and son together – with Gausbert and Bonizo, judge (son of Fulbert of good memory who was also a judge), guardian, and advocate of those who are here present, state whether that monastery belongs to me and the emperor and his realm with the area around it and all the aforesaid property within and without the city of Pavia, serfs and bondmaids, freedmen both male and female, pertaining and belonging to the same monastery, just as I have enumerated them here, for they seek to chal-

[58] *Protospatharius*, a high-ranking *spatharius*, originally a bodyguard of the Byzantine emperor. The term came to be extended to important officials at court with mainly honorific significance. The use of this title is one of the many examples of Greek influence on Otto III.

lenge us or encroach upon me and on the same lord emperor and his realm.'

After the same Lanfranc, judge and advocate, made this statement, Countess Rotlind and Hubert the deacon, mother and son, were given a chance to reply, and Gausbert and Bonizo, their judge, guardian, and advocate, set forth their case:

'Indeed, as to your claim to the monastery with the surrounding area around it, situated within this city dedicated to the Lord Saviour and St Felix and called Regine, together with the dwellings, ramparts, chapels, mills, fisheries, and all things including serfs and bondwomen, freedmen and freed women, pertaining and belonging to the same monastery, which you Lanfranc, judge and advocate, have named here, we are not denying your claim nor that of the emperor and his realm, nor can we attempt to do so, for we cannot do it lawfully. The property belongs to that realm by law and does not and cannot belong to us. We cannot have it or claim it or own it legally since we do not have any diploma or any deed nor can we have, with which we can challenge or encroach upon the rights of the emperor and his realm, but, as we have said, the property belongs to his realm and ought to be by law.'

And thus Rotlind and Hubert the deacon, mother and son, officially renounced their claim.

Moreover, at the same time Countess Rotlind and Hubert the deacon, mother and son, and Gausbert and also Bonizo, their judge, guardian, and advocate, swore that if in their lifetime or that of their sons or daughters or of their heirs or representatives or any person under their control should venture to assert a claim, bring an action, or reopen the case against the judge advocate Lanfranc or against the emperor and his realm concerning anything belonging to the same monastery or its surroundings and all the aforesaid property within the city as well as outside, serfs and bondwomen, freedmen and freed women, pertaining and belonging to the same monastery; or if his rights to the property are ever challenged again, or if a diploma, deed, or any sort of muniment should turn up which they have had anything to do with and if this can be proved, then they promise to make restitution – Countess Rotlind and Hubert the deacon, mother and son – and if the sons or daughters of the same Rotlind or their heirs or representatives should initiate legal proceedings as regards the rights of the emperor or his realm in this matter, they will have to pay double of all the property within the city as well as outside, in proportion as it may have increased in value in the course of time and according as it may be appraised, and this property shall be an equivalent portion of land with serfs and bondwomen, freedmen and freed women, and moreover as a penalty for having violated this, a fine of 1,000 pounds of the best gold, 10,000 pounds of silver.

When this was finished and the admission of having been beaten as stated above, it seemed to the judge [Lanfranc] and the assessors that justice had been done to them [Rotlind and Hubert], inasmuch as their suit was justly decided, that is, the suit of mother and son and Gausbert, their guardian and advocate, by confession and acknowledgement that they were beaten, and inasmuch as Lanfranc, judge and advocate, in behalf of the realm was supposed to have and hold the said monastery with the surrounding territory, with all dwellings, ramparts, chapels, and everything within this city and outside, serfs and bondwomen, freedmen and freed women pertaining and belonging to the same monastery; and so they decided that the defendants, Countess Rotlind and Hubert the deacon, mother and son, and Gausbert, their lawyer and advocate, should drop their claim and hold their peace.

So the case was finished. And we have ordered that a record of it be drawn up so as to protect the rights of the realm. I Giselbert, notary and judge of the sacred palace, in accordance with the above-said decree of the lord emperor and the order of the count palatine and judge, have drawn up two identical copies of the text, in the sixth year of the empire of the aforesaid Lord Otto III, fourteenth day of the month of October, the fifteenth year of the indiction.

I Otto, *protospatharius* and count palatine, had it drawn up. I Alberic, judge and legate of the lord emperor, was present. I Arman, judge of the sacred palace, was present. I Ebbo, judge of the lord emperor, was present. I Gerolimus, judge of the sacred palace, was present. I Andreas, judge of the sacred palace, was present. I Sigefred, count of the sacred palace, was present, SYGEPHREDOUS [in Greek characters]. I Almo, judge of the sacred palace, was present. I Walfred, judge of the sacred palace, was present. Waltari, judge of the lord emperor, was present, OUUALTHARU [in Greek characters].

26. Henry II confirms immunity to the abbey of St Gall but demands participation in the election of abbots (Zürich, 17 June 1004): DH.II.76, from *MGH Diplomata*, III, *Heinrici II. et Arduini diplomata*, ed. H. Bresslau, 2nd unaltered edn, Berlin, 1957, 96–7.

In the name of the holy and indivisible Trinity. Henry, by God's grace king of the Franks and Lombards. To all our pious faithful, future as well as present, let it be known that the venerable abbot of the monastery of

St Gall, Burchard by name, came to us, presenting to our eyes diplomas of our lord and predecessor of blessed memory Otto III, emperor augustus, and of other kings and emperors, in which it was found written down how they received the aforesaid monastery and all things belonging to it under royal and imperial immunity of his protection.[59]

For the stability of the matter he asked our highness if we would renew it. Granting assent to his pious request and at the same time considering the documents of our predecessors under immunity of the holy place, we decree and establish that the aforesaid monastery should retain its immunity, just as the text of the diplomas written in that place reports so that the monks coming together in that monastery according to the rule of St Benedict have the right of electing an abbot among themselves, *the king's choice however taking precedence*,[60] and that likewise the monastery, together with the persons attached to it both within and without, and also the lands cultivated and uncultivated belonging thereto justly and legally as a donation, subject to us and our successors by the will of God and His saints is not to be disturbed or troubled by any person superior or inferior, nor should it suffer the burden of any decree or prosecution.

But the same abbot, without the obstacle of any contradiction, is permitted to govern his monks with rules, to give orders to the family, to order the affairs of the monastery, and to govern the provision of its counsel in all things both within and without properly, suitably, and advantageously.

Also the lawsuits and claims of the monastery, if the need arises, may be examined through compulsory oath, the officials and advocates of the monastery – when the affairs of the same place require – having received our permission to exercise the law themselves.

Therefore, as stated above, the aforesaid place being under our protection is to remain secure from any vexation of foreign inquisition or tax levy so that the servants of God living there may continually pray to Almighty God for us and for the stability of our realm without any outside disturbance.

And in order that this diploma of our concession may remain in force through the course of future times, we have corroborated it by signing it with our hand, and we have ordered it to be marked with the imprint of our seal.

[59] '*Immunitas* in late Roman law meant the freedom of imperial domains from certain taxes and duties (*munera sordida*). Like so many other components of Roman culture it too penetrated the legal system of the Frankish empire founded by Clovis.' For a detailed study of the development of the concept under the Carolingians and Saxons, see Stengel, *Zur mittelalterlichen Geschichte*, pp. 30–68.

[60] The clause in italics is an addition of Henry II. The document upon which this diploma is based (DO.III.145) does not contain it.

Sign of Lord Henry, most invincible king.

I Egilbert, chancellor, have verified it for Willigis, archchancellor.

Given the fifteenth day before the kalends of July in the year of the Incarnation of the Lord 1004, the first year of the indiction, in the third year of Lord King Henry II; carried out at Zürich; under favourable auspices in the name of God, amen.

27. The Synod of Frankfurt confirms the bishopric of Bamberg, founded according to papal arrangement by Henry II after concluding an exchange treaty with Bishop Henry of Würzburg (Frankfurt, 1 November 1007): DH.II.143, from *MGH Diplomata*, III, 169–72.

In the year of the Incarnation of the Lord 1007, the fifth year of the indiction, kalends of November, in the sixth year of the reign of the most pious and serene Henry II, a great synod was held and celebrated in Frankfurt for the status and augmentation of our Holy Mother Church.

For the same King Henry, great and peaceable, trusting in God and conscientious towards men, while he pondered again and again with magnanimous deliberation of mind how he might be most pleasing to God, determined in the course of his cogitation with the highest inspiration of the divinity that he would choose God as his heir and make a donation by charter, setting up out of all his hereditary property a bishopric in honour of St Peter, prince of the apostles, in a certain place named Bamberg where he had hereditary property from his father, so that the paganism of the Slavs would be destroyed, and the memory of the name of Christ would always be remembered there.

But since he did not have a diocese in that place, while celebrating Holy Pentecost at Mainz in the sixth year of his reign, he acquired from Bishop Henry of Würzburg by solid legal transfer a certain part of the diocese of Würzburg, namely, the county called Regnitzgau and a certain part of the territory called Volkfeld situated between the rivers Urach and Regnitz, giving in exchange to the church of Würzburg 150 manses in the district called Meiningen and in adjacent places, with the consent and approval of the venerable prelates, in first place Henry, bishop of the church of Würzburg; Willigis, reverend archbishop of Mainz, Burchard of Worms, Walter of Speyer, Werner of Strasbourg, Adalbero of Basel, Lambert of Constance, Ulrich of Chur, Archbishop Liudulf of Trier, Theodoric of Metz and Berchtold of Toul, Heimon of Verdun, Archbishop Heribert of Cologne, Notker of Liége, Erlwin of Cambrai, Archbishop Tagino of Magdeburg, and Hildolf of Mantua.

Indeed, the most glorious King Henry, having carried out his vow with the consent of the said bishops, sent to Rome two of his chaplains, Alberic and Ludwig, with a letter from Henry, bishop of Würzburg, that they might better establish the undertaking according to Roman authority.

Indeed the Roman pontiff and universal Pope John [XVIII], inspecting the letter of request from the aforesaid Bishop Henry and rejoicing in the devotion of the most conscientious King Henry, held a synod in the basilica of St Peter, and to confirm the bishopric of Bamberg he had a privilege drawn up and corroborated by apostolic authority, writing to all the bishops of France and Germany that they should corroborate and confirm the bishopric with equal and joint authority.

Wherefore the venerable prelates, meeting in council at Frankfurt as said above, undertaking to read the privilege with the greatest veneration, and being obedient to apostolic authority with devoted minds, have unanimously praised and jointly corroborated it.

I Willigis, archbishop of the holy church of Mainz, who presided at the same synod for the Roman Church, was present and have signed. I Rethari, bishop of the church of Paderborn, was present and have signed. I Megingaud, bishop of Eichstätt, was present and have signed. I Lambert, bishop of Constance, was present and have signed. I Arnulf of Halberstadt, was present and have signed. I Ulrich, bishop of Chur, was present and have signed. I Burchard, bishop of Worms, was present and have signed. I Werner, bishop of Strasbourg, was present and have signed. I Walter, bishop of Speyer, was present and have signed. I Bruno, bishop of Augsburg, was present, assented, and signed. I Liudulf, archbishop of Trier, was present and have signed. I Berthold, bishop of Toul, was present and have signed. I Heimo, bishop of Verdun, was present and have signed. I Hartwig, archbishop of Salzburg, was present and have signed. I Christian, bishop of Pavia, was present and have signed. I Gebhard, bishop of Regensburg, was present and have signed. I Egilbert, bishop of Freising, was present and have signed. I Adalbero, bishop of Brixen, was present and have signed. I Heribert, archbishop of Cologne, was present at the vote of the synod and have signed. I Suidger, bishop of Münster, was present and have signed. I Ansfrid, bishop of Utrecht, was present and have signed. I Thietmar, bishop of Osnabrück, was present and have signed. I Tagino, archbishop of Magdeburg, was present and have signed. I Hildiward, bishop of Zeitz, was present and have signed. I Burchard, archbishop of Laon, was present and have signed. I Baldolf, archbishop of Tarentaise, was present and have signed. I Anastasius, archbishop of the Hungarians, was present and have signed. I Adalbero of Basel was present and have signed. I Hugo of Genoa have signed. I Henry of

Lausanne have signed. I Eckhard of Schleswig have signed. I Alberic, bishop of Como, was present and have signed. I Richolf, bishop of the church of Trieste.

28. Henry II renews his document of 1007 about the settlement of the dispute over Gandersheim between Archbishop Willigis of Mainz and Bishop Bernward of Hildesheim (Werla, 1013): DH.II. 255, from *MGH Diplomata*, III, 293–6.[61]

In the name of the holy and perpetual Trinity – Father, Son, and Holy Spirit. Henry II, by God's grace king. To all the faithful, lasting welfare and peace in Christ.

Being the servant of Jesus Christ and of my Lord God and being a son of His maidservant, recognizing that we have reached the height of terrestrial government (however insignificant it may be) not by our merits, but only because of our respect for divine piety, we have decided to devote our whole will and ability to the divine spirit and genius of the Christian religion, and as we have promised the bishops and principally our spiritual father, Archbishop Willigis, we will be zealous to glorify the Church of God and the priests of Christ and to exalt them by the most vigilant devotion according to our knowledge and power.

Thus, thinking to proceed against the ancient enmity between the well-known and eminent bishops, to wit, W., archbishop of Mainz, and Bernward of Hildesheim, a bishop proven of equal faith and charity, and anxiously turning over in our mind how we might recall them to harmony, fearing that it would be difficult, because the archbishop had often been admonished by the Apostolic See and the imperial majesty that he should stop his attack on the church at Gandersheim, yet he could not be persuaded, still at last, because we have such great regard for both of them, we have brought up the case in front of the bishops who have come to us at Pöhlde at Christmas, and we urged them thus to charity and harmony, with the result that they promised to obey us and the decision of the bishops in all things.

Next, we announced that the church there belonging to the said monastery, which was without benediction beyond a reasonable time and against our will, having been rebuilt, is to be consecrated on the second day before the ides of January.

Also, B., our faithful bishop, at our urging, called Archbishop W. and

[61] This diploma replaced one that was issued in January 1007, after the church was consecrated. The original document was destroyed in a fire at Gandersheim in January 1013.

all the bishops to help him, so that harmony and unanimity might be shown between dissident brothers by the grace of God so that the solemn office of dedication might be carried out with the greatest charity, the archbishop assuming that nothing was in his purview unless Bishop B. conceded it to him.

For, as before, we do not evade the truth out of reverence or for the sake of the archbishop; indeed we have confirmed the opinion of Bishop B. with a powerful ordinance because in the judgement of all the situation became clear, until by joint common persuasion the archbishop came to the clergy and the people with us and when a speech was made conformable with Catholic doctrine before the door and when limits had been established to the district covered by the donation, as is the custom, he publicly acknowledged that the monastery had been possessed legitimately from its origin by Bishop B.'s predecessors without any contradiction; afterwards he recalled his office and in order that neither he nor his successors could at any time have a claim or revindication to the aforesaid church with its boundaries, he turned over the bishop's crozier which he had customarily wielded to us who corroborated, to the bishops who were the authors, and to Bishop B., saying,

'I concede to lawsuit and right, brother, in those things in which I have up to now persisted, and since I know I cannot canonically compete for this church or its boundaries either on my own part or that of my successors without your counsel, I recognize the full power of yourself and your successors with regard to it, and before Christ, in the presence of our lord king, and also with the witness of our brothers I transfer the property both on my part and that of my successors; and in order that no appeal at law may be carried out in the future by me or my successors, I give you this crozier as a sign of my sworn promise.'

After this the church was consecrated on the appointed day, and on the next day the veiling of the nuns of God was celebrated, the venerable Bishop B. being the master of ceremonies.

And because I desire perpetual peace for the Church of God, I have had this document drawn up and strengthened by the imprint of my ring and have corroborated it with my signature.

Sign of Lord Henry, most invincible king.

Gunther, chancellor, verified it for Archchaplain Erkambald.[62]

Given_____[space was never filled], the eleventh year of the indiction, in the year of our Lord's Incarnation 1013, in the eleventh

[62] This archchaplain is the same Erkambald who as abbot of Fulda was the recipient of Doc. 24. He was selected to succeed Willigis as archbishop of Mainz in 1011. Note that in Doc. 29, issued in 1017, Erkambald has achieved the title of archchancellor.

year of the reign of Lord Henry II, carried out at Werla; under favourable auspices, amen.

I Henry II, by God's grace king, consenting to this reconciliation and document, rejoicing in the sign of the Holy Cross, have signed. I Willigis, by God's grace archbishop of the see of Mainz, rejoicing in this Catholic and canonical reconciliation and pledge, have signed with the sign of the cross. I Tagino, archbishop of the holy church of Magdeburg, have signed with the sign of the Holy Cross. I Rethari, bishop of the holy church of Paderborn, have signed. I Bruno, bishop of the holy church of Augsburg, have signed. I Theodoric, bishop of the holy church of Minden, have signed. I Arnulf, bishop of the church of Halberstadt, have signed. I Bernger, bishop of the church of Verden, have signed. I Aeggilhard, bishop of the church of Schleswig, have signed. I Hildeward, bishop of the holy church of Zeitz, have signed. I Wigo, bishop of the holy church of Brandenburg, have signed. I Aerlugin, bishop of the church of Cambrai, have signed. I Bernhard, duke of Westfalia, have signed. I Herman, duke of the Swabians, have signed. I Burghard, count palatine, have signed. I Count Henry have signed. I count Sigifred have signed. I Count Aeggilhard have signed. I Count Gero have signed. I Count Theodoric have signed. I Count Cristan have signed. I Count Geuuzo have signed. I Count Bodo have signed. I Count Liudulf have signed. Count Dodico. I Count Sigubodo have signed. I Count Udo have signed. Sigifrid. Count Bernhard. I Count Hermann have signed. I Herp, son of Aegizo, have signed. I Count Hernust have signed.

29. Henry II bestows the abbey of Helmarshausen on the episcopal church at Paderborn (Leitzkau, 11 July 1017): DH.II.371, from *MGH Diplomata*, III, 474–6.

In the name of the holy and indivisible Trinity. Henry, by God's grace emperor augustus of the Romans.

The statutes of the canons, being established not by the mouth of men but by the spirit of God, enjoin the bishops to visit the cloisters of monks frequently, and if they find anything there outside the rule, they are to put a stop to it and correct the situation.

Vigilantly contemplating these things and lightening our burdens in the course of this life by imposing them on the bishops, we for the sake of charity, without which a rich man is a pauper – with the intercession of our most beloved wife Kunigunda, empress augusta, then with the intercession of Archbishops Erkambald of Mainz, Poppo of Trier, Gero

of Magdeburg, Unwan of Bremen, and of Bishops Arnold of Halberstadt, Eppo of Bamberg, Theodoric of Metz, Henry of Würzburg,
Theodoric of Münster, Henry of Parma, Theodoric of Minden,
Thiemo of Merseburg, Eric of Havelberg, and also of the lay people,
Duke Bernhard, counts Siegfried and Edzico – have granted as a property
an abbey by the name of Helmarshausen with all of its appurtenances
movable and immovable to the see of Paderborn established in honour
of St Mary and of St Kilian and St Liborius, which Bishop Meinwerk
has charge of with the signs of acquisition at present, and we have handed
it over by our right and dominion into the right and dominion of him to
be disposed of and possessed by the bishop with complete power according to the rule of St Benedict.

And in order that this diploma and deed of our donation should remain solid and unshaken, having corroborated it with our own hand and
having confirmed it with the imprint of our seal, we have ordered it to
be sealed below.

Seal of Lord Henry, most invincible emperor augustus of the Romans.
Gunther, chancellor, verified it for Archchancellor Erkambald.

Given the fifth day before the ides of July, the twelfth year of the
indiction, in the year of our Lord's Incarnation 1017, in the sixteenth
year of the reign of Lord Henry II, fourth of the empire; carried out
at Leitzkau.

30. Henry II regulates the redress of grievances and the punishment
of disputes and feuds between the people belonging to the monasteries
of Fulda and Hersfeld (Bamberg, 9 March 1024): DH.II.507, from
MGH Diplomata, III, 648–50.[63]

In the name of the holy and indivisible Trinity. Henry, by God's grace
emperor augustus of the Romans. To all the faithful present and future
we desire it to be noted how constant complaint has alarmed us on account of the numerous and frequent disputes between the family of
Fulda and that of Hersfeld, which now have grown so bad that there
have even been innumerable homicides committed between them, and
hence the greatest possible damage has been suffered by both churches.

Therefore, in order that such boldness of so great presumption
should not remain any longer between the two families without a fitting
revenge, we have drawn up a decree in the form of this diploma upon

[63] Bresslau's edition has been improved by Hans Weirich in Urkundenbuch
der Reichsabtei Hersfeld, I, 1, Veröffentlichungen der Historischen Kommission
für Hessen und Waldeck, XIX, 1, 1936, 161–5.

the advice and consent of both abbots, Richard of Fulda and Arnold of Hersfeld, as follows:

First of all injustice which has remained uncompensated for a long time on both sides is to be fully corrected by the advocates and provosts of each place.

And henceforth if any member of the family of either church should pursue and assail any servant of St Boniface or St Wigbert, and through bold daring with an armed band should break into either his courtyard or his house in order to kill or plunder, and if he should either run away or if he were not perchance at home or if [the victim] gets free from that power or attack somehow or other, let the skin and hair of whoever was a leader or principal of this bold invasion be removed, and, moreover, let him be scratched and burned well on both cheeks with a white hot iron, and let his henchmen be deprived of skin and hair.

However, if the victim is killed there, then all those who took part in this murder or invasion are to undergo the punishments stated above.

And if he who is killed and those who do the killing are from the family of one and the same church, they must each pay the wergild of the slain man and everything owed, just as they have done so far, to their own church.

If, however, he who is killed is from one family and the murderers are from another, the author of the homicide alone shall pay the wergild for the others.

And if someone is slain in whatever place from one or the other family, unless he who committed the murder has witnesses worthy of credit or is able to prove by means of a white-hot iron that he did it because he could not otherwise have escaped alive from the attack of the other, he is to undergo the said punishment. On the other hand, if he can prove this, nothing may be allowed except what the same church has legally held up to now.

The advocate in whose jurisdiction this has taken place is faithfully to carry out this decree with the knowledge of both abbots and in the presence of their commissioners. And if the advocate, corrupted by a bribe or motivated by pity, should seek to avoid this decree by any sort of trickery, he will lose our grace and the advocacy, unless he dares to swear on the holy relics that he can nowhere apprehend the murderer or intruder; and still he should apprehend him as soon as possible.

And if the advocate in whose area this took place could not or would not apprehend the criminal, let the faithful of the other abbot apprehend him if they can and present him to the commissioners of both abbots to carry out the aforesaid punishment.

And in the case of chamberlains and butlers and other honoured servants of both abbots, we have decided that if any of them should do
such a thing, he should undergo the aforesaid punishment according
to the will of the abbot or else pay ten pounds of *denarii*.

And I desire this and strongly command in order that no one should
dare to renew the dispute which has been clearly and legally defined
once and for all.

But if the aforesaid abbots wish to nullify this decree, each is to pay
me or my successor two pounds of gold; and yet they may not carry out
their impulse.

And in order that this regulation may remain stable and unshaken,
we have ordered this diploma to be marked with the impression of our
seal.

Sign of Lord Henry, most invincible august emperor of the Romans.
Ulrich, chancellor, verified it for Archchaplain Aribo.

Given in the year of our Lord's Incarnation 1024, in the twenty-
second year of the reign of Henry, emperor augustus, in the eleventh
year of his empire, the seventh year of the indiction; given the seventh
day before the ides of March; carried out under favourable auspices at
Bamberg.

31. Wipo, On the election and consecration of Conrad II (1024):
from *The Deeds of Conrad II (Gesta Chuonradi II imperatoris)*, from
Imperial Lives and Letters of the Eleventh Century, trans. Theodor E.
Mommsen and Karl F. Morrison, New York, 1962, pp. 57–68.

In the year 1024 from the Incarnation of the Lord, the Emperor Henry
II, although sound of mind, was taken with an infirmity of the body, the
which prevailing he departed this life the III of the Ides of July [July
13]. The empire was sound, its affairs well ordered; and after long
labour, he had finally begun to reap the ripe fruit of peace. His body was
taken for burial from Saxony to a place which is called Bamberg, where
he himself had founded with good zeal and industry an episcopacy
distinguished with every ecclesiastical appurtenance. At its dedication,
he associated with himself the apostolic Lord Pope, Benedict [VIII] by
name, by whose authority he confirmed with a state covenant charters
for the protection of the place. In a short time after the death of the
emperor, the commonwealth, so to speak, desolate through the loss of
its father, began to stagger. From this happening all the best men had
fear and anxiety that the empire was in danger, but the worst prayed
that this were so. Divine Providence, however, gave the anchors of the
Church into the charge of bishops and such steersmen as were needed

at that time to take command in guiding the fatherland without jettison into the harbour of quiet. For when the emperor died without children, every man of very great power among the secular princes strove by force rather than by the qualities of his character either to become the man [of the state] or by some pact or other to become second to the first. Consequently discord fell upon almost the whole kingdom, to such a degree that in many places there would have been slaughters, arsons, and plunders, had this fury not been checked by the resistance of eminent men. The Empress Kunigunda, though deprived of her husband's strength, nevertheless by the counsel of her brothers, Theodoric, bishop of Metz, and Hezzilo, duke of Bavaria, succoured the commonwealth to the best of her ability and with serious thought directed the power of her talents and mind to the restoration of the empire.

This state of affairs demands that I mention the names of some of the greatest men, bishops as well as secular princes, who thrived then in the kingdom – by whose counsels the realm of the Franks was wont to elect kings – so that those things which I am about to say may not seem to have come about as if by chance, but rather in order that that which is seen to have been done by the advice of the most prudent be believed useful, honest, and the best thing.

At that time, Aribo ruled the archdiocese of Mainz, a Bavarian by birth, noble and wise, apt in royal councils; Pilgrim held the archdiocese of Cologne, a relative of Aribo the archbishop, provident and fit for that office. Poppo governed the archdiocese of Trier, a brother of Duke Ernst [I], a pious and humble man, who at that time had under his guardianship Duke Ernst [II], a son of his brother, with the dukedom of Alemannia. Theodoric, noble and valiant in virtue, possessed the episcopacy of Metz. The generous Bishop Werner was in charge of the bishopric of Strasbourg, zealous in divine and secular duties. Mazelinus, wise and faithful in ecclesiastical offices, sat in the see of the church at Würzburg. Eberhard ruled the episcopacy of Bamberg, the first bishop of that church, a man in character and customs most indispensable to the commonwealth. Heimo was leader of the church at Constance, a man wise in God, modest and provident for the affairs of this world. Bishop Bruno ruled Augsburg, brother of Emperor Henry, useful and outstanding in character, if it [that is, his good character] had not been obscured by the hate with which he opposed his brother, the emperor. Archbishop Gunther of good memory, gentle and good before God and men, brother of Counts Ekkehard and Herman, ruled the church at Iuvavenia, which they called in the vernacular Salzburg. Gebhard, outstanding because of his benevolence, was bishop of the church at Regensburg. Bishop Egilbert, provident governor of his clergy and people, ruled the church at Freising.

N

Together with these men, many other bishops and abbots from these same regions were present [at the election of Conrad] to name each of whom would produce distaste for this work. I have avoided mentioning the prelates of Saxony, since biographical information which may appropriately be added to their names is hidden from me, although I have assumed without any doubt that they, too, were present at those supreme affairs and that they gave counsel and succour. I pass over Italy, because her princes were unable to come to the regal election on such short notice. Afterwards, meeting the king in the city of Constance with the Archbishop of Milan and other princes, they were made his men and vowed fidelity to him with a ready spirit.

These were the dukes, on the other hand, contemporaries of the above-mentioned men: Benno, duke of Saxony; Adalbero, duke of Istria; Hezzilo, duke of Bavaria; Ernst, duke of Alemannia; Frederick, duke of the Lotharingians; Gozilo, duke of the Ripuarians; Cuono of Worms, duke of the Franks; Udalric, duke of Bohemia.

Of course, Burgundy was not yet dependent upon the Roman Empire, as it is now. The fact, however, that it has now been subjected is credited to the glory of three kings. Emperor Henry II sought first to subject it and persevered successfully in this effort. Then Emperor Conrad with a spirited onslaught ejected the Latin Franks [that is, the French] from it and subjected it. Finally, King Henry III, pious, pacific, the Fine Line of Justice, governed magnanimously the same Burgundy in war and peace. I shall commemorate in another place the things which he did there by Divine Providence in the councils of peace, as in those of war, in councils and assemblies which I myself occasionally attended.

Now I return to the principal subject. We hear nothing of Hungary in the stated time, however, which the same King Henry III subdued with a noble and wondrous victory and, after the victory, made secure for himself and his successors with very wise counsel.

The above-mentioned bishops and dukes and the other powerful persons, thinking that in no other way could they avoid the threatening peril better or more quickly, strove with the greatest resourcefulness and with memorable industry to the end that the commonwealth might totter no longer without a ruler. The expedient of letters and envoys made it possible to weigh private counsels and the opinions of individuals as to the man to whom each would consent, to whom he would object, or whom he wanted for his lord; nor was this done in vain. For it is the part of foresight to prepare within for that which is needed without; and counsel before action is the seed of the following fruit. That is to say, you wait for help from another in vain if you do not know what you want. Taking counsel secretly in difficult affairs; deliberating by stages, from one point to the next; acting swiftly will have a good outcome. At last, the day had been agreed upon, and the place designated; there was a public assembly the like of which I do not remember ever having seen before. I will not put off writing about the thing worthy of memory which was done in this assembly.

Between the confines of Mainz and those of Worms, there is a place which could accommodate a very large crowd by virtue of its size and flatness; and some island retreats were near by, thus making it safe and suitable for the consideration of secret matters. But I leave it to the topographers to speak more fully of the name and situation of the place, and I return to [my] undertaking.

While all the magnates, and, so to say, the valour and vitals of the kingdom, had convened there, they pitched camps on this side and in the region about the Rhine. As it [the Rhine] separated Gaul from Germany the Saxons, with their neighbours, the Slavs, the eastern Franks, the Bavarians, and the Alemanni, convened from the German side; and from Gaul, the Franks who lived above the Rhine, the Ripuarians, and the Lotharingians were joined together. An affair of supreme importance was in question; there was hesitation in view of the possibility of an indecisive election. Hung between hope and fear, as relatives together, so, too, members of the same households long explored alternate desires among themselves. For there was to be deliberation, not about a middling matter, but about one which, unless considered with very great zeal in a fervent breast, might be terminated to the ruin of the whole body of the kingdom. And, to use common proverbs: 'Food cooked well delights the mouth; food taken raw leads to peril.' And, as they say, 'Medication to be put in the eyes has to be seen to carefully.' When, in this fashion, a long disputation took place as to who ought to rule; and when age – too immature or, on the other hand, too greatly advanced – rejected one, untested valour, another; and a proven state of insolence, some others, few were chosen among many, and from the few two only were singled out. On them rested at last, in an instant of unity, the final examination of the greatest men, long contemplated with the utmost diligence.

Two Conrads were there, of whom one, since he was of the greater age, was named Cuono the Elder; but the other was called Cuono the Younger. Both were very noble men in German Francia, born of two brothers, one of whom was called Hezil and the other Cuono. We learn that these [latter] were born of Otto, duke of the Franks, with two others, Bruno and William. Of these, Bruno, having become pope of the Apostolic See of the Roman Church, was called by a changed name Gregory [V]; and William, made bishop of the Strasbourg church, exalted it in a wondrous way. Although the two aforesaid Cuonos were, as has been said, very noble on their fathers' parts, they were not at all less outstanding on their mothers' sides. Matilda, the mother of Cuono the Younger, was born of the daughter of Conrad, king of Burgundy. Adelaide, mother of Cuono the Elder, sprang from a very noble family of the Lotharingians. This Adelaide was the sister of Counts Gerhard and Adelbert, who, always contending with kings and dukes, to the end scarcely gave assent to the cause of their relative, King Conrad. Their forefathers, it is said, came from the ancient family of the Trojan kings, who submitted their necks to the yoke of the Faith under St Remigius the Confessor.

The rest of the nobility vacillated long between these two men – that is, the elder and the younger Conrad. And although almost everyone chose the elder Conrad by hidden counsel and eager desire because of his valour and probity, nevertheless everyone dissembled his opinion cleverly because of the power of the younger, lest they [the two men] come to strife through their ambitious desire of the honour. But finally by Divine Providence, it happened that they came into common agreement with the stipulation, fitting enough in such a doubtful matter, that if the greater part of the people should acclaim one of them, the other should yield to him without delay.

I think it a worthy thing to say by what method the elder Cuono disclosed his character, not because he despaired of ruling, as he already perceived that the assent of God was breathed into the hearts of the princes, but so that he might strengthen the spirit of his kinsman that it might be less perturbed amidst the new state of affairs. Therefore, he addressed them with this most outstanding speech.

'In prosperous affairs, the most becoming happiness neither exceeds the measure of gravity nor allows anyone to be ungrateful for benefices received; and, just as in adverse affairs pernicious pusillanimity draws man to the worse things, so in favourable affairs honourable pleasure leads him to the better: the fruit of felicity, once born, is of little value if it does not feed with joy well-tempered the spirit of the one who tends it.

'Thus, I feel that the vigour of my spirit is increased with great rejoicings, since in so great a gathering the common consent looked first to us two alone, to us, one of whom it may place in the regal dignity. But we ought not to think that we surpass our relatives either in nobility or possessions or that we have especially merited something worthy of such great veneration. It ill behoves us to extol with empty words; our ancestors preferred to advance their glory with deeds rather than with pronouncements. Among equals it will become any men to be content in the common life. But whatever that is, in which we are thought more competent for some undertaking than others, let us render thanks for it to God, its author. We must take thought, therefore, lest we who, by consent of others, are thought worthy of so great an honour seem unworthy of this favour through our own – indeed, through familial – discord. For it is exceedingly foolish to make use of the power of others instead of one's own.

'In any election, no man is allowed to pass judgement on himself, although [he may pass judgement] on another. If, indeed, anyone were permitted to pass judgement on himself, how many kinglings, not to say kings, might we see? Ours was not the power to narrow the choice for this office from many to two. Prayers, zealous efforts, the consensus of Franks, Lotharingians, Saxons, Bavarians, and Alemanni gave to us their good will, so to speak, as to the shoot of the root; just as to one house, so to an indissoluble friendship. No one will suppose that men bound together by so many reasons can be separated by enmity.

'It befits as many things as nature has bound together to be in harmony – nature who joins to herself the friendship of kinsmen. But if, on the other hand, we reject because of some obstacle the things offered by others – that is, if we come into mutual discord – it is certain that the people will then wish to desert us and to seek for themselves some third man. And not only will we be deprived of the supreme dignity, but – and this is more detestable to all good men than death – we will fall into the reputation of baseness and jealousy, as though we were unable to uphold the high character of so great a position of command and – this I think a great crime among relatives – as though one were unwilling to yield for the honour of the other.

'The greatest dignity, therefore, the supreme power, will abide as yet about us, and it has so come to us that, if we wish, it may rest upon one of us. For this reason, it seems to me, if this dignity remain joined on one of us, that the other is not deprived in any way of sharing this same honour. For just as to the forebears of kings, although they may not all be kings, a certain derivative honour is transferred, so also those who are chosen and nominated before others for a position of power, although they may not come into it, nevertheless will not lack entirely a certain honour born from the fact that they were not accounted unworthy of the greatest dignity. Besides (if kinsmen of kings be honoured because of their royal relations), since everyone wishes to regard us as we, in the spirit of harmony, would regard each other, and since the advancement of the one depends upon the other in this fashion: who could be more happy than we, if one reign, and the other through his good will, step forth as though alone to aid the one ruling the commonwealth? Let us, therefore, be careful that we not give preference to an outsider instead of to a relative, to something uncertain instead of to something certain, lest this day, hitherto happy and joyful enough because of such a judgement freely given, bring a long time of misfortunes for us, if we begrudge between us the favour conceived by so great a people.

'So that this may not come to pass on my part, most beloved of all my kinsmen, I want to say what I think concerning you. If I learn that the spirit of the people wants you, that it earnestly desires you for a lord and king, by no perversity will I divert this good will from you. Rather I shall elect you as much more avidly than the others as I should hope to be more pleasing to you than they. If, however, God should look to me, I do not doubt that you will render in turn what is due to me.'

To these words, the younger Cuono answered that this whole resolve would be agreeable to him, and he promised in the most certain terms that he would render all fealty owed to the king, to him as to his dearest kinsman, if the call to the supreme power should come to him. Amidst these words, the elder Cuono, with many looking on, leaned forth a little and kissed his kinsman. By this kiss it was first discovered that each of them has made his peace with the other. Hence, after the affirmation of this token of concord, the princes sat down together, and a very large crowd stood immediately at hand: Each man rejoiced that the time was at hand when he was allowed to bring forth openly what he had long covered in his heart. The archbishop of Mainz, whose opinion had to be taken before all, asked by the people what was seemly to him, with a full heart and a happy voice, acclaimed and elected the elder Cuono as his lord and king, and rector and defender of the fatherland. The other archbishops and the remaining men of holy orders unhesitatingly followed him in this vote. The younger Cuono, who had been negotiating for a short time with the Lotharingians, returned suddenly and elected him as lord and king with the greatest good will. The king, taking him by the hand, made him sit beside him.

Then, one by one, men from each of the several realms repeated the same words of election again and again; there was a shout of acclamation by the people; all consented unanimously with the princes in the election of the king; all eagerly desired the elder Cuono. On him they insisted; him they placed without any hesitation before all the mighty lords; him they judged to be most worthy of the regal power; and they demanded that there be no delay of his consecration. The abovementioned Empress Kunigunda graciously brought forth the regal insignia which the Emperor Henry had left to her and supported him for governance as far as lay within the authority of her sex. I believe that the good will of heavenly powers, indeed, was not absent from this election, since among men of singular power, among so many dukes and margraves, he was elected without malice, without controversy; he, who, although he was inferior to no one in family and in valour and in allodial goods, nevertheless in comparison with such men held of the state but little in fief and in power.

Although the archbishop of Cologne and Duke Frederick, with certain other Lotharingians, departed belligerent, as was said, on the younger Cuono's account (but, in fact, at the instigation of the devil, the enemy of peace), they nevertheless returned swiftly to the favour of the king, with the exception of those whom the common state of death had caught. Whatever he ordered, they accepted gratefully. And Archbishop Pilgrim, as if in emendation of his former wrong, besought the king that he be allowed to consecrate the queen in the church at Cologne.

Of her I am going to speak subsequently. Now I shall return to the king. Truly, by the assent of God was he elected whose later acknowledgement by men as king had been foreseen by God. For he was a man of great humility, provident in counsel, truthful in statements, vigorous in deeds, not at all greedy, the most liberal of all kings in giving. I shall speak afterwards more fully of his habits. This, however, must be said here, that he could never have failed to become a prince – and the greatest prince – in whom was the strength of the greatest virtues. For since it has been written, 'Humility surpasses glory', he to whom the queen of virtues adhered surpassed rightly the glorious of this world. It was not, therefore, in accord with divine law for anyone on earth to fight against him whom omnipotent God had predestined to govern all.

When the election was over, everyone, with the greatest eagerness, hastened to follow the king to Mainz, where he was to receive the most holy unction. They went rejoicing; the clergy chanted psalms, the layfolk sang, each in his own fashion. At no time have I found that God received such great praises from men on one day in one place.

If Charlemagne had been present, alive, with his sceptre, the people would not have been more eager, nor could they have rejoiced more at the return of so great a man than at the first coming of this king. The king arrived at Mainz. And there, received with due honour, he waited devoutly for his consecration, [as one] desirable to all. When the archbishop of Mainz and all the clergy solemnly prepared themselves to bless him on the day of the birth of St Mary, the archbishop delivered this sermon to the king during the sacred offices of regal unction:

'All power of this transient age is derived from one most pure font. It is usually the case, however, that when several rivulets spring forth from the same source, at one time they are turbulent, at another, clear, while at their head, the font stays fast in its purity. In the same way, inasmuch as the human state dares to set creator and creation side by side for comparison, we have the power to conjecture in a similar way about

God the immortal king and about earthly kings. For it has been written: "All power is of God." When this omnipotent king of kings, the author and the beginning of all honour, pours the grace of some dignity upon princes of the earth, in so far as it is in accord with the nature of its origin, it is pure and unstained. When, however, it has come to those who wield this dignity unworthily and pollute it with pride, malice, lust, avarice, wrath, impatient wilfulness, and cruelty, they will serve the perilous potion of iniquity to themselves and to all subject to them, unless they purge themselves by doing penance. O let the whole Church of the saints pray and intercede before God that the dignity which is offered pure today by God to our present lord and king, Conrad, be preserved inviolate by him as far as is humanly possible.

'Our sermon is with you and for you, O Lord King. The Lord, who elected you to be king over His people, has wished first to test you and to have you rule afterwards. For he scourges all whom He received. He sees fit to assail the one whom he has wished from an earlier time to receive; it pleases Him to humble him whom He has designed to exalt. So God tried Abraham His servant and glorified the one tried. So He permitted David, his bondman, to suffer the wrath of King Saul, persecution, injuries, the haunts of the desert, flight and exile – David whom afterwards He made the most glorious king in Israel. Blessed is he who suffers trial, since he will receive the crown. Not without cause has God exercised you, He has sweetened that which was to come to fruition within you. He permitted you to lose the favour of your predecessor, the Emperor Henry, and to receive the same again, that now you may know how to be merciful to those who lose your favour; you have suffered injuries that now you may know how to be merciful to those who sustain injuries. Divine Piety has been unwilling for you to be without preparatory discipline, so that after this instruction from heaven you might take up the Christian empire. You have come to the highest dignity: you are the vicar of Christ.

'No one but his imitator is a true ruler. It is necessary that in this "throne of the kingdom" you reflect on the perpetual honour. It is great felicity to rule in the world, but the greatest is to triumph in heaven. Although God requires many things of you, He wishes most of all that you render judgement and justice, and peace for the fatherland, which always looks to you; and [He wishes] that you be the defender of churches and clerics, the guardian of widows and orphans. With these and other good [works] your throne will be firmly established here and forever.

'And now, Lord King, all Holy Church asks with us your favour for those who hitherto have transgressed against you and have lost your favour through some offence. Of these, there is one, Otto by name, a noble man, who offended you. We pray your clemency for him and for all the rest, that you may grant pardon to them for the love of God which has changed you today into another man and has made you a sharer of His will, to the end that He may deign to repay you in kind for all your transgressions.'

During this sermon, the king, moved by compassion, sighed and, even more (how could it be believed ?), broke into tears. Thereupon, as the bishops and dukes with all the people petitioned, he pardoned all whatever transgressions they had done against him.

The whole people received this gratefully. All cried out for joy when the piety of the king had been manifested: Beast-like would have been the man who could not be moved to tears that such great power ignored such great wrongs. And although he would have been able to avenge his wrongs, even if he had never become king, nevertheless he was not led by reliance in such great power to reserve anything for vengeance.

When the divine offices and the regal consecration had been performed most fittingly, the king began the procession. And, as is read of Saul the king, he returned with the holy company to his chamber with an eager countenance and a noble step, as though he went higher 'than any of the people from his shoulder and upward' and as if [his bearing] had been transformed. . . . After that he was received with regal magnificence at dinner and consumed this first day of royal splendour as was most suitable for his office.

32. Conrad II confirms the estates of Colmar and Hüttenheim and a manse at Bohlsbach to the cloister at Peterlingen (Payerne) as well as the right of free election of abbots (Mainz, 9 September 1024): DK.II.1, from *MGH Diplomata*, IV, *Conradi II. diplomata*, ed. H. Bresslau, 2nd unaltered edn, Berlin, 1957, 1–2.

In the name of the holy and indivisible Trinity. Conrad, by God's grace king.

If we confirm and corroborate by our royal authority those things for the holy venerable places which have been arranged there by the faithful, we are certain that we shall doubtless obtain support in the present as well as in the eternal life.

Therefore let all of the faithful of the holy Church of God and of us, both present and future, know that the venerable abbot Odilo of the holy church of the Everlasting Virgin Mary located at Peterlingen, with all of his congregation of brothers devoutly serving God there and also Holy Mary, approached our highness, bringing to our presence diplomas, corroborated by the authority of our most pious predecessors Emperors Otto I, Otto II, and Otto III, and also the invincible Henry [II] of divine memory, which contained a text telling how our predecessors [granted and gave] those things which had been granted and given by the most noble Duke Rudolf [of Burgundy] to the aforesaid church of Mary, the Holy Mother of God, and for the use and provision of the monks serving there, to wit, the estates of Colmar and Hüttenheim with all their appurtenances, and one manse in the village of Bohlsbach bestowed upon the same monastery by the above-mentioned emperor Henry, with a humble request for justice that we should take care to corroborate by our new charter all the aforesaid things given and legally belonging to the same church, situated in Alsace and in the county of Count Otto.

Giving our assent to their request we have thus decreed and under immunity of our protection through the force of this our diploma we have included all the above-mentioned things legally belonging thereto, ordering by our royal authority that freely, safely, and perpetually remote from the disturbance of all, they should belong to the said church and that they should serve the daily use of the brothers dwelling there now and in the future under the rule of the abbot.

Moreover, it is permitted to the aforesaid Abbot Odilo and his successors in the afore-mentioned places to appoint an advocate of their choice so that he may not have any power there of his own beyond what the abbot or his successors grant him with the consent of the brothers.

And in order that this record of our protection remain stable and unshakeable, we have ordered the diploma to be marked by the imprint of our seal, corroborating it with our own hand.

Sign of Lord Conrad II, most invincible king.

Ulrich, chancellor, verified it for Archchaplain Aribo.

Given the fifth day before the ides of September in the year of our Lord's Incarnation 1024, the seventh year of the indiction, in the first year of the reign of Lord Conrad II; carried out at Mainz; under favourable auspices.

33. Under the chairmanship of Conrad II and his son Henry, the claims of Duke Adalbero of Carinthia to *fodrum* and other services from the church of Aquileia are refused (S. Zeno near Vernoa, 19 May 1027): DK.II.92, from *MGH Diplomata*, IV, 125–7.

In the name of the Lord. When Lord Conrad, by God's grace emperor augustus, presided in court in the portico of the gallery of S. Zeno in the county of Verona, together with his son Henry, to do justice to individuals and to decide claims, present with them were Poppo, archbishop of Trier, Wecellinus, bishop of Strasbourg, Bruno of Augsburg, Meinwerk of Paderborn, Vermund, bishop of Constance, Ulrich of Trent, Roger of Treviso, Albuin of Belluno, Rigizo of Feltre, Helminger of Ceneda – bishops of the saints of God – Margrave Hugo, Count Agizardus, Count Poppo, Count Arduin, Count Meinhard, Count Orekcerio, Count John, Count Magifred, and Count Regimbald, Beuo, Rafald, Ingelram, Arpo, Bernard, Alberic, Remego, Iscledo, Rozzo, Naldipsi, and Arnald – judges of the sacred palace – Acilin de Turre and Hubert, brothers; Luitfred, Papo, and Gualterus, brothers; Hermerard, Arduin, Regenald, son of a certain Leo; Azo and Glopo, brothers; John and Paganolus, brothers, and sons of Walpert; Wulfrad, son of Agichard; Walpert and Alderin, brothers, and sons of Ulrich; Azo, son of Varientus, and the rest.

Lord Poppo, patriarch of Aquileia, coming into their presence in that place, with Walpert, his advocate of the same church and on the other side Lord Adalbero, duke of Carinthia, together with Count Wecellinus, his advocate, who is also called Walpoto.

When they had come together there and had made claims on both sides, Duke Adalbero with his advocate Wecellinus said that from the freeholds, castles, and villages and from all dependants, servile as well as free, belonging to the holy church of Aquileia and the inhabitants over and above the dependants of the same church, his duchy should be paid *fodrum* and *angaria*[64] or public service, that is, bread and wine, meat and grain, and other services and public duties.

To this Lord Patriarch Poppo and his advocate Walpert replied that it was not true that from the estates and all the above items they owed *fodrum* or anything of those things which he had mentioned before, to dukes or margraves or counts, to local judges [*sculdasiis*], to police officials [*decanis*], or to manorial bailiffs [*saltariis*].

Then the aforesaid advocate Walpert coming there, through the judgement of the judges, with four oath-helpers – Varientus, Hubert, Tubert, and Cono, armed retainers of the church of Aquileia – who so swore concerning the estates, castles, villages, and all of the aforesaid appurtenances of the holy church of Aquileia, the inhabitants both bond and free, that neither *fodrum* nor duties nor any of the other things said above ought to pertain legally to dukes, margraves, counts, local judges, police officers, or manorial bailiffs nor ought they to make any distraint in the same place.

And the lord patriarch with his advocate Walpert replied: 'We have and possess on the part of St Mary and St Hermagoras of the church of

[64] *Angaria* was the service of transporting goods or messages.

Aquileia freeholds, castles, villages, and *massaricias*[65] and everything
including the inhabitants belonging to the same church.

'And if any man wishes to say anything against us and against the
church of Aquileia, we are prepared to stand in court with him and
come to a legal settlement; and what more, we ask, might Lord Duke
Adalbero say together with Count Wecellinus his advocate, concerning
the freeholds or castles or villages or other legal rights of the holy church
of Aquileia either involving *fodrum* or any aforesaid procurement of
victuals [*gaforium*]; we ask if he wishes to say more or contest anything
or not.'

To this Duke Adalbero and his advocate Count Wecellinus gave
assurances: 'We say and strongly praise what is worthy and just, that
concerning the freeholds, castles, dwellings, *massaricias*, and appurtenances of St Mary and St Hermagoras and the inhabitants belonging to
them, bond as well as free, nothing legally belongs either to us or other
dukes or margraves or counts or local judges or police officers or
manorial bailiffs, but everything is the property of the church of
Aquileia.'

Moreover, in this place and at the same court of law, Duke Adalbero
with his advocate Count Wecellinus pledged to pay 100 pounds of the
best gold to Lord Poppo, patriarch, and Walpert, his advocate, or to the
church at Aquileia dedicated to St Mary and St Hermagoras, and
acknowledging that his heirs, representatives, and offspring should pay
the same if they ever presume to bring a suit or to challenge the claim of
Poppo the patriarch or of anyone else concerning the afore-mentioned
matters and that they should waive the claim and remain content for all
time, and if any accomplices try to go against this, they should all pay
the same and waive the claim.

When this was so decided, it seemed to be just to all the above-
written auditors; they also judged that after the acknowledgement and
evidence of Lord Poppo, patriarch, and of Walpert, advocate of the
church of Aquileia, and also of Duke Adalbero and Count Wecellinus,
advocate of his duchy, henceforth in the future the lord patriach with
his advocate Walpert should have and hold the same freeholds with
dwellings, castles, villages, and *massaricias*, and with all those inhabitants, free as well as unfree, pertaining to the same church, with *fodrum*
and everything written above from Duke Adalbero and his advocate,
Count Wecellinus, without any inquisition; and this Duke Adalbero
with his advocate, Count Wecellinus, promised that they would thenceforth waive the claim and remain content for all time.

So the case is finished, and the present record excellently demon-
strates how it was carried out.

[65] Estates tenanted by a class of dependants higher than a serf.

I Arnold, notary and judge of the sacred palace, have written this diploma by command of the aforesaid emperor and by order of the judges, and I was present in the first year of the same Lord Conrad, by God's grace emperor augustus, in Italy, on the fourteenth day before the kalends of June, the tenth year of the indiction.

34. In an imperial document Bishop Kadeloh of Naumburg secures certain concessions for merchants from Grossjena (Memleben, 1033): DK.II.194, from *MGH Diplomata*, IV, 258.

In the name of the holy and indivisible Trinity.

Be it known to all men present as well as to all those of the following era that I, Kadeloh, by God's grace bishop of Naumburg both on authority of the glorious emperor Conrad and on the consent of the brothers Herman and Ekkehard, who by paternal hereditary raised this place to episcopal rank, have conceded as a donation to the merchants of Grossjena on account of their spontaneous pledge to leave their own place and to emigrate here that whatever any of them possesses in the way of enclosure with household and farm buildings, he may keep by continuous right without paying taxes; and thereafter he may have the right of doing whatever he wishes with it, under the condition that he swear to me upon the law of all businessmen of our region and that he freely follow my successors afterwards in the observances of all merchants.

For the sake of this matter I sought royal support, and I obtained his flowing munificence for all so that he might bring them under the law of the tribes. He favoured this easily with his usual benevolence granting by royal power the right of going out from this place and returning, and he confirmed it by this imperial edict.

And in order that it remain acceptable and immutable for all time, he ordered the charter of this grant to be subscribed and to be confirmed by the impression of his seal.

Carried out at Memleben; under favourable auspices.

35. The *Constitutio de feudis*; Conrad II makes a law about legal relations of feudal tenants in Italy (at the siege of Milan, 28 May 1037): DK.II.244, from *MGH Diplomata*, IV, 335-7.

In the name of the holy and indivisible Trinity. Conrad, by God's grace emperor augustus of the Romans.

To all of our faithful of the holy Church of God future as well as present we wish it to be known that in order to reconcile the minds of lords and knights so that they may always be mutually harmonious and may faithfully and steadfastly serve us and devotedly serve their over-lords, we order and have powerfully decreed that no knight of bishops, abbots, abbesses or margraves, counts, or of all who now hold a bene-fice from our royal property or from that of the Church or may hold one or who unjustly lost one hitherto, whether of our major vassals or of their knights, should lose his benefice without a fault being proved and demonstrated unless in accordance with the constitution of our prede-cessors and the judges of their peers.

If a dispute emerges between great vassals and knights, although the peers adjudge that the knight ought to be deprived of his benefice, and if the knight should say this was done unjustly or out of hatred, he may keep his benefice until he comes with his overlord and peers into our presence, and there the case shall be settled justly.

If the peers of the accused fail to award judgement to the great lords, the accused may hold his benefice until he comes into our presence with his overlord and peers.

Moreover, if either a great lord or a knight is condemned, and he decides to come to us, he should notify the one with whom he has had the dispute six weeks before he begins the journey. This applies to our great vassals as well.

Concerning lesser vassals in the realm, however, their case shall be settled either before great lords or before our *missus*.

We also decree that when any knight of a great or lesser vassal dies, his son may have his benefice; but if he had no son and left a son of his son, he may similarly have the benefice, when the custom of the great vassals of giving horses and arms to his overlords has been observed.

If, perchance, he has not left behind a son of his son, and he has a legitimate brother on the paternal side, if he [the surviving brother] has offended his overlord and wishes to satisfy him and become his knight, he may have the benefice that was his brother's.

Moreover, we altogether forbid that any lord presume to make an exchange either of a *precarium* or a *libellum*[66] out of a benefice of their knights without their consent. Indeed, let no one dare to divest them illegally of their property which they hold by proprietary right[67] either through charters or through a regular *libellus* or through other precarial contract.

[66] *Precarium, libellum*: two types of precarial land. *Precaria* (fem. sg.) and *libellus* (masc. sg.) designated the deed or contract stipulating the kind of tenure granted.

[67] Note that allodial land, i.e. land held 'by proprietary right', still existed side by side with land held through various types of feudal contract.

We wish to have *fodrum* from the castles which our ancestors had, but that which they did not have, we in no way demand.

If anyone breaks this command, he is to pay 100 pounds of gold, one-half to our treasury and one-half to the one to whom the damage was done.

Sign of Lord Conrad, most serene emperor augustus of the Romans.

Kadeloh, chancellor, verified it for Herman, the archchancellor.

Given the fifth day before the kalends of June, the fifth year of the indiction, in the year of our Lord's Incarnation 1037 and in the thirteenth year of Lord Conrad, eleventh of the empire; carried out at the siege of Milan; under favourable auspices, amen.

36. Conrad II gives to the episcopal church at Cremona the movable and immovable property of Adam of Cremona, the murderer of the cardinal deacon Henry, who was under the emperor's protection (1937): DK.II.252, from *MGH Diplomata*, IV, 348–9.

In the name of the holy and indivisible Trinity. Conrad, by God's grace emperor augustus of the Romans.

If we have felt compassion for the miserable and unfortunate ones of the holy Church of God and for its pastors and have been zealous in granting gifts by which the same holy Church ought to be elevated and supported, we do not doubt at all that the status of our empire will be strengthened and enlarged and beyond this that the reward of eternal life will be extended to us.

For in truth we have learned that a certain man of Cremona, Adam by name, puffed up by the spirit of pride and spurred on by diabolic boldness, murdered a certain cardinal deacon by the name of Henry, a most able servant of the holy church of Cremona, whom we had taken under the protection of our power with all his possessions both movable and immovable, [the murderer] thereby depreciating the reverence of our majesty, and by killing this servant of the church, capable in all things, he caused more harm than we can reckon.

Therefore we wish it to be known to all the faithful of the holy Church of God, both present and future, that by the intercession of our beloved wife, Empress Gisela, in order that the church should recoup in part the injury from the death of its servant and in order that the contagion of so great a crime should nowhere become a habit, we have granted all the land which the aforesaid Adam appeared to hold within the city of Cremona and outside throughout the area of the whole diocese, and all the property movable and immovable which he possessed, to the aforesaid holy church of Cremona to have and to hold by proprietary right through this our diploma, and we have conveyed it into the jurisdiction and domain of the aforenamed church by our imperial authority, on condition that our faithful beloved Hubald, venerable bishop of the same church, as well as his successors, may perpetually do whatever seems right to them for the good of the church concerning all the property, movable and immovable, of the aforesaid murderer.

Moreover, concerning all the properties and all the possessions movable and immovable of the said murderer, we have also ordered on imperial authority that no duke, margrave, count, viscount, judge, *sculdahis*,[68] or any person of our realm great or small, shall presume by any ruse or subterfuge to dispossess or disturb the holy church of Cremona and Hubald, bishop of the same see, and his successors.

If anyone indeed should rashly violate this diploma of ours, which we can hardly believe would happen, let him know that he shall pay 200 pounds in the best gold, half to our treasury and half to the church and its rector, to whom the injury was done.

In order that this be diligently believed and observed by all, we have decreed that a document of this edict of ours be made, and we have ordered it to be marked with the impression of our seal, corroborating below with our own hand.

Sign of Lord Conrad, most serene emperor augustus.

37. Conrad II orders Roman judges to use Roman law when deciding cases involving a Lombard as plaintiff or defendant if they are tried in Roman territory (1038): DK.II.275, from *MGH Diplomata*, IV, 381.

Conrad, emperor augustus, to the Roman judges. Having heard that there has been a controversy which has hitherto existed between you and the Lombard judges and has not been settled and is without termination, we decree that from now on when trials take place within the walls of Rome or even outside in territory belonging to Romans, and either the plaintiff or the accused is a Lombard, they are to be settled by you only according to Roman laws and are not to be revived at any time.

[68] See note 23 above.

38. Henry III restores a fief to the monastery of Hersfeld, which had been taken away by Conrad II (Goslar, 5 January 1043): DH.III.100, from *MGH diplomata*, V, *Heinrici III. diplomata*, ed. H. Bresslau and P. Kehr, 2nd unaltered edn, Berlin, 1957, 127.[69]

In the name of the holy and indivisible Trinity. Henry, by God's grace king. May all of our faithful of Christ, future as well as present, know on account of the salvation of the soul of our pious father Emperor Conrad and on account of the steady and faithful service rendered to us by the venerable Abbot Meginher of the holy church of Hersfeld and on account of the assiduous prayers of the monks serving God there, we have granted a fief to the said abbot and the brothers, which our father of happy memory removed from there and gave to Count Otto. Now that Countess Irmingard [his widow] has died, we have returned it to them by our royal munificence so that the said abbot and brothers serving God there may henceforth have free power of holding, granting, exchanging, bestowing by precarial contract, or whatever they wish to do with it. And in order that this deed of our donation remain stable and unshaken, we have ordered it signed and sealed with the imprint of our seal.

I Adalger, chancellor, have verified it for Bardo, archchancellor.

Given the nones of January in the year of our Lord's Incarnation 1043, the eleventh year of the indiction, in the fifteenth year of Lord Henry III's ordination, fourth of the reign; carried out at Goslar; under favourable auspices, in the name of God, amen.

39. With Henry III and his chancellor presiding in royal court, a dispute between Bishop Bernard II of Ascoli and Albasia, wife of Pandulf, over a farm and a castle is decided in favour of the bishop (S. Marotto, 1047): DH.III.188, from *MGH Diplomata*, V, 236-7.

When in the name of God in the county of Fermo in a place which is called S. Marotto the emperor Lord Henry presided at a *placitum* along with Henry, chancellor of the sacred palace, in order to hear cases and render judgement, presiding with him were Bonusfilius, an imperial magnate and resident of Pavia; Hugo, son of Grimoald; Trasmund, son of Taselgard; Atto, son of Odemund; Giselbert, son of Giselman; Bishop Ezemanus of Fermo; Bishop Sigeman of Foligno; Folcho, son

[69] I wish to express my thanks to Dr Kurt-Ulrich Jäschke of the Institut für Mittelalterliche Geschichte in the University of Marburg for bringing this diploma to my attention.

O

of Alberic; Hugo, son of Peter; Lado, son of Carbonus; and many more. And Bishop Bernard II of Ascoli and his advocate Ansus came before them and said:

'My lord and emperor, on several occasions now I have complained to you about Albasia, wife of Pandulf, as regards the estate of Helicetum and the castle of Corata and everything that belongs to them, which she is holding unjustly and in defiance of my rights and refuses to hand over.'

When the emperor heard this, he asked Albasia about her claim to this property.

She replied that her husband had acquired it by exchange with Atto, son of Chonus.

Then the emperor asked the aforesaid judge [Bonusfilius] what the law prescribed in such cases.

The judge said, 'Lord, ask her where the donor is and whether she has any witnesses.'

Then the emperor asked her if she had either donor or witness.

Albasia replied, 'I am unable to produce donor or witness here because although I asked you to send them a summons, they were not willing to appear with me in your presence.'

When the emperor heard this, he asked the judge what the law prescribed, and the judge Bonusfilius answered, 'Lord, the law is that you make her renounce her possession of the property in favour of the aforesaid bishop, that you uphold the claim of the bishop against Albasia, and that you make a perpetual grant to the aforesaid bishop and his advocate.'

When the lord emperor heard that, he had the aforesaid Albasia renounce the aforesaid things to the aforesaid bishop as the aforesaid judge had decided, and by the staff which he held in his hand, the aforesaid emperor bestowed the aforesaid things on the aforesaid bishop and the aforesaid advocate of the aforesaid bishopric in perpetuity.

Moreover, he placed the bishop under his protection and also the aforesaid estate of Helicetum and the aforesaid castle with their appurtenances so that henceforth no one might dare to divest, molest, or disturb the said bishop or his successor or a representative of the said bishop without legal judgement.

If anyone does this, let him know that he must pay 100 pounds of gold, half to our treasury and half to the aforesaid bishop or his successors. And they had this document drawn up as a record of the case.

I Folcho, notary of the sacred palace, have written it by command of the aforesaid emperor and by order of the judges in the year of the

Incarnation of our Lord Jesus Christ 1047, the fifteenth year of the indiction, in the first year in which it pleased God for Henry II to rule.[70] This was done in the county of Fermo at S. Marotto; in the name of God, under favourable auspices, amen.

I Henry, emperor, have signed.

I Henry, chancellor, have signed.

I Bonusfilius, imperial judge and resident of Pavia, was present.

I Adamo, judge of Fermo, was present.

I Adelbert, judge, have signed.

I Hugo, judge of Ravenna, was present.

I Bonushomo, judge, have signed.

40. Henry III orders that no secular or regular clergy and no nun shall be forced to take an oath in criminal or civil cases, but that all religious persons should take an oath through the intermediary of their advocates (Rimini, 3 April 1047): DH.III.191, from *MGH Diplomata*, V, 239–42.

Henry II, by God's grace emperor augustus. To everyone:

Since the laws warn that no cleric should presume to take an oath, yet it is elsewhere found written that all principal persons at the beginning of a law suit take an oath forswearing calumny, the matter comes into doubt in some laws drawn up by experts whether clergy ought to take an oath or perhaps delegate this office to other persons.

Because that rescript where clergy are forbidden from taking an oath seems to have been promulgated by the august Theodosius for his praetorian prefect Taurus concerning the clerics of Constantinople, it is therefore not thought to pertain to other clerics. Therefore in order that this doubt be completely removed, we have decreed that that rule of the divine Theodosius be thus interpreted so that it be judged to pertain generally to the clerics of all churches.

Yet when the divine Justinian legally decreed that it is necessary that canons of the fathers have the force of law, and it is found in some canons of the fathers that clergy dare not take an oath, it is fitting that all the clerical order should undoubtedly be considered to be immune from having to take an oath.

[70] Henry III is called the second here because he is now emperor (the coronation took place in Rome on Christmas Day, 1046), and only Henry II (1002–1024) qualified as an emperor of the same name, Henry the Fowler never having received the imperial crown. Cf. Doc. 38, issued in 1043, where he is called Henry III, since he was the third Henry to be king of the Germans.

Therefore we decree, with regard to both divine and human law, and we determine irrevocably by means of imperial authority that no bishop, priest, or cleric of whatever rank, abbot, monk, or nun should be compelled to swear an oath in any controversy either criminal or civil for any reason whatsoever, but may delegate this duty to the appropriate advocate.

Given the third day before the nones of April [in the year of the Lord's Incarnation 1047; carried out] at Rimini.

41. Henry III permits the inhabitants of Val Scalve to trade in iron and frees them from customs, *fodrum,* and other public duties in exchange for a yearly payment of 1,000 pounds of iron to the royal court at Darfo (Mantua, 1 May 1047): DH.III.199, from *MGH Diplomata,* V, 255-7.

In the name of the holy and indivisible Trinity. Henry, by God's grace emperor augustus of the Romans.

May all of the faithful of the holy Church of God and of us, both present and future, know that we have made a grant by means of our diploma for the love of God and the salvation of our soul, and as we were able justly and legally, we have granted to all men living in Val Scalve the opportunity and dispensation of trading and of selling their iron or whatever they wish through the vastness of our empire to Kreuzberg[71] and La Cisa[72] without contradiction or molestation of any mortal man or a duty of any royal exaction beyond 1,000 pounds of iron, which they have supplied up to now and must give henceforth every year to our royal estate called Darfo [Dervio] on the conditions and following the custom and habit of their ancestors or predecessors. Therefore no duke, margrave, bishop, count or any other person of our realm, great or small, shall dare to bring a dispute or force or any charge against the men dwelling in the aforesaid Val Scalve or shall presume to exact either a toll or *fodrum* or any public duty from them or their heirs, except as we have decreed above.

If anyone is a violator of this diploma, let him know that he must pay 100 pounds of the best gold, half to our treasury and half to the aforesaid men or their heirs.

[71] Kreuzberg (Monte Cruciam in the diploma) is an Alpine pass north of Aquileia on the Drave River.

[72] La Cisa (formerly Mt Bardonis) is a pass in the Apennines about 50 miles east of Genoa, elevation 3,410 feet. Thus the territory described to the iron-workers of Como in the diploma as 'the vastness of our empire' seems to consist of a triangle superimposed on north Italy alone.

In order that this be more truly believed and diligently observed by all, we have ordered this diploma to be marked with the impression of our seal, confirming with our own hand.

Sign of Lord Henry II, most invincible emperor augustus of the Romans.

I Henry, chancellor, have verified it for Herman, archchancellor.

Given the kalends of May in the year of our Lord's Incarnation 1047, the fifteenth year of the indiction, in the eighteenth year of Lord Henry III's anointment, eighth of his rule, the first year of his reign as emperor; carried out at Mantua; in the name of God, under favourable auspices, amen.

42. Henry III outlaws the crimes of poisoning and assassination in Italy (Zürich, 17 June 1052): DH.III.293, from *MGH Diplomata*, V, 397–9.

Henry II, by God's grace emperor augustus of the Romans. To all Lombards.

It seems proper that the imperial skill should take care of the public welfare so that it is attended to in the present in so far as one may diligently provide those things which will be useful and beneficial for future generations.

Moreover, this is properly enough done when the reward of virtue is given to the good but also revenge suitable for punishing the wicked, as an example for others.

But since the human race excels everything that is in the world, care is to be taken particularly concerning its welfare in so far as it is more manifest that Almighty God also sent his only Son to earth from the eternal seat of His divinity for our redemption.

Therefore since we have heard that many have died from pain, poison, and other kinds of clandestine homicide, we have issued a law about it, approved by the consent and authority of bishops, margraves, counts, and many others of our faithful when we sat in council at Zürich at the universal convention of Lombards.

Whoever kills someone by poisoning or any means of clandestine homicide or is an accomplice will incur the death penalty and lose his right to all property, movable and immovable, so that the amount of ten pounds is paid first to the relatives of the dead man as a legitimate wergild, half of which remains with the same relatives and the other half comes into the royal treasury.

If anyone should wish to deny either the perpetration of, or the connivance at, the aforesaid crime, he will receive a similar sentence unless he defends himself – if he is free by means of a duel, if he is unfree by means of ordeal

Moreover, we wish and we ordain by our imperial authority that whoever offers refuge or any kind of help to men accused of the said crime, all of his property is to come into the royal treasury, and he runs the risk of our indignation and that of all our people.

Given at Zürich on the fifteenth day before the kalends of July, the fifth year of the indiction.

43. Henry III forbids certain types of marriage (Zürich, 1052): DH.III.294, from *MGH Diplomata*, V, 399–400.

Henry II, by God's grace emperor augustus of the Romans. To everyone.

Since the care of imperial office has been entrusted to us by the providence of divine piety, we believe we should be continually solicitous of those things which pertain to the Christian religion and to the cult of justice.

Therefore, when we attended a universal meeting of all of our faithful Italian magnates at Zürich, where the question of illegal marriages was considered, we put forth this opinion, with the counsel of our princes, archbishops, bishops, margraves, counts, and with the judgement of our judges or with the consent of all those passing judgement: we have confirmed by the highest authority all those things which the holy canons or the sacred laws of our predecessors set forth, and we also add by our imperial right that whoever marries or betrothes a woman whether of legal age or below legal age, if he should die, none of his near relatives is permitted to marry his widow or fiancée.

If anyone should do this – woman as well as man – let them be disinherited by this law, and half of all their property shall come into the royal treasury, while the other half goes to the near legal relatives by hereditary right.

And whoever is born from this sort of marriage, let him be disinherited by this law just as his parents are.

44. Henry IV gives several farms to the monastery of SS. Simon and Jude at Goslar with their revenue as it was paid to the brothers in the days of Henry III (Kessel, 17 September 1057): DH.IV.27, from *MGH Diplomata*, VI, Pts I and II, 33–4.

In the name of the holy and indivisible Trinity. Henry, by God's grace king.

We do not doubt that if we are willing to bestow some of our wealth on those places devoted to the divine religion, it will redound to the prosperity of us and the state of our realm. Therefore we wish it to be known to the faithful of Christ and of us, future as well as present, how – upon the intercession and petition of our most beloved mother Agnes, empress augusta, and of the venerable archbishop Anno of Cologne for the salvation of the soul of our most kind father of happy memory, Henry, third king and second emperor [of that name], in the place Goslar at the altar consecrated in honour of the holy and indivisible Trinity and of the Saints Simon and Jude Eucharius Valerius Maternus and of all saints – we have given and granted as a property certain freeholds with the revenues that go with them, which the brothers serving there had in the time of our father and which was paid to them, with this stipulation that the abbot of the brothers have free power henceforth of doing whatever he likes concerning the aforesaid freeholds and revenues for the use of the brothers serving God and his saints there day and night.

And in order that this our royal donation remain stable and unshakeable for all time we have ordered this diploma to be written and signed by our own hand, as is seen below, corroborating by the impression of our seal.

Sign of Lord Henry IV, king.

I Winithere, chancellor, have verified it for Archchancellor Liutpold.

Given on the fifteenth day before the kalends of October in the year of our Lord's Incarnation 1057, the tenth year of the indiction, in the fourth year since the ordination of Lord Henry IV, first of his reign; carried out at Kessel; under favourable auspices, in the name of God, amen.

45. Henry IV confirms for Count Ernest of Austria the privileges of emperors Julius Caesar and Nero (spurious; Dürrenbuch, 4 October 1058): DH.IV.42b, from *MGH Diplomata*, VI, Pts I and II, 52–4.[73]

In the name of the holy and indivisible Trinity, amen. Henry, by God's grace king augustus of the Romans, son of the former Lord Henry of blessed memory, emperor of the Romans.

Since it is fitting that the imperial highness admit the just petitions

[73] For a discussion of the history of forged Austrian privileges including this one, see *Urkundenbuch zur Geschichte der Babenberger*, ed. Heinrich Fichtenau, IV, 1, Vienna, 1968, p. 20, n. 576, and Alphons Lhotsky, *Privilegium maius*, Österreich Archiv, Vienna, 1957, especially pp. 20–1.

of eminent men and noble princes also by consideration of their intercessors, we have admitted through the portals the requests of the most famous and noble Lord Ernest, margrave of Austria, the foremost and most faithful prince of the holy Roman Empire, and of the most generous lady, Lady Agnes, empress of the Romans, our most beloved mother, co-petitioner of the same, wishing to allow them a favourable hearing, since the prince of the said empire [Ernest], has procured honours and advantages and may continue to do so. In this very year he fought the pagans three times and drove them from those lands with the mighty help of divine assistance. The requests of this prince require that we perpetuate by a diploma of confirmation the grants or privileges conceded by the ancient emperors of the pagans to his [Ernest's] noble margraviate of Austria, the texts of whose privileges follow. The text of the first privilege runs thus:

'We Emperor Julius, we Caesar and worshipper of the gods, we highest imperial augustus on earth, we supporter of the whole earth, grant Roman grace and our peace to you, the zone of that Eastern Land, and to its inhabitants. We command you through our triumph to obey our uncle, the distinguished senator, since we have given you to him and his heirs and the descendants of his house as a feudatory possession to be held in perpetuity, bequeathing to him and his posterity forever that we ought not to set up any power over them, and therefore we grant to him and the said successors all uses of the renowned Eastern Land. Moreover, we have taken the same man, our uncle, and all his successors into the most secret Roman advisory council so that from now on no standing business or case may be made without their knowledge. Carried out at Rome, capital of the world, on Venus's day in the first year of our reign and in the first year of gold exaction.'

And the text of the second privilege runs:

'We Nero, friend of the gods and one who displays faith in them, preceptor of Roman power, emperor and Caesar and augustus. We have deliberated with all our senate that that Eastern Land ought to be tax exempt before other lands because she and her inhabitants laudably shine forth before all those who are subjects of the Roman Empire. On account of this we say that that same land will be perpetually exempt and absolved of all tribute and tax which is imposed now or in the future by the imperial power either by us or our successors or anyone else. We also wish that the same land should remain forever free. We order by Roman power that the abovenamed land should not be disputed with any enmity at all, and if anyone moreover should go against this, as soon as he has perpetrated this, he is to be under the ban of the Roman

Empire and never leave it thenceforth at any time. Given at the Lateran
on Mars's day, that great god.'

On account of this, we the aforesaid King Henry have observed and
called to mind that men who persist in unfaithfulness give documents
to other men who are of the same faith and belief but which may be useless and fruitless to those men and tribes who believe in Jesus Christ,
and useless to their lands. On account of this, we have corroborated to
that generous prince the aforesaid Ernest, margrave of Austria, and
his heirs and to the land of Austria, and we have had these diplomas
renewed which were written in the language of the pagans and which we
have converted and translated into the Latin tongue, so that these
diplomas may bring honour and fruitfulness to the aforesaid margrave
Ernest and to his land Austria and to his heirs and successors if this or
a similar diploma is given to him by the divine and Christian emperors.

Moreover, we have observed with the pure desire of our mind that
the aforenamed illustrious prince Ernest, margrave of Austria, is so full
of merit and so worthy, that the holy Roman Empire should be helpful
to him. Since he is situated and established in a border area of Christianity and always promotes and exercises the works of our Lord Jesus
Christ, we give and grant to him as a help and subsidy those bishoprics
with all their goods which are, and have been, called up to now from
ancient times Ivvavia [Salzburg] and Lavreacensis [Lorch] so that the
abovenamed margrave Ernest and his successors ought to be advocates
and lords over them in the land of Austria.

Moreover, we concede and grant that grace to the named Ernest and
his descendants and to the land of Austria that they should be able to
wield the sword of justice and the banner or standard of the royal land
before the empire and before the whole world and people, for he and
his land have ever more frequently sprung forth laudably in the service
of God and appeared gloriously.

And in order that this diploma of donation should remain stable and
unshaken for all time, we have ordered that this deed be signed by our
own hand, as appears below, corroborating by the impression of our
seal.

Sign of Lord Henry IV, king.

I Gebhard, chancellor, have verified it for Archchancellor Liutpold.

Given the fourth day before the nones of October, in the year of our
Lord's Incarnation 1058, the eleventh year of the indiction, in the fifth
year of the ordination of Lord Henry IV, king, in the second year of the
reign; carried out at Dürrenbuch; in the name of God, under favourable
auspices, amen.

46. Henry IV confirms to the archiepiscopal church of Hamburg–
Bremen certain forests and allows the dependants of the church to
sell their property among themselves (Regensburg, 26 October 1063):
DH.IV.115, *MGH Diplomata*, VI, Pts I and II, 151–2.

In the name of the holy and indivisible Trinity. Henry, by God's grace
king.

Since it is supposed to be the duty of the royal office to serve everyone's right, still the rights of the church appear to need our special
attention because if sinning is more tolerable against man than against
God, if no sin is committed, it is all the more reverently favoured by
God than by men.

Indeed, since we wish to imitate the footsteps of the preceding fathers
in augmenting church property and in retaining what has been augmented, we ought to protect as much as we can in our power, in so far
as our young age – striving for manly strength, hoping to advance –
may both attain the glory of giving in the sight of God and not let slip
the grace of confirming gifts among men.

Therefore we wish it to be known to all of the faithful of Christ and
of us, future as well as present, how our beloved and faithful Adalbert,
archbishop of the holy church of Hamburg, approached the serenity of
our clemency, with the request that we confirm and amplify the forest in
Eiterbruch and the other surrounding woods, which our grandfather Conrad of holy memory, emperor augustus, granted to the aforesaid holy
church of Hamburg as a property by perpetual right. Therefore, having
inclined to his request we have joined to the aforementioned forest whatever hunting can be done between the rivers Warmenau, Weser, Ollen, and
Hunte, except Dimusi; we have handed it over to the aforesaid church
as a property under the ban of royal protection, the contradiction of all
present and succeeding parties being removed.

Moreover, we add to the same church a forest on our property situated
in the district of Ammer in the county of Margrave Udo to be retained
perpetually by right of possession.

Moreover, when that same archbishop was making the request, we
conceded to all the male and female serfs of the holy church of Hamburg
that whatever they might acquire outside church property in the way
of lands or dependants, they have free power of inheriting, possessing,
selling, or granting or doing whatever has been determined for them
within the church property so long as it is among the family of the same
church.

Moreover, by royal munificence we confirm freedom and all goods
to the same church that our predecessors since Charles the Great,
whether emperors of the Romans or kings of the Franks, have granted

to the aforenamed church up to our time, and we grant to it the having for all time and the possession by perpetual right through our diploma, including parish churches, tithes, lands cultivated and uncultivated, county revenues, market-places, mintage, toll-houses, and forests with all advantages which in any way can issue or be assessed. The possibility of us and our successors and all mortals great and small disturbing the same has been removed.

And in order that this mandate of our donation, concession, and confirmation remain stable and unshaken for all time, we have ordered this written diploma to be signed by our hand, as is seen below, and to be strengthed by the impression of our seal.

Given the seventh day before the kalends of November in the year of our Lord's Incarnation 1063, the second year of the indiction, in the ninth year of the ordination of Lord King Henry IV, seventh of the reign; carried out at Regensburg; under favourable auspices, in the name of God, amen.

47. Adam of Bremen, The downfall of Archbishop Adalbert (1063–72): from *History of the Archbishops of Hamburg–Bremen* (*Gesta Hammaburgensis ecclesiae pontificum*), trans. Francis J. Tschan, New York, 1959, pp. 143–8, 154–6, 164–79, 184–5.[74]

. . . our metropolitan, striving only for earthly fame and glory, thought it improper to elevate anyone associated with him. Although he drew many needy persons into his following, he regarded it as something of a reflection on himself for either the king or any of the great to favour them. As he put it, 'I myself can reward these people as well or better'. Therefore only a few among his following attained to the heights of the episcopate through his favour. Many, however, if only they were apt of speech or adroit at service,[75] were showered with enormous riches. Hence it was that, to catch at worldly glory, he took into his confidence men of various kinds and of many arts, but chiefly flatterers. He drew

[74] The notes to this selection are all taken from Tschan's translation.

[75] Scholium: Among them was the foreigner Paul, a convert from Judaism to the Christian faith, who had, I do not know whether out of avarice or out of a desire for knowledge, wandered into Greece. When he returned thence, he attached himself to our prelate. He boasted that he was so adept at many arts that he could in the course of three years make learned men of persons ignorant of letters and render fine gold from copper. He easily persuaded the archbishop to believe everything he said, topping all his lies with the statement that he would soon have the public money at Hamburg coined of gold and bezants paid out instead of *denarii*.

their burdensome throng along with him to court and through the diocese
or wherever else he journeyed, protesting that he was not only not put
to inconvenience by the great multitude of travelling companions but
even found it diverting. The money he received from his people or from
friends or also from those who frequented the palace or who were
answerable to his royal majesty, that money, I say, even though it
amounted to a very large sum, he promptly dispersed to disreputable
persons and hypocrites, healers and actors and others of that sort.
Unwisely, to be sure, he thought that the favour of such persons would
either make him the only one accepted at court or give him preferment
before all as the first lord of the palace, and that in this way he might
accomplish what he had in mind about the advancement of his church.
When, moreover, he adopted as his vassals all the honourable and
distinguished men in Saxony and in other parts by giving many of them
what he had and by promising the rest what he did not have, he bought
an empty title to vainglory at great loss to his body and soul. Indeed, the
archbishop's manners, corrupted thus from the beginning, in the course
of time and towards the end became even meaner.

Puffed up, therefore, by the great honours then accorded him at
court and now hardly tolerant of his destitute diocese, he came to
Bremen with a great number of armed men, as was usual, and loaded
new taxes on the people and country.[76] At this time were erected the
strongholds which most of all fired our dukes to wrath.[77] He ceased to
take the interest he previously had in establishing holy congregations.
Marvellous, to be sure, were the man's strength of purpose and his
impatience with idleness, which would never let him tire, though he
was occupied at home and abroad with so many tasks. Although this
wretched bishopric had often before been in distress because of the
enormous costs of his expeditions and his extraordinary activities at a
ravenous court, it was now unmercifully impoverished for the building
of canonries and strongholds. He even planted gardens and vineyards
on arid land. Although he put ineffectual effort into many things he
tried, it was nevertheless his desire to reward magnificently the labour
of all who gratified his wishes. Thus the man's lofty mind contended
against the nature of the land. There was nothing splendid anywhere
which, if he got knowledge of it, he did not also wish to possess himself.
From a long and careful probing into the causes of his distemper, I
have concluded that this knowing man was brought to this weakness
of spirit by the worldly glory which he esteemed too highly. It was that

[76] Probably in the fall of 1063, on his return from the Hungarian expedition.
The following January, Adalbert was at the court again.
[77] Probably in the course of 1063. They were levelled again within the next
two years.

which, when his worldly enterprises prospered, lifted him up to a pride whose quest for glory knew no bounds but which in times of adversity depressed him more than it should and gave free rein to his anger or worry. And so, in what is good, when he was compassionate, as well as in what is bad, when he was in a passion – in both he exceeded measure.

In proof of this statement I present the fact that in his fierce anger he struck some persons with his hand so that blood came, as he did in the case of the provost and others. But in his compassion, which in this case is better called prodigality, he was so profuse that – in his estimation a pound of silver was like a penny – at times he ordered a hundred pounds lavished upon ordinary persons, and more upon those of greater importance. Hence it happened that whenever he was angry, everyone fled him as if he were a lion, but when he was calm he could be caressed like a lamb. Very quickly, also, could either his friends or strangers by praising flatter him out of a rage into cheerfulness and then, as if changed from the man he had been, he started smiling upon his panegyrist. We often saw the opportunity to do this seized by the sycophants who flowed from different parts of the earth into his quarters as into a cesspool. In his judgement princes needed such men in order to obtain the esteem of the world. The moment anyone was better known at court or to the king, he was honoured by being received into the circle of his intimates; the rest he let go away with presents. The ambition to be on intimate terms with him lured even respectable persons and men conspicuous in the priestly order to this most disgraceful business of flattery. Finally, we have seen one who did not know how to flatter, or perhaps would not, shut out of doors as if he were witless or stupid. It was one might say:

Let him who would be just from court depart [Lucan] and

Informer will he be who speaks the truth [Juvenal]. Liars at last prevailed so much among us that they who spoke the truth would not be believed even under oath. With persons of this sort, then, was the bishop's house filled.

In addition to these persons there came daily other mountebanks, parasites, interpreters of dreams, and newsmongers who gave out that the stories they had made up and trumpeted to us for the sake of winning favours had been revealed to them through angels. Already they publicly prophesied that the patriarch of Hamburg – for such he preferred to be called – would soon become pope, that his rivals would be driven from court, even that he would for a long time govern the state by himself, and that he would live to so ripe an age that he would exceed fifty years in the episcopate; finally, that through this man a golden age would come upon the earth. Although, indeed, these predictions had been fabricated by the sycophants and were put forth for the

sake of gain, the bishop for all that thought everything was true, as if it
had been cited down from heaven, and he drew from the Scriptures
that certain signs about things there were to happen were given to men
either in dreams or omens or everyday conversational expressions or
unusual manifestations of the elements. Therefore, he is said to have
formed the habit of being entertained with fables when he went to bed,
with the interpretation of dreams when he awakened, even of taking
the auspices whenever he undertook a journey. At times, also, he gave
up a whole day to sleep and kept vigil during the night, either playing
at dice or sitting at table. When, however, he reclined at table, he commanded everything to be set before his guests in cheerful abundance.
Now and then he himself got up from the repast without having eaten,
but he always had some persons at hand whose duty it was to receive
the guests as they arrived, taking particular care that they did not lack
anything. Hospitality he furthermore extolled as a virtue of the highest
order, which, though it is not without its divine reward, often also wins
the greatest possible applause among men. As he reclined, however, he
took pleasure not so much in food or drink as in witticisms or the histories of kings or the rare sayings of philosophers. But if he was by
himself, which rarely happened, that he might be alone and without
guests or royal legates, then he would waste his leisure with fables and
in reveries, always, however, with continent speech. Rarely did he admit
minstrels whom, however, he considered needful at times in order to
lighten his anxious cares. As for pantomimes, who made a practice of
entertaining the common folk by obscene movements of their bodies, he
drove them absolutely from his presence. Physicians alone ruled with
him. For others access was difficult. Only if a matter of grave importance
required it were some laymen admitted. Hence it also came to pass that
we saw the door of his chamber, which at first had been open to every
stranger and pilgrim, later so closely guarded that legates on important
business and persons of consequence in the world at times had to wait
unwillingly a week before the doors.

At dinner, furthermore, he had a way of criticizing eminent men,
noting foolishness in some, avarice in certain others, reproaching
many, too, for the meanness of their origin. But all he charged with
infidelity, for the reason that they were ungrateful to him, who had
lifted them out of the dunghill, and to the king, whom he himself alone
loved, whose rule he alone evidently protected for the sake of what is
right, not for the sake of his own advantage. His proof of this was that
whereas they, baseborn that they were, were ravishing the goods of
others, he, noble that he was, was lavishing his own; this was the clearest
indication of his nobility. With defamatory invective of this sort he
abused each in turn, finally sparing no one if only he might exalt himself

above all. Briefly, therefore, one must say that for the mere sake of the worldly glory in which he delighted this man forswore all the virtues of which he was in the beginning possessed. Such traits of his and many others of like nature were evinced at the time when his superstition or his boasting or, I might better say, his thoughtlessness bore him much bad repute and the hatred of all mortals, but especially that of the great nobles.

. . . .

I confess that I shudder to reveal everything as it happened, for the reason that these were only the first stages of our sorrows, and grave vengeance followed. From that day, therefore, our good fortune changed to ruin, everything turned out adversely for us and the church, so that everyone hissed our bishop and his followers as they would heretics. But he paid little attention to what all were saying. At the same time, also, he gave up looking after his domestic concerns. He passionately devoted his whole being to the court and [in 1065] rushed headlong after glory for the reason he himself gave: that he was striving for primacy in the control of the affairs of state because he could not bear to see his lord and king fall captive into the hands of those by whom he was being plundered. He had already attained the consulship. With his rivals removed, he alone now held the citadel of state, yet not without the envy that always follows hard upon glory. At this time our metropolitan is also said to have contemplated the renewal of a kind of golden age in his consulate, by extirpating from the city of God all who work iniquity, evidently those especially who had laid hands on the king or had plundered the churches. Since nearly all the bishops and princes of the realm were afflicted with guilty consciences, they were unanimous in their hatred and conspired to destroy him so that the rest should not be imperilled. They all met together therefore, at Tribur [13 January 1066] and, since they had the support of the king's presence, drove our archbishop from court as if he were a magician and seducer. So much was his hand 'against all men, and all men's hands against him' that the end of the controversy reached the point of bloodshed.

Now, when our dukes heard that the archbishop had been expelled from the senatorial order, they were filled with great joy and thought that the time to take vengeance on him was also at hand, to deprive him of his bishopric altogether, declaring, 'Raze it, even to the foundation thereof', and cut him 'off out of the land of the living' [Ps. 136:7]. Thus, many were their plots, many their taunts against the archbishop, who, because he had no safer place, stayed then in Bremen as if he were besieged and hemmed in by a watchful enemy. Although all the duke's vassals derided the pastor and the church and the people and the sanctuary, still Magnus[78] raged more than all the others and boasted that the taming of the rebel Church had been at length reserved for him.

And so to the duke's son Magnus collected a multitude of brigands and undertook to attack the church, not in the manner in which his forebears had operated but by attacking the person of the pastor of the church. Evidently to put an end to the long-drawn-out contest he sought either to maim the bishop in his members or utterly to destroy him. The latter, nevertheless, did not lack craft in protecting himself, but he got absolutely no aid from his vassals. As he was at that time hard pressed by Duke Magnus, the archbishop secretly fled by night to Goslar and stayed there half a year in the security of his estate at Lochtum. His stronghold and revenues were plundered by the enemy. Caught in this distressful noose, the archbishop concluded what was an ignominious but necessary alliance with his oppressor, thus turning his enemy into his vassal. The archbishop presented him in benefice with over a thousand hides of church lands – on the condition, to be sure, that Magnus was without all subterfuge to revindicate and defend the rights of the Church to the counties of Frisia, of which Bernhard [Count of Werl] retained one and Egbert [Count of Brunswick and margrave of Meissen] another against the bishop's will. Thus, in fine, was the bishopric of Bremen divided into three parts. Since Udo held one part and Magnus another, barely a third remained to the archbishop. For all that, he later apportioned this third part among Eberhard[79] and other sycophants of the king, keeping almost nothing for himself. The episcopal estates and the tithes of the churches,[80] from which the clergy, the widows, and the needy ought to have been supported, all now fell to the use of laymen, so that to this day courtesans and brigands live luxuriously on the goods of the church, the while holding the bishop and all the ministers of the altar in derision. From these great gifts, as can today be seen, this alone accrued to the archbishop: Udo and Magnus refrained from expelling him from his bishopric; the others, indeed, gave him nothing by way of service except the empty title of 'lord'.

.   .   .   .

The archbishop stayed at Bremen[81] at this time and, since he had nothing left, lived off the plundering of the poor and the property of the

[78] The son of Ordulf [Billung], who did not become duke [of Saxony] until after his father died, 28 March 1072.

[79] Probably count of Nellenburg.

[80] Scholium: A tithe of all the bishop's living and service was, according to law, daily rendered to his chaplain for the support of the infirm and the needy and for the care of pilgrims. But the chaplain fraudulently kept back much for his own use, reserving nothing for the poor.

[81] This chapter covers the years 1066–9.

holy congregations. A servant of his, a certain Suidger, administered the principal provostship of the bishopric. When, after the property of the brethren had been squandered, this man was deposed for the murder of a deacon and, on being again restored, had nothing with which to render service to the brethren and his lord, he fled the archbishop's wrath, smitten with fear. And so the provostship, returned into the bishop's power, was then deplorably torn to pieces by vicars who sought the 'things that are their own' [Phil. 12:42; I Cor. 13:5]. The several communities fared in like manner. While the bishop was angry with the provosts, they raged among the people and dissipated all the property of the church. From this destruction escaped only the xenodochium [an asylum for strangers, the poor, and the sick] which, founded by Saint Ansgar and afterwards cared for by succeeding fathers, remained whole and entire until the last days of the Lord Adalbert. But then, indeed, a certain episcopal vicar of our own, as it were a 'faithful and wise steward' [Luke 12:42], was appointed to watch over the alms of the poor. I dare not say what a sin it is to defraud the poor of their substance, for some canons call it a sacrilege, others murder. This only is it allowable to say with the good leave of all the brethren: that in all seven years which the archbishop still lived, absolutely no alms were dispensed from that famous and opulent hospital of the church of Bremen. And this seemed the more lamentable and inhuman because a period of famine ensued and many poor people were found dead everywhere in the streets. While our pastor was so intent upon the court, his most holy vicars ravaged the Lord's sheepfold, going through the bishopric like wolves and sparing therein only places in which they found nothing to carry away.

At that time one might see the deplorable tragedy at Bremen in the distress of the citizens and the knights and the storekeepers, and, what was more serious, likewise in that of the clergy and of the nuns. To the guilty, indeed, misfortune evidently came with justice, that they might be rebuked, but to others not so. In the first place, then, if a rich man was reputed innocent, he was ordered to do something nearly impossible to make him guilty. If he ignored the order, or stoutly declared compliance with it to be impossible, he was immediately stripped of all his belongings. If he presumed to murmur, he was thrown into chains. One beheld some plied with the lash, many put in prison, some driven from their homes, very many sent away into exile. And, as it happened when Sulla was victorious in the civil war, one of the mighty, often without the archbishop's knowledge, condemned another whom he regarded as his enemy for a private grudge, as if on the archbishop's order. Then, indeed, as if no sex or class should be immune from such wantonness, we also beheld even frail women stripped of their gold and garments, and the perpetrators of the infamous spoliation live with priests and

P

bishops. Again, we learned that of those who were robbed of their property or who were too severely pressed by the quaestor, some were so much affected with anguish that they lost their minds; and some, formerly rich people, went begging from door to door. Although this quest for plunder reached all who were subject to the bishop, it also did not pass by the merchants who resorted to Bremen from every part of the world with the usual wares of trade. The execrable imposts levied by the episcopal vicars compelled them all to leave, often without anything. And so it is plain why to this day the city lacks citizens and the market merchandise, especially since if anything of ours remained untouched it was altogether consumed by the duke's servants. Although all these outrages had often been perpetrated before even while the archbishop was present, they became intolerable when he was away and after the day of his expulsion.

At the expense of much effort and the lavishing of many gifts to no purpose, the metropolitan at length accomplished his wish in being restored to his former place at court after he had been expelled for a period of three years [1069-71]. Soon also, as his affairs prospered, he attained the height of power, that is the regency, after he had been seven times consul. On gaining the position of dignity in which he could display the greatness of his soul, he resolved that now he must walk circumspectly with respect to the princes, in order not to offend them as he had before. On this account he desired first to be reconciled with the bishop of Cologne, then with the others against whom he had sinned – or, rather, who plainly had sinned against him. After these hindrances had been removed, he was not idle in behalf of his church, for the exaltation of which he seemed to be as wanton in the lavish expenditure of money as in his intrigues at court. At this time he acquired Plisna, Duisberg, Groningen, and Sinzig. Wildeshausen, a provostship in the vicinity of Bremen, he almost had in his hands; also Harsfeld, very near Hamburg. Furthermore he also designed, if he had lived longer, to subject the bishopric of Verden to our metropolis. Finally, he now worked openly to establish a patriarchate at Hamburg, and to do many other great and incredible things about which more than enough has been said above.

The prelate's renown was enhanced by the fact that in the year in which he was consul [1071] that famous conference of Caesar with the king of the Danes was held at Lüneburg to embarrass the duke. Military measures against the Saxons were there agreed upon under cover of an alliance. That same year the first conspiracy formed against the king was suppressed. In consequence of this insurrection Duke Otto and Magnus,[82] after devastating Saxony for a year, at length

[82] Doubtless Otto of Nordheim and Magnus of Saxony.

surrendered themselves into the king's power on the advice of the prelate. The king gave Otto's duchy to Guelf; our archbishop recovered the property of the church that Magnus previously held.

Placed thus at the very pinnacle of glory, he would still not withdraw from the business of the state though he was often afflicted with bodily ills. From the Rhine to the Danube and thence back into Saxony he would go with the king,[83] carried on a litter. Some say it had been agreed, on the solemn promise of the king, that all the desires of the archbishop's soul in respect of Lorsch and Corvey and other matters were to be confirmed for him at Utrecht on the Rhine when the princes met there the following Easter. Others assert that the archbishop was led on by crafty delays on the part of the king to accept in donation of his church twice as much, wheresoever in the realm he wished, on condition, namely, that he would forego Lorsch. But he began to be obstinate, replying that he would have nothing else. In the end he sank, his efforts frustrated, losing both his life and Lorsch, along with the rest of the property of the church.

Of his imminent death there were very many signs and forebodings, so dreadful and unusual that they terrified us and, apparently, the bishop himself; so striking and plain were they that anyone who considered at all closely his stormy ways and uncertain health would say that doubtless the end was at hand. Although, indeed, the man's behaviour had always been different from the deportment of ordinary mortals, towards the end – especially after the day of his expulsion and after the devastation of his diocese, which attended it – his ways seemed altogether inhuman and intolerable and alien to himself. After that day, I say, he was more perturbed by shame, indignation, and grief than is seemly for a wise man, because he found no way of recovering the property of the church. I dare not say he was insane from overmuch anxiety about his multifarious difficulties, but his mind was affected. At a distance, some of the things he did from this time on could indicate a wandering mind or foolishness; in my opinion, 'the mad Orestes himself would swear' they 'were the signs of madness' [Persius *Satires* III. 118]. For example, there is the fact to which we have referred, that he spent whole nights awake and whole days asleep. Moreover, he turned away from hearing the truth to fables and dreams; likewise, he slighted the alms for the poor and distributed everything he could get among the rich, particularly among sycophants; and again, there is the fact that there was nothing left because, after the property of the church had been

[83] Henry IV, accompanied by Adalbert, spent Christmas, 1071, at Worms on the Rhine and moved thence to Regensburg on the Danube by way of Lorsch. From there they went to Utrecht by way of Goslar in Saxony for the conference held at Easter 1072.

squandered, he lived off the plunder of the wretched and the lawful income of the holy congregations. Again, in making a tenancy of a provostship and a provostship of a hospital he was not unlike one 'who tears down in order to build and exchanges the square with the round' [Horace *Epistles* I. i. 100]; again, provoked to anger more easily than was usual, he struck some with his hand until blood came; and in exasperating many with abusive words, he dishonoured himself not less than them. Towards the end he was so entirely changed from his own self and so impaired of his former virtue that none of his associates, nor he himself, could fully make out what he wished or did not wish. Still, his eloquence was to the very end such that in hearing him speak one would be very quickly persuaded that everything he did was wholly reasonable and well judged.

While reports of this sinister change, or aberration, and of the very evident degeneration of this distinguished man were being spread into every country of the world on the wings of his fame, his noted brother, namely, the count palatine Frederick, came, as I recall, as far as Lesum to caution him. But since his admonitions about matters that touched the bishop's honour or welfare proved vain, the count went away sad, accusing Notebald[84] and his sort of circumventing the illustrious man with their trickeries and of disordering his mind by their counsels. These were his words, but we saw the archbishop himself at that time sink so low in repute that he was said to have given himself up to the magic arts. I call to witness Jesus and His Angels and all His saints that the man was free and guiltless of this crime, especially since he himself often declared that magicians and fortune tellers and men of that sort must be punished with death. But because it is written, 'With the holy, thou wilt be holy; with the perverse thou wilt be perverted',[85] I am of the opinion that at first he lapsed from the accepted state of rectitude and then broke down altogether, either because of the malice of those who he believed were true to him or because of the molestation of the enemies who were assailing his church. Broken at length by the violence of his disordered ways and battered at the same time by reverses in his outer fortunes, he began to weaken also in body like a ship buffeted by the seas. And while he was trying to recover his health with the aid of physicians, his infirmity soon became so much more serious from his repeated trials of medicaments that, as he lay in a coma at the point of death, hope was given up. At that time, too [1069], he suffered a severe fall from his horse as he was on his way to court.[86] With

[84] Scholium: Notebald was a magician, a flatterer, and a most brazen liar.

[85] II Kings 22:26–7.

[86] Scholium: From that time he abstained from the reheated salt baths which he had been used to taking almost daily and from many other practices which he noticed were objectionable to the people.

Hezekiah, then, he wept with much weeping, promising God amend-
ment of his life. Oh, the wonted clemency of Christ! He forthwith
recovered. In the three whole years during which he still lived many, but
not all, the promises he had made were fulfilled.

In those days there came up a certain woman who had the power of
divination. She publicly declared to all the people that the archbishop
would pass away suddenly within two years unless, indeed, he was
converted. Physicians attested that statement. But there were with the
bishop others, false prophets, who made promises of a far different
kind, and in them he had greater faith. They, in truth, foretold that he
would live so long as to make all his enemies his footstool, and that this
bodily infirmity would then be followed by perfectly good health and
much success in his affairs. The most intimate of all was Notebald who
had often predicted for the archbishop many things that had turned out
true, but who from the first word to the last deceived his believer. At
that time[87] we saw in Bremen crosses sweating tears; we saw hogs and
dogs desecrating the church so boldly that they could with difficulty be
driven from the very foot of the altar. We saw wolves howling in packs
in the suburbs of our city, vying with horned owls in horrific contest.
And although the bishop eagerly heeded dreams, everyone pointed in
vain to these signs as referring to him. The dead never spoke so intimately with the living. Everything forboded the bishop's death. Now,
the same year in which the metropolitan died Hamburg was burned and
twice pillaged. From that time on the victorious pagans had either been
killed or led into captivity, the province was reduced to a wilderness, so
that you might say peace also was taken from the land at the good
shepherd's end. Fourteen days before his death [c. 2 March 1072] he
lay down at Goslar and, as was his way, would take neither potions nor
bleedings. For that reason, he was seized with a very severe spell of
dysentery and worn down to the very bones. Alas, he still was entirely
unmindful of his own salvation! He carried on the business of the state
to his very dying hour. Werinhar, the archbishop of Magdeburg, and
other brethren were at hand, asking to be admitted. How they had
offended him I do not know. He ordered his doors closed to them on
the plea that he was unfit to be seen by anyone on account of the un-
cleanness of his sickness. Visiting the sick man was conceded only to the
king whom he loved devotedly to the very end. Reminding him, therefore, of his fidelity and long service, the archbishop with much sighing
commended his church and the property of the church to him.

Eventually the fateful day arrived, marked by Egyptian darkness,[88]

[87] In 1072, after Adalbert's death. Cf. Vergil *Aeneid* I.402, IV.462, XI.243,
XII.862; *Georgics* I.486. The winter of 1071–2 was severe.

[88] Since there was no eclipse on 16 March 1072, and since no other natural

on which the great prelate Adalbert was touched by the imminent call of bitter death. Even he sensed that the dissolution of his body was at hand, as much because of his want of strength as by his premonition of the indications described. But as the physicians hesitated to make the truth known[89] and only Notebald gave assurance of life, the knowing man lay uncertain and forgetful of self between the hope of living and the dread of dying. Alas, he did not take notice that 'The day of the Lord shall so come, as a thief in the night', and 'When they shall say, peace and security; then shall sudden destruction come' [I Thess. 5:2–3], and other passages in which the Gospels enjoin us to watch, as they say 'You know not the day nor the hour' [Matt. 25:13]. In this connection I recall the observation of a certain holy man, that I cannot without tears adapt to this place. 'Now', he said, 'the sinner is stricken, now he is forced to depart unrepentant so that dying he forgets himself, who while he lived had forgotten God.' In this manner did the glorious metropolitan, still hopeful of the present life, lie alone in his agony and breathe forth his spirit on the sixth ferial day, at noon [Friday, 16 March 1072], as his friends sat down to eat, and with a moan

> Life passed indignant to the shades below
> [Vergil, *Aeneid* XI.831, XII.952].

Alas, that I might write better things about so famous a man who loved even me and was so illustrious in his life. But I am afraid, because it is written, 'Woe to you that call evil good'; also let him perish 'that put darkness for light'.[90] It seems to me hazardous for us to have to flatter either in writing or in speech a man who was undone by adulation while he lived. Nevertheless, some assert that a few spectators were at hand as he lay thus alone. In their presence he did bitter penance in his last hour for all the vexation he had caused by his deeds. He wept and wailed that he had misspent his days and then at last understood how petty, in reality how miserable, is the glory of our dust, 'For all flesh is as grass; and all the glory thereof as the flower of grass' [I Peter 1:24].

Oh, how false is the good fortune of mortal life! How much to be

phenomenon is recorded, the expression must refer to the darkness of the ninth plague of Egypt. Exod. 10:21–2.

[89] Scholium: Adamatus, a physician of Salernitan origin, is said to have informed the archbishop three days in advance that the end of his death was very near at hand. But he disregarded this warning and gave heed only to Notebald, because the latter promised him that the hour for his turning point would soon come.

[90] Scholium: As one reads in the book of Esther: 'While with crafty fraud they deceive the ears of princes that are well meaning and judge of others by their own nature. Now, this is proved both from ancient histories and by things which are done daily, how the good designs of kings are depraved by the evil suggestions of certain men.'

shunned the courting of honours! Of what avail to you now, O venerable father Adalbert, are the things you always prized, the glory of the world, multitudes of people, exalted nobility? Forsooth, you lie alone in your high palace, abandoned by all your followers. Where now are the physicians, the sycophants, and the tricksters who used to concur with you in the desires of your heart, who swore you would recover from this sickness, who reckoned you would live to a ripe old age? As I see, they were all your companions at table and did not abide in the day of distress. There are left only the needy and the pilgrims, the widows and the orphans, and all the oppressed to confess that they have been desolated by your death. With them we can also truthfully affirm that no one henceforth will compare with you in benignity and generosity towards pilgrims, in the defence of the holy churches, and in reverence for all the clergy, or in withstanding so much the plundering of evildoers of might and the presumptions of the proud; and, finally, that no one may be found readier with all manner of counsel in the wise disposition of divine and human affairs. If, indeed, anything appears reprehensible in your ways, that is due to the wickedness of those in whom you trusted more than was right or to those whose enmity you bore for the sake of the truth. For by their plottings they perverted your laudable character, making of a good nature one that was bad. It behoves us, therefore, to pray the most merciful Lord to indulge you 'according to the multitude of His mercies' and to give you [a] place in eternal bliss through his merits of all His saints to whose patronage you always devoutly commended yourself.

Our most illustrious metropolitan Adalbert died on the seventeenth day before the kalends of April in the tenth indiction. That was the year of our Lord Jesus Christ one thousand and seventy-two, the eleventh of Pope Alexander, the seventeenth of King Henry the Fourth [actually the sixteenth].[91] Except for books and relics of saints and sacred vestments, almost nothing was found in the man's treasure chest. Nevertheless, the king received all these effects and he took also the hand of Saint James the apostle along with the documents of the church. This hand the bishop had been given by a bishop Vitalis of the Venetians while he was in Italy.[92]

Midst the great bewilderment of the whole realm the archbishop's body was borne from Goslar to Bremen, and at length on the tenth day, that is, the feast of the Annunciation of the Blessed Mary [25 March],

[91] Scholium: In this year also, in which he departed this life, when he went out for the last time and thereafter did not return, he held a chapter at Bremen with the brethren, at which he deposed the deacon Liudger for a murder of which he stood accused. And on this occasion he delivered a sermon about chastity, at the end of which he made terrible threats.

[92] Vitalis Orseolo, bishop of Torcello (1037?-48).

in the presence of a seemly gathering of people, it was placed in a sepulchre in the middle of the choir of the new basilica that he himself had built. Nevertheless, there are those who affirm that he had previously often asked to be entombed in the metropolitan city of Hamburg which, like his predecessors, he had with all affection always esteemed deserving of honour. For while he still lived he would often spend the whole summer there and with great pomp celebrate the principal feasts. There, furthermore, he would at the proper times very often make promotions in the ecclesiastical ranks with solemn reverence throughout. There he was in the habit of appointing the time and place at which our dukes of the neighbouring Slavic peoples or other legates from the arctic nations could meet him. Such esteem had he for the ruined city and such love for the exhausted mother that he said in her was fulfilled the prophecy which runs: 'Rejoice thou barren that bearest not . . . for many more are the children of the desolate, more than of her that hath a husband' [Gal. 4:27].

They say that he took to his bed, from which he was unable to rise, only three days before he died. So resolute of will was the man that he never would have anyone help him, never emitted a moan, when he was in a state of the uttermost bodily prostration. But as he lay at the point of death and felt that the hour of his summons was at hand, he repeated with frequent sighs: 'Woe is me, unfruitful and miserable one who went through so much wealth for nothing. I could have been blessed indeed if I had distributed to the poor what to my sorrow I parted with for the sake of earthly glory. However, I now call Him to witness, whose eye considers the most hidden parts, that the purpose of my heart was wholly the exaltation of my church. Although she may appear to have been very much reduced because of my guilty demands or the overpowering hatred of my enemies, still I give thanks that more than two thousand manors have accrued to the church from my inheritance or through my efforts.' From this confession of the sage man one can discern that if in some respects he sinned as a man, he repented many times of his mistakes as a good man.

Of this characteristic I cite as one instance that in the beginning of his career, when he was a very proud man, he antagonized many people because of his arrogance. For this reason, too, and because he gloried in his noble rank, he made a remark which it were better he had not uttered; namely, that all the bishops who had presided before him had been obscure and ignoble persons, that he alone stood out by right of his family and wealth, worthy, then, to have been chosen for a greater see or for the apostolic chair itself. As he boasted more than once to this effect, he is said to have been terrified by an ominous vision. Because of its significance and because we gained knowledge of it from a reliable source, I do not forbear adding it here. And so in the dead of night he saw himself transported into the choir of the church where Mass was to be celebrated. His fourteen predecessors [correctly, fifteen] stood in their places in the order of succession, so that the last, the one who had preceded him, Alebrand, carried out the rite that usage had fixed for Masses. When the Gospel had been read and the priest of God turned about to receive the oblations of the offerers, he came to the lord Adalbert, who stood in the last place of the choir. Looking upon Adalbert then with earnest eyes, he rejected his oblation with the words, 'You, a noble and distinguished man, can have no part with the lowly.' And with these words he withdrew. From that hour Adalbert was truly sorry for the remarks he had inconsiderately made, held all his predecessors in extraordinary reverence, and with many a sigh he made it known that he was not worthy of the company of holy men. Hence also he soon ordained that the brethren and poor be given the amplest meals from the income of the Bramstedt estate on the anniversary day of each of his predecessors – something it had previously not at all been customary for any bishop to do.

He left behind also many other signs of his repentance and conversion, among them the noteworthy one that, after the devastation of his church and the day of his expulsion, although he survived it for five years, he never used the baths, never was cheerful of countenance, rarely showed himself in public or at a banquet unless he went to court or unless a feast day required it. Oh, how often did we see that face drawn by sorrow whenever he thought of the devastation of the church or when he saw the devastators in person! On the feast day of the Lord's nativity Duke Magnus[93] was present and a great multitude of guests also was assembled. When the feast was over, the happy company, as was the custom, voiced its applause. The archbishop, however, was not a little displeased at this. Nodding, therefore, to our brethren who were also present, he instructed the cantor to intone the antiphon: 'Sing ye to us a hymn.'[94] And when the laymen again broke into applause, he had the clergy begin: 'We looked for peace, and it did not come.' But when they howled in their cups still a third time, he was much irritated, ordered the table cleared, and in a loud voice announced, 'Turn again our captivity, O Lord,' and the choir responded, 'as a stream in the south.' Leading the way into the chapel, with us following behind, he wept bitterly. 'I shall not cease weeping', he said, 'until "the just judge, strong and patient", shall liberate my, or rather His, Church

[93] On a Christmas after Adalbert's fall and before his restoration, 1066–9; but Magnus was then not yet duke. Adam doubtless was present.
[94] Ps. 136:3. The chants that follow must have been from the psalms Adam said Adalbert had selected.

which He beholds, with its pastor despised, torn pitifully by wolves.'
Then was fulfilled the yearning of those who said: 'Let us possess the
sanctuary of God for an inheritance'; and, 'Let us abolish all the festival
days of God from the land'; and, 'Let us destroy them, so that they be
not a nation: and let the name of Israel be remembered no more'. 'Arise,
why sleepest thou, O Lord?' and, 'Cast us not off to the end', because
'the pride of them that hate thee ascendeth continually'. 'Have mercy
on us, O Lord . . . for we are greatly filled with contempt.' 'Because they
have persecuted him whom Thou hast smitten; and they have added to
the grief of my wounds.' These and other laments of compunction we
often heard from him, even that he many times longed to become a
monk. Sometimes, also, he wished he might merit dying in the ministry
of his legateship either in Slavia or in Sweden or in remotest Iceland.
Often, too, he was so willed that without hesitation he fain would even
have been beheaded in the confession of Christ for the sake of the truth.
Still, God who knows all the hidden things comprehends whether he was
better in His sight than he appeared before the eyes of men. 'For man
seeth those things that appear, but the Lord beholdeth the heart' [I
Kings 16:7].

.   .   .   .

The archbishop was actuated by the same complaisant zeal toward the
legates of the Roman See, whose patronage and companionship he
cultivated to the highest degree of friendship. At the same time he prided
himself on having only two masters, that is, the pope and the king, to
whose dominion all the powers of the world and of the Church of right
were subject, and he truly regarded these two with fear and honour.
This was evident in the fidelity which the man observed so completely
towards each that he put nothing above the apostolic authority, contended that the ancient and honourable prerogatives of the Apostolic
See must be preserved in their entirety, and held that its legates were to
be received with the greatest respect. Of the regard in which he held the
imperial majesty his bishopric gives proof. On this account especially
was he destroyed, that neither the threats nor the blandishments of
the princes could swerve him from his fidelity towards the king.
The royal power, however, is an object of fear for the wicked. Hence it
is also that many plots used to be hatched in the kingdom. With these,
nevertheless, he would not even by word have anything to do. For his
fidelity he was indeed rewarded by the king in being appointed chief
steward in the palace. By royal gift he gained much property for the
church at Bremen, about which we have given a more detailed account
above. By the pope, indeed, he was rewarded with the stately privilege
of having the apostolic lord confer his own plenary rights upon him and

his successors, to such an extent that he might, frequently against the will of the kings, establish bishoprics throughout the whole north in places that seemed suitable and consecrate as bishops those men from his own chapel whom he wished elected.

48. Henry releases the citizens of Worms from the customs due at six toll stations (falsified;[95] Worms, 18 January 1074): DH.IV.267 *MGH Diplomata*, VI, Pts 1–2, 341–3.[96]

In the name of the holy and indivisible Trinity. Henry, by God's grace king.

It is fitting for the royal power and piety to respond to the service of all men with appropriate benefices, so that those who show themselves more prompt in devoted service may rejoice to be judged more eminent and more worthy too of remuneration for service.

We have judged the inhabitants of the city of Worms worthy of not the least but the greatest special reward, indeed worthier than all the citizens of any other city since we have learned that they were loyal to us with especially great fidelity in the worst turmoil of the kingdom and since we did not bring them to this extraordinary fidelity by our speech or written words or by the words of our legate. We say it is extraordinary because they alone were loyal to us, rushing as if to death against the general will, while all the princes of the realm were raging against us, having abandoned the ties of fealty. For when each city was closed as if precisely at our arrival while sentinels were stationed in shifts and while they encircled the cities to be protected by fire and sword night and day, Worms alone facilitated our arrival with support of arms by the general approval of all her citizens.

Therefore let those who were the advance guard in devotion to service be the first to receive the rewards of service. Let those who excelled all in preserving the bond of fealty be an example to everyone of the response due for service. Let the inhabitants of all cities rejoice

[95] The word used to describe this diploma by the *MGH* editor is *verunechtet*. 'As opposed to patent forgery [*Fälschung*], falsification [*Verunechtung*] of a document signifies a partial alteration of the original text of the document – sometimes deliberate, sometimes not (that is, the result of faulty scribal transmission) – brought about by the omission, change, or addition of individual words or characters.' See Renate Klauser and Otto Meyer, *Clavis mediaevalis*, Wiesbaden, 1962, p. 262.

[96] This diploma is today guarded in the city archive of Worms 'as if it were the crown jewels'. See Rudolf Pörtner, *Das Römerreich der Deutschen*, Düsseldorf, 1967, p. 347.

in the hope of royal munificence, which the citizens of Worms have obtained as a result of this event. May all learn to keep faith with the king by imitating those who proved their good will in the service of the king. To be sure, this service can be expressed with few words, but in considering what they did I do not count it light but worthy of gratitude and honour.

Since indeed the ⟨Jews and other citizens⟩ of Worms[97] have had to pay a toll, which is called *zol* in the Teutonic language and which is everywhere consigned to the royal power – to wit, when they travel by Frankfurt, Boppard, Hammerstein, Dortmund, Goslar, and Enger – we grant to the citizens of Worms that they no longer must pay the toll, and we have corroborated it in the presence of our princes, namely, Liemar, metropolitan of Hamburg, Eberhard of Naumburg, Bishop Dietrich of Werden, Bishop Herman of Bamberg, Bishop Burchard of Basel, and in the presence of our other faithful of Christ.

We ask and we obligate for the desired stability of their deed that none of our successors – kings or emperors – be willing to invalidate this charter remitting the aforesaid toll; whoever invalidates us in this (God forbid) may know that he is discredited and whatever he has done.

Therefore we have left this document of bestowal for every generation, future as well as present, which we have ordered to be drawn up and subscribed with our hand, as is seen below on this diploma, and marked with the impression of our seal.

Sign of Lord King Henry IV, humble and most invincible.

I Adalbero, chancellor, have verified it for Archchancellor Siegfried.

Given the fifteenth day before the kalends of February in the year of our Lord's Incarnation 1073 [*sic*], the twelfth year of the indiction, in the eighteenth year of the ordination of Lord King Henry IV, the seventeenth of the reign; carried out at Worms: under favourable auspices, in the name of God, AMEN [in Greek capitals].

49. Anon., The early years of Henry IV, from *The Life of Henry IV (Vita Heinrici IV imperatoris)*, from *Imperial Lives and Letters of the Eleventh Century*, trans. Theodor E. Mommsen and Karl F. Morrison, pp. 105–9.

When Emperor Henry whom we discuss here, still a boy, succeeded in

---

[97] The words in brackets ⟨*Iudei et coeteri*⟩ were added at the beginning of the thirteenth century, according to the editor of the diploma. This falsification was possible because there was a gap left after the list of towns that was probably intended to accommodate other town names. Though the forger attempted to

the kingship his father, the most glorious Emperor Henry III (for while he was still a boy his father yielded to nature), war did not disturb the peace; trumpet calls did not break the quiet; rapine was not rampant; fidelity did not speak falsely – since the kingdom yet held to its former state. Justice was still full of its own vigour; power was still full of its own right. Agnes, the most serene empress, a woman of manly disposition, sustained greatly this happy state of the kingdom, she who together with her son with equal right governed the commonwealth. But since immature age inspires too little fear, and while awe languishes, audacity increases, the boyish years of the king excited in many the spirit of crime. Therefore, everyone strove to become equal to the one greater than him, or even greater, and the might of many increased through crime; nor was there any fear of the law, which had little authority under the young boy-king.

And so that they could do everything with more license, they first robbed of her child the mother whose mature wisdom and grave habits they feared, pleading that it was dishonourable for the kingdom to be administered by a woman (although one may read of many queens who administered kingdoms with manly wisdom). But after the boy-king, once drawn away from the bosom of his mother, came into the hands of the princes to be raised, whatever they prescribed for him to do, he did like the boy he was. Whomever they wished, he exalted; whomever they wished, he set down; so that they may rightly be said not to have ministered to their king so much as to have given orders to him. When they dealt with the affairs of the kingdom, they took counsel not so much for the affairs of the kingdom as for their own; and in everything they did, it was their primary concern to put their own advantage above everything else.

This was certainly the greatest perfidy, that they left to his own devices in his boyish acts him who ought to have been kept, so to speak, under seal, in order thus to elicit from him what they strove to obtain.

But when he passed into that measure of age and mind in which he could discern what was honourable, what shameful, what useful, and what was not, he reconsidered what he had done while led by the suggestion of the princes and condemned many things which he had done. And, having become his own judge, he changed those of his acts which were to be changed. He also prohibited wars, violence, and rapine; he strove to recall peace and justice, which had been expelled, to restore neglected laws, and to check the license of crime. Those accustomed to

copy the style of the chancery notary, his handiwork can be spotted because he used darker ink and left too much space between words. Another clue is that the Jews are not mentioned in the dispositive part of the charter: 'we have granted to the citizens of Worms' (Uvormatiensibus . . . remisimus).

crime whom he could not coerce by edict, he corrected, more mildly, indeed, than the wrong demanded by the stricture of the law and the legal prerogative of the Curia. Those men called this not justice, but injury; and they who had cast law aside disdained to be bound by law, just as they who were racing through every impiety, disdained to suffer the reins, and they gave their attention to plans by which they might either kill him or deprive him of his office, not remembering that they owed peace to their citizens, justice to the kingdom, fidelity to the king.

Therefore the Saxons, a hard people, harsh in wars, as rashly inclined to arms as bold, making for themselves a claim to pre-eminent acclamation by having undertaken the furious raid, suddenly rushed upon the king with arms. The king considered it dangerous to engage in conflict with a few against innumerable armed men and escaped with difficulty; he preferred life to praise, safety to the changes of fortune. When the Saxons thus saw that their undertaking had not answered to their desires – O inhuman mind, O shameful vengeance! – they disinterred the bones of the son of the king[98] (for he had not yet been made emperor). The king, aroused by these two most heavy wrongs, led an army against that people, fought, and was victorious. He was victorious, I say, over the armed host set up against him, not against the stubborn resistance which had been built up. For although he conquered those gathered in battle, put the conquered to flight, followed hard on the fugitives; although he laid waste their goods, destroyed their fortifications, and did everything which is to the victor's taste – for all that, they could not be forced to surrender. After he had departed thence and had, in a short time, restrengthened his army, he moved against them a second time. Since they mistrusted their own forces, most gravely shaken as they were in the earlier war, they decided on what was the next best thing to safety – to give themselves up. They hoped that the king would be content with surrender alone and would grant his pardon easily. But the outcome was far different from what they had hoped. For the king sent those who had been sentenced to exile into other lands where, under close confinement, they awaited the edict of release.

From this exile, some slipped away in flight; others were released by their guards through bribery. When they had returned to their country and their homes, they bound themselves together in a new conspiracy, pledging that they were ready to die before being cast down again in surrender. But their conspiracy became even stronger, for some Lombards, Franks, Bavarians, and Swabians adhered to them after exchanging the faithful assurance that they would batter the king with wars on every hand.

[98] At the Harzburg, 1074. The body of Henry's brother, Conrad, also buried at the Harzburg, was likewise disinterred [Morrison's note].

They saw, however, that the king would be touched by wars, not cast down; vexed, not conquered; indeed, his strength until that time was unassailable. In order to extenuate his resources, they fabricated and wrote up criminal charges against him mixing true things with false – the worst and most foul which hate and spiteful malice could devise and which, if I were to put them down, would make me ill in writing and you, in reading them. Thus they accused him before the Roman pontiff, Gregory, saying that it was not seemly that so profligate a man, known more by crime than by title, should rule, most of all since Rome had not conferred the regal dignity upon him; that it was necessary that her right in setting up kings be returned to Rome; and that the pope and Rome, according to the counsel of the princes, should provide a king whose life and wisdom would be congruent with so great an honour.

The pope, deluded by this act of stealth and, at the same time, urged on by the honour of creating a king, which they had thrust upon him in a spirit of deception, bound the king with the ban and commanded the bishops and the other princes of the kingdom to withdraw themselves from communion with the excommunicated king: [He announced] that he would go very soon into the German regions, where one might deal with ecclesiastical affairs, and most especially with the problems of the kingship. Nay, he even added this: he absolved all who had vowed fealty to the king of their oath, so that this absolution might force against him those whom the obligation of fealty held. This deed displeased many – if one may be displeased with what the pope does – and they asserted that what had been done was done as ineffectually as illicitly. But I should not dare to present their assertions, lest I seem to rebut with them the act of the pope.

Soon most of the bishops, those whom love as much as those whom fear had drawn to the side of the king, fearing for their office, withdrew their assistance from him. This also the greater part of the great nobles did. Then, indeed, seeing that his cause was set in the narrows, the king conceived a plan as secret as astute and seized upon a sudden and unexpected journey to meet the pope. And with one deed he did two – namely, he both received the loosing of the ban and cut off at mid-point a conference of the pope with his adversaries which he had suspected. As for the criminal charges placed upon him, he answered little, since he averred that it was not for him to answer the accusation of his enemies, even though it were true.

What did it profit you to have done this, to the end that he might be bound with the ban, when loosed from the ban he is free to use mightily his might ? What did it profit you to have accused him with fabricated crimes, when he should have scattered your accusation with easy response, as the wind [scatters] the dust ? Nay more, what madness armed you against your king and the ruler of the world? Your conspiratorial malignity profited nothing, accomplished nothing.

Whom the hand of God had established in kingship, yours could not cast down. Where was the fidelity which you vowed to him? Wherefore were you forgetful of the benefices which he conferred upon you with regal liberality? Use sane counsel, not rage, to the purpose that you repent you of the undertaking, lest perchance coming upon you more strongly, he may conquer you and crush you with his feet, and lest that vengeance rage which may show to future ages what the royal hand can do. At least, you, O bishops, see 'lest ye perish from the just way'; see lest you transgress your promises of fidelity. Otherwise, you yourselves know what will overtake you.

50. Helmold of Bosau, The public penance of Henry IV, from *The Chronicle of the Slavs (Chronica Slavorum)*, trans. Francis Joseph Tschan, New York, 1935, pp. 107–9.

A few days later the Saxon princes were released from captivity, contrary to the wish of the king. They returned to their own homes but from that time on never trusted the promises of the king.[99] The princes of the Saxons also sent an account of what had been happening to the Apostolic See, complaining to the most reverend Pope Gregory that the king contemned the divine law and deprived the churches of God of all liberty of canonical election by appointing their bishops and forcibly seating the bishops whom he chose; moreover, that after the manner of the Nicolaitans[100] he had made a public prostitute of his wife, subjecting her by force to the lust of other men, and that he had done many other things which seemed improper and hard to understand. Much moved by zeal for justice, the pope consequently sent legates to summon the king to a hearing by the Apostolic See. After he had disregarded a second call and a third call, the king finally accepted the advice of his intimates, who feared that he might *rightfully* be deposed from the kingship, and went to Rome,[101] where he yielded himself to the pope's

[99] As a matter of fact Henry IV announced a policy of reconciliation at the diet held at Goslar, Christmas, 1075. Thompson (*Feudal Germany*, I, 214–16) is of the opinion that his policy might ultimately have been successful if the Saxons had not been drawn into the investiture contest which immediately followed. Helmold's account of this contest in this and the following chapters departs far from fact. On the attitude of the Saxon historians and their reliability see Meyer von Knonau, *Heinrich IV*, IV, 541–6. [The notes in this section are those of Tschan.]

[100] Cf. Rev. 2:6, 15.

[101] Correctly to Canossa, 25–8 January 1077. Henry IV had been excommuni-

judgement upon the crimes of which he stood justly accused. Therefore, he received injunctions not to depart from Rome for a whole year, not to mount a horse, but in mean attire to make the round of the thresholds of the churches, through prayer and fasting bringing forth fruit meet for repentance. And the king was content humbly to abide by this sentence.

Now when the cardinals and those who were of the Curia saw that the mighty were beginning to tremble in fear of the Apostolic See and that those stooped who bear up the world, they suggested to the pope that he transfer the kingdom to another man, saying that it is not meet that one convicted of public crimes should rule. When the pope accordingly inquired who in Germany was worthy of so high a dignity, Rudolph, the duke of the Swabians, was indicated because he was, indeed, an upright man, a lover of peace and most favourably disposed towards the work of the priesthood and of the churches. To him the lord pope sent a golden crown inscribed with this verse:

The Rock gave Rome to Peter, the Pope gives you the Crown.[102] And he instructed the archbishops of Mainz and Cologne[103] and the other bishops and princes to assist Rudolph's cause and to establish him in the kingship. As many, therefore, as received the word of the lord pope elected Rudolph king, and the Saxons and Swabians joined his party. The other princes and the cities along the Rhine and all the Franconian people did not accept him because they had pledged themselves to Henry and would not break their oath. Henry in the mean time tarried at Rome, obedient to his injunctions and without knowledge of the evil that was being done him.

cated and suspended from the kingship the year before. The papal injunctions given by Helmold are a fabrication.

[102] *Petra*, 'the Rock', refers to Christ. Cf. Matt. 16:18. This verse is cited also by Otto of Freising, *Gesta Friderici I imperatoris*, i, 7, and in Sigebert of Gembloux, *Chronographia*, 1077.

[103] Respectively Siegfried (1060–84) and Hidolph (1076–8). For the alignment of the factions in the struggle after Rudolph's election at Forchheim in March 1077, see Thompson, *Feudal Germany*, I, 224–7.

Bibliographical Envoi

The charge of impressionism can certainly be levelled at the preceding collection, just as of any other anthology. Whole campaigns, intrigues, and rebellions have been disregarded. Genealogies have been purged of all but the most significant members in order to keep an uncomplicated picture before the reader. The alternative was not to tell all – that would have run to twenty volumes – but to recount other events while suppressing some of those included here. Anyone other than myself would have made a different selection, just as I might make another if the book were undertaken at another time. I have already given my explanations of the emphasis of the book in the Preface. To make up for the major lacunae, I here offer a selection of works to which the reader can refer.

One of the most important aspects of the period 919–1075 is that the Germans formed an empire which then expanded to dubious proportions, dubious, that is, for the later welfare of the state. Germany's lack of geographical barriers allowed her frontiers, in the words of A. J. P. Taylor, to go in and out 'like a concertina'. The political results of outward expansion under the later emperors were disastrous. Because the possibility of encroachment upon her neighbours was so very attractive, the historians of the Second Reich took partisan delight in extolling or condemning the territorial ambitions of the Saxons, the Salians, and especially the Hohenstaufen. The resulting war of *Grossdeutsch v. Kleindeutsch* in the nineteenth and twentieth centuries is outlined in Heinrich Hostenkamp, *Die mittelalterliche Kaiserpolitik in der deutschen Historiographie seit v. Sybel und Ficker*, Historische Studien, no. 255, Berlin, 1934. A good introduction to the topic in English can be found in Robert Edwin Herzstein, *The Holy Roman Empire in the Middle Ages: Universal State or German Catastrophe?* Problems in European Civilization, Boston, 1966, and London, Harrap, 1966 with selections from Sybel, Ficker, Brackmann, and Below, among others.

H. A. L. Fisher's two-volume study *The Mediaeval Empire*, London, 1898, is not especially recommended. Though one of the few early treatments in English, it is a bit dull. Another older work in English is that of James Bryce, *The Holy Roman Empire*, which originally appeared in 1864. Bryce, though dated in his interpretations, is eminently readable and still quite useful. The work is now available in paperback (New York, Schocken Books, 1961, and London, Macmillan, 1968). Hans Kohn, the editor, omitted the last two chapters (added by Bryce in the edition of 1904) covering the revival of the empire in the nineteenth century, on the grounds that they 'no longer show the penetrating insight of the preceding chapters. They are filled with the spirit of an unfounded optimism about the trends which led to the renewal of the imperial idea, an optimism typical of British liberal thought in the second half of the nineteenth century as it contemplated developments on the European continent' (p. xxxi). However, these chapters do show something about nineteenth-century historiography, and it is a pity that they were purged.

A curious fact of mid-twentieth century history of the medieval period is that Germany seems to have fallen into a void. It is not unusual to find the Germans featured as marauding barbarian invaders in the late Roman Empire or as incompetent, politically divided princelings in the later Middle Ages, while the great period of Ottonian and Salian creativity is virtually passed over in silence (for example, Scott–Hyma–Noyes, *Readings in Medieval History*, New York, 1933 and 1961, and Donald A. White, *Medieval History: A Source Book*, Homewood, Illinois, 1965). This de-emphasis shows up in general works on European history by non-German specialists. Two English-speaking historians made significant contributions to German medieval history after World War I – James Westfall Thompson and Geoffrey Barraclough, whose works are cited in the Introduction. English and American scholars working in Church history have shed light on Germany through their research on papal and ecclesiastical problems. See especially the works of Gerhart Ladner, Walter Ullmann, and Karl Morrison.

My complete neglect of the art works of the Saxon and Salian period does not mean that I underrate their importance. On the contrary, I think they are both historically significant and visually exciting. But it is usually unsatisfactory to read any sort of art criticism without copious illustrations. That was outside the scope of this book.

A good survey with handsome illustrations covering European art of the period is John Beckwith, *Early Medieval Art*, New York, 1964, and London, Thames & Hudson, 1964. For photographs of the principal architectural monuments see Louis Grodecki, *L'Architecture ottonienne*, Paris, 1958, and for plans and maps of the royal strongholds see *Deutsche Königspfalzen*, 2 vols, Veröffentlichungen des Max-Planck-Instituts für Geschichte, Vol. II, Pts 1 and 2, Göttingen, 1963–5.

Perhaps the most stimulating treatment of art works is Percy Ernst Schramm, *Herrschaftszeichen und Staatssymbolik*, 3 vols, Stuttgart, 1954–6. Such items as crowns, coins, seals, sceptres, and battle standards are examined for their symbolic significance. Schramm's work in conjunction with Florentine Mütherich is also excellent: *Denkmale der deutschen Könige und Kaiser*, Veröffentlichungen des Zentralinstituts für Kunstgeschichte in München, II, Munich, 1962, a large work with black and white photographs of manuscript illuminations, coronation regalia, burial ornaments, and other imperial artifacts.

Art works commanded by Bishop Bernward of Hildesheim are illustrated in vol. III of Francis J. Tschan, *Saint Bernward of Hildesheim*, Notre Dame, 1952.

TE DUE